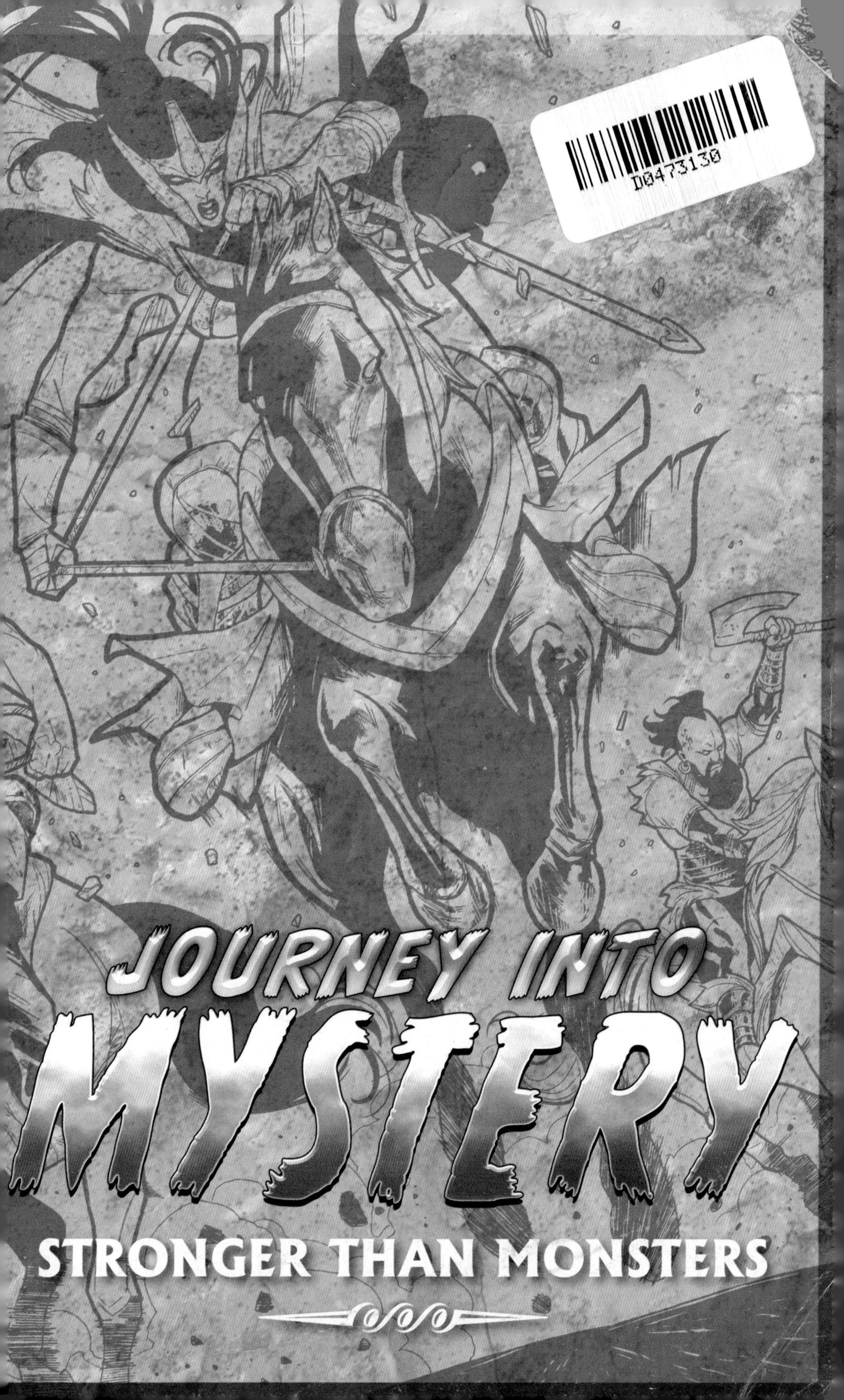

JOURNEY INTO MYSTERY

STRONGER THAN MONSTERS

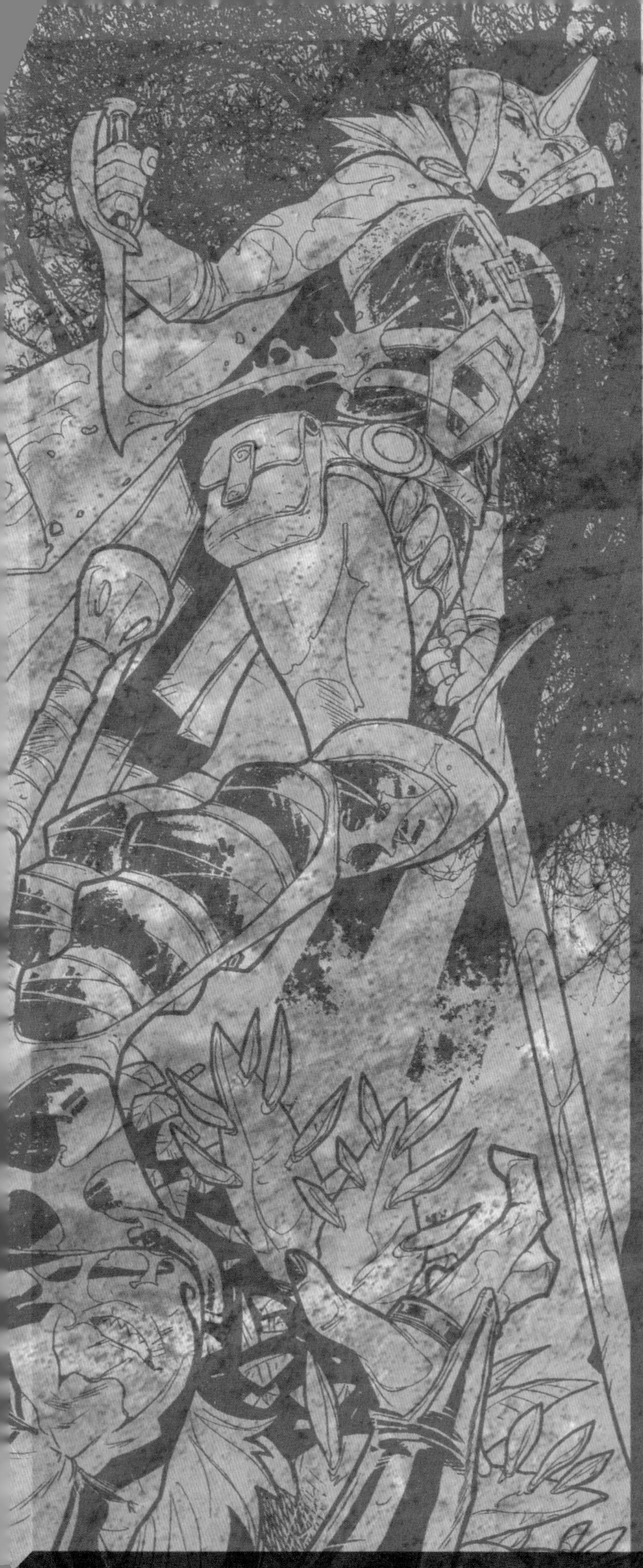

COLLECTION EDITOR
CORY LEVINE

ASSISTANT EDITORS
ALEX STARBUCK
NELSON RIBEIRO

EDITORS,
SPECIAL PROJECTS
JENNIFER GRÜNWALD
MARK D. BEAZLEY

SENIOR EDITOR,
SPECIAL PROJECTS
JEFF YOUNGQUIST

SVP OF PRINT & DIGITAL
PUBLISHING SALES
DAVID GABRIEL

BOOK DESIGN
JEFF POWELL
CORY LEVINE

EDITOR IN CHIEF
AXEL ALONSO

CHIEF CREATIVE OFFICER
JOE QUESADA

PUBLISHER
DAN BUCKLEY

EXECUTIVE PRODUCER
ALAN FINE

JOURNEY INTO MYSTERY FEATURING SIF VOL. STRONGER THAN MONSTERS. Contains material original published in magazine form as JOURNEY INTO MYSTER #646-650. First printing 2013. ISBN# 978-0-7851-6108- Published by MARVEL WORLDWIDE, INC., a subsidiary MARVEL ENTERTAINMENT, LLC. OFFICE OF PUBLICATIO 135 West 50th Street, New York, NY 10020. **Printed in the U.S.A.** ALAN FINE EVP - Office of the President, Marvel Worldwide, Inc. and EV & CMO Marvel Characters B.V.; DAN BUCKLEY, Publisher & President - Print, Animation & Digital Divisions; JOE QUESADA Chief Creative Officer; TOM BREVOORT, SVP of Publishing DAVID BOGART, SVP of Operations & Procurement, Publishing C.B. CEBULSKI, SVP of Creator & Content Development DAVID GABRIEL, SVP of Print & Digital Publishing Sales; JI O'KEEFE, VP of Operations & Logistics; DAN CARR, Executiv Director of Publishing Technology; SUSAN CRESPI, Editor Operations Manager; ALEX MORALES, Publishing Operation Manager; STAN LEE, Chairman Emeritus. For informatio regarding advertising in Marvel Comics or on Marvel.co please contact Niza Disla, Director of Marvel Partnerships, ndisla@marvel.com. For Marvel subscription inquiries, pleas call 800-217-9158. **Manufactured between 4/3/2013 an 5/6/2013 by QUAD/GRAPHICS, VERSAILLES, KY, USA.**

10 9 8 7 6 5 4 3 2 1

JOURNEY INTO MYSTERY

STRONGER THAN MONSTERS

WRITER
KATHRYN IMMONEN

ARTIST
VALERIO SCHITI

COLOR ARTIST
JORDIE BELLAIRE

LETTERER
VC'S CLAYTON COWLES

COVER ARTIST
JEFF DEKAL

ASSISTANT EDITOR
JACOB THOMAS

EDITOR
LAUREN SANKOVITCH

#646

MARVEL COMICS PRESENTS

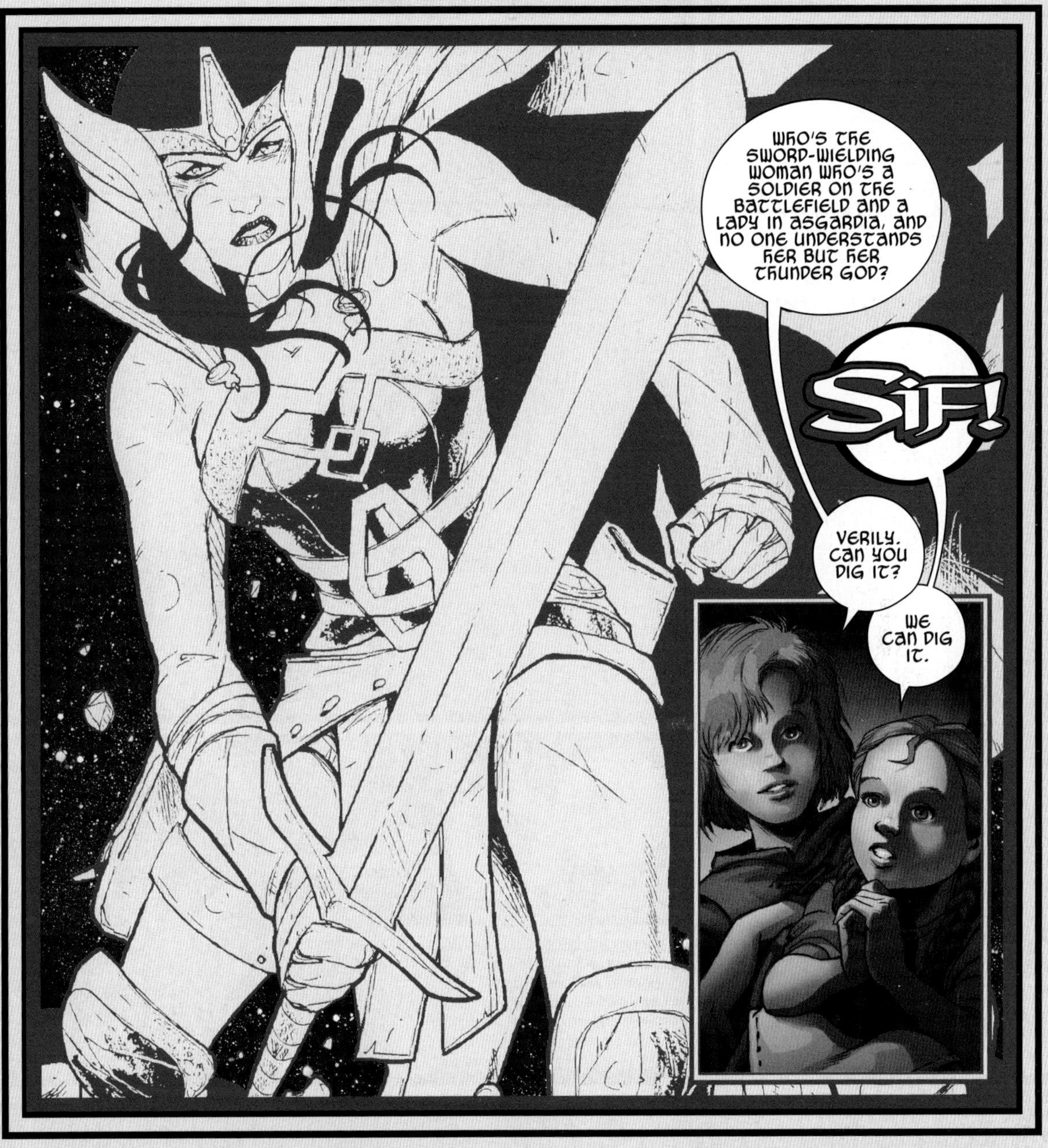
WHO'S THE SWORD-WIELDING WOMAN WHO'S A SOLDIER ON THE BATTLEFIELD AND A LADY IN ASGARDIA, AND NO ONE UNDERSTANDS HER BUT HER THUNDER GOD?
SIF!
VERILY. CAN YOU DIG IT?
WE CAN DIG IT.

JOURNEY INTO MYSTERY

STRONGER THAN MONSTERS, PART 1 OF 5

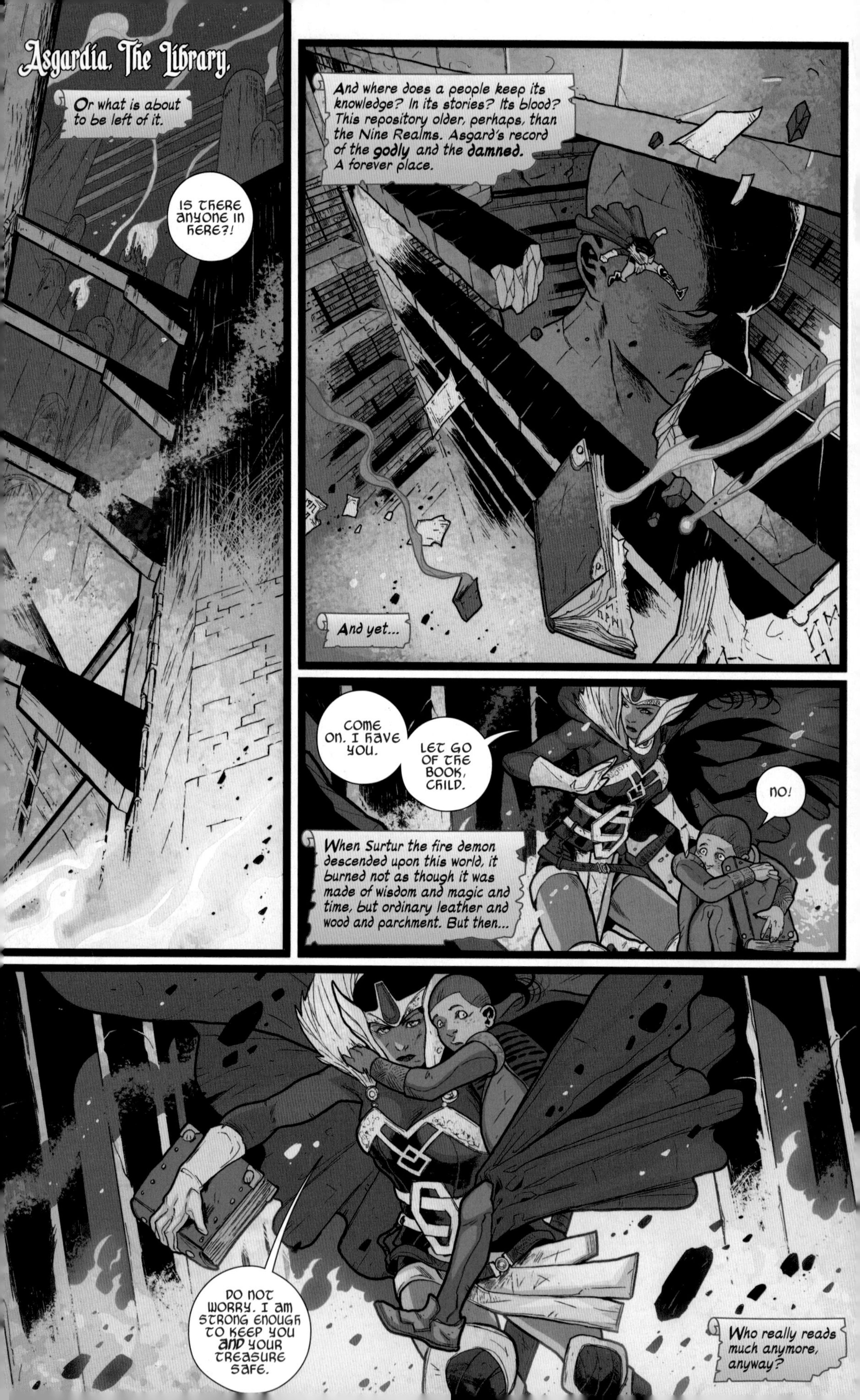

Asgardia. The Library.
Or what is about to be left of it.
IS THERE ANYONE IN HERE?!
And where does a people keep its knowledge? In its stories? Its blood? This repository older, perhaps, than the Nine Realms. Asgard's record of the godly and the damned. A forever place.
And yet...
COME ON. I HAVE YOU.
LET GO OF THE BOOK, CHILD.
NO!
When Surtur the fire demon descended upon this world, it burned not as though it was made of wisdom and magic and time, but ordinary leather and wood and parchment. But then...
DO NOT WORRY. I AM STRONG ENOUGH TO KEEP YOU AND YOUR TREASURE SAFE.
Who really reads much anymore, anyway?

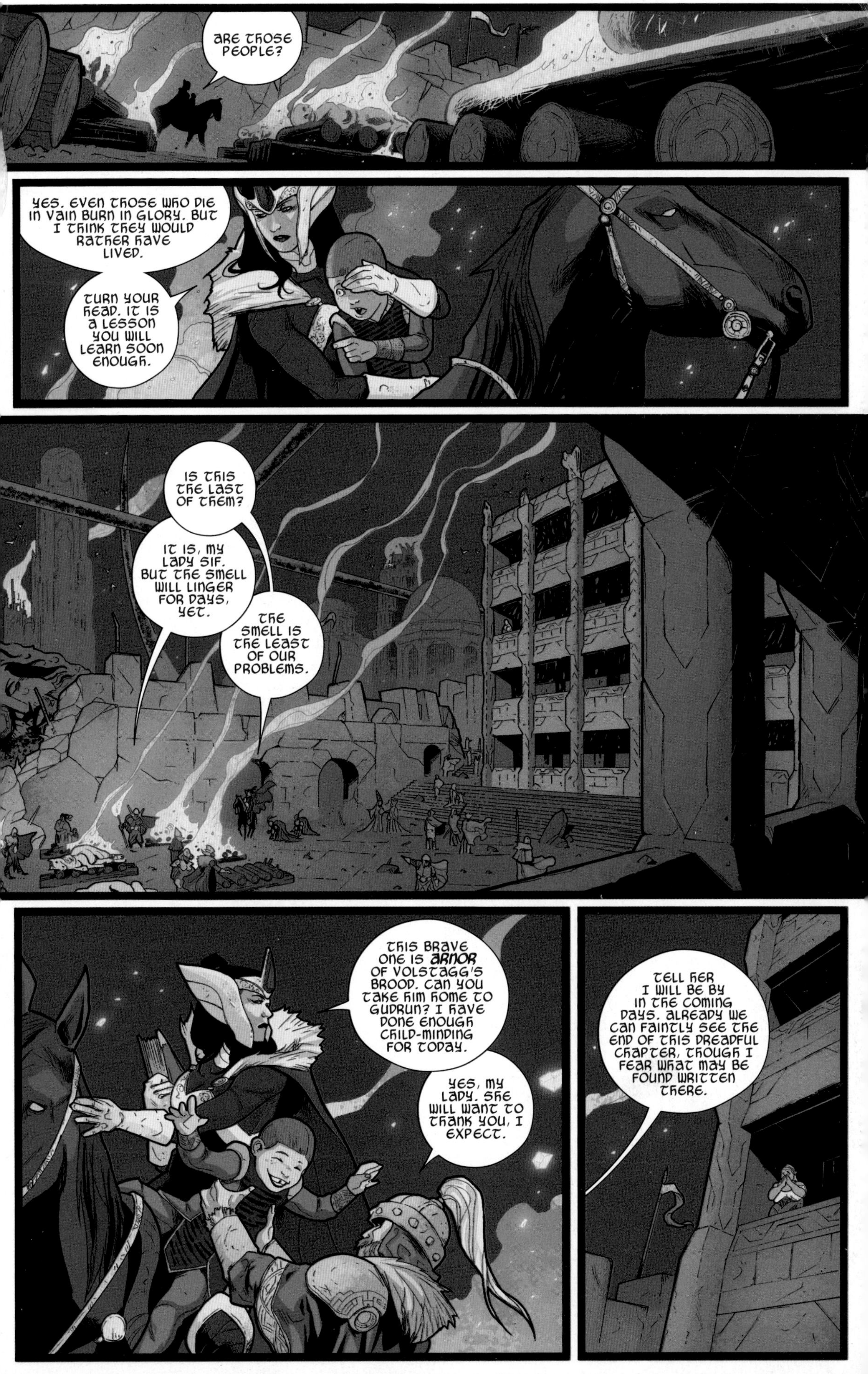
ARE THOSE PEOPLE?
YES. EVEN THOSE WHO DIE IN VAIN BURN IN GLORY. BUT I THINK THEY WOULD RATHER HAVE LIVED.
TURN YOUR HEAD. IT IS A LESSON YOU WILL LEARN SOON ENOUGH.
IS THIS THE LAST OF THEM?
IT IS, MY LADY SIF. BUT THE SMELL WILL LINGER FOR DAYS, YET.
THE SMELL IS THE LEAST OF OUR PROBLEMS.
THIS BRAVE ONE IS ARNOR OF VOLSTAGG'S BROOD. CAN YOU TAKE HIM HOME TO GUDRUN? I HAVE DONE ENOUGH CHILD-MINDING FOR TODAY.
YES, MY LADY. SHE WILL WANT TO THANK YOU, I EXPECT.
TELL HER I WILL BE BY IN THE COMING DAYS. ALREADY WE CAN FAINTLY SEE THE END OF THIS DREADFUL CHAPTER, THOUGH I FEAR WHAT MAY BE FOUND WRITTEN THERE.

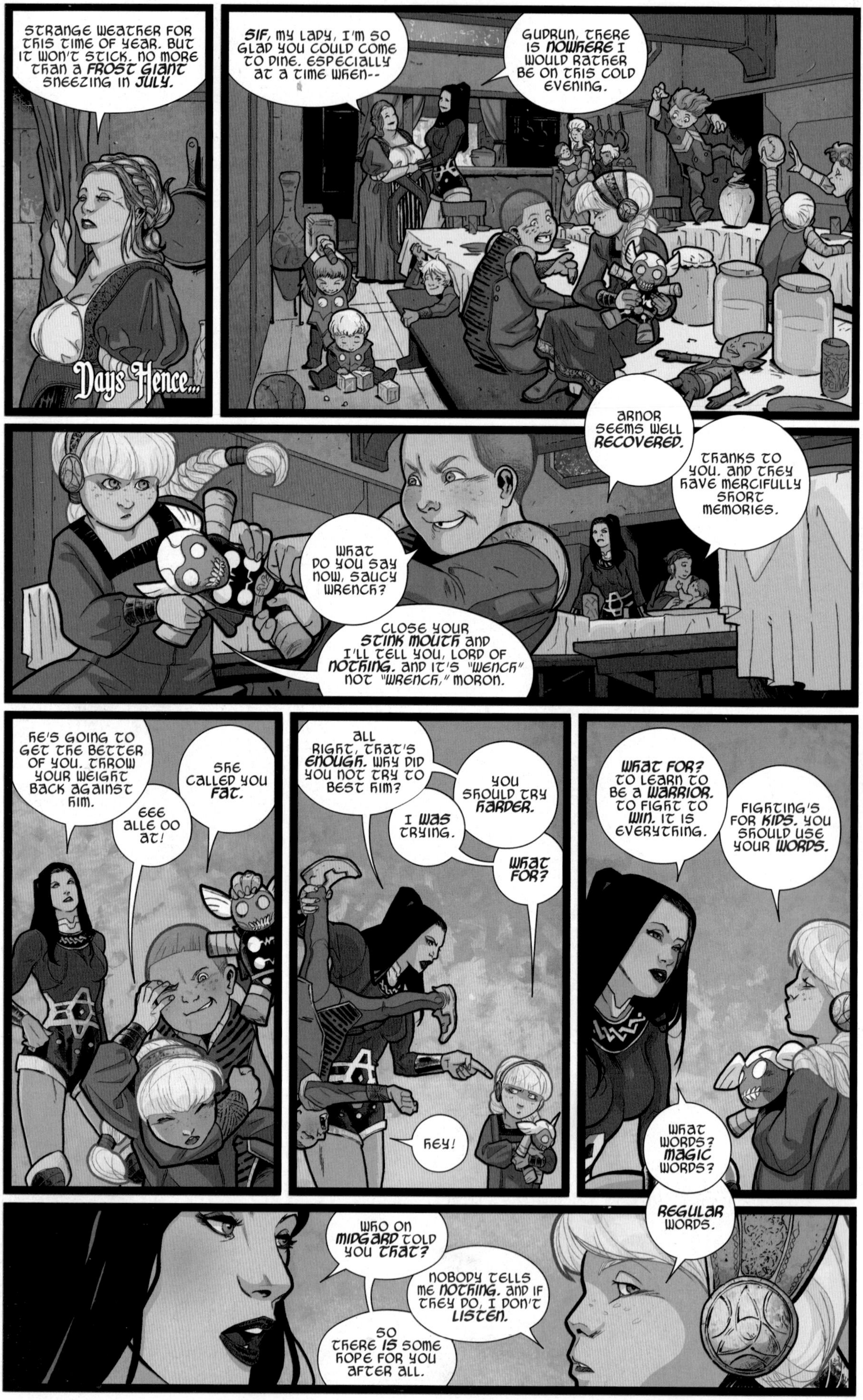
STRANGE WEATHER FOR THIS TIME OF YEAR. BUT IT WON'T STICK. NO MORE THAN A FROST GIANT SNEEZING IN JULY.
Days Hence...
SIF, MY LADY, I'M SO GLAD YOU COULD COME TO DINE. ESPECIALLY AT A TIME WHEN--
GUDRUN, THERE IS NOWHERE I WOULD RATHER BE ON THIS COLD EVENING.
ARNOR SEEMS WELL RECOVERED.
THANKS TO YOU. AND THEY HAVE MERCIFULLY SHORT MEMORIES.
WHAT DO YOU SAY NOW, SAUCY WRENCH?
CLOSE YOUR STINK MOUTH AND I'LL TELL YOU, LORD OF NOTHING. AND IT'S "WENCH" NOT "WRENCH," MORON.
HE'S GOING TO GET THE BETTER OF YOU. THROW YOUR WEIGHT BACK AGAINST HIM.
EEE ALLE OO AT!
SHE CALLED YOU FAT.
ALL RIGHT, THAT'S ENOUGH. WHY DID YOU NOT TRY TO BEST HIM?
YOU SHOULD TRY HARDER.
I WAS TRYING.
WHAT FOR?
HEY!
WHAT FOR? TO LEARN TO BE A WARRIOR. TO FIGHT TO WIN. IT IS EVERYTHING.
FIGHTING'S FOR KIDS. YOU SHOULD USE YOUR WORDS.
WHAT WORDS? MAGIC WORDS?
REGULAR WORDS.
WHO ON MIDGARD TOLD YOU THAT?
NOBODY TELLS ME NOTHING. AND IF THEY DO, I DON'T LISTEN.
SO THERE IS SOME HOPE FOR YOU AFTER ALL.

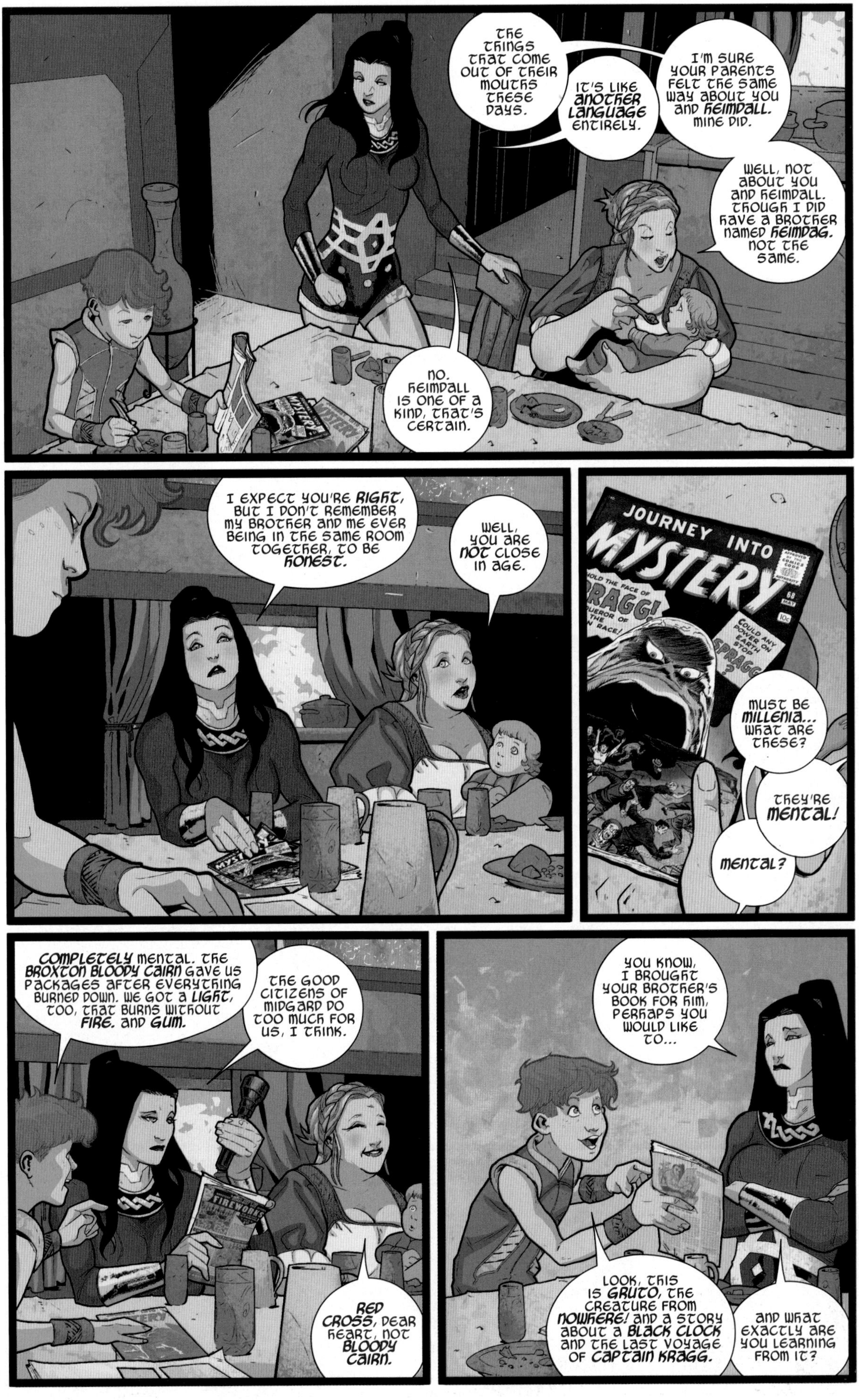
THE THINGS THAT COME OUT OF THEIR MOUTHS THESE DAYS.
IT'S LIKE ANOTHER LANGUAGE ENTIRELY.
I'M SURE YOUR PARENTS FELT THE SAME WAY ABOUT YOU AND HEIMDALL. MINE DID.
WELL, NOT ABOUT YOU AND HEIMDALL. THOUGH I DID HAVE A BROTHER NAMED HEIMDAG. NOT THE SAME.
NO. HEIMDALL IS ONE OF A KIND, THAT'S CERTAIN.
I EXPECT YOU'RE RIGHT, BUT I DON'T REMEMBER MY BROTHER AND ME EVER BEING IN THE SAME ROOM TOGETHER, TO BE HONEST.
WELL, YOU ARE NOT CLOSE IN AGE.
JOURNEY INTO MYSTERY
68
MAY
10¢
COULD ANY POWER ON EARTH STOP SPRAGG?
MUST BE MILLENIA... WHAT ARE THESE?
THEY'RE MENTAL!
MENTAL?
COMPLETELY MENTAL. THE BROXTON BLOODY CAIRN GAVE US PACKAGES AFTER EVERYTHING BURNED DOWN. WE GOT A LIGHT, TOO, THAT BURNS WITHOUT FIRE. AND GUM.
THE GOOD CITIZENS OF MIDGARD DO TOO MUCH FOR US, I THINK.
RED CROSS, DEAR HEART, NOT BLOODY CAIRN.
YOU KNOW, I BROUGHT YOUR BROTHER'S BOOK FOR HIM, PERHAPS YOU WOULD LIKE TO...
LOOK, THIS IS GRUTO, THE CREATURE FROM NOWHERE! AND A STORY ABOUT A BLACK CLOCK AND THE LAST VOYAGE OF CAPTAIN KRAGG.
AND WHAT EXACTLY ARE YOU LEARNING FROM IT?

HE CAN KEEP HIS OLD BOOK. LOOK, *SPRAGG!* *CONQUEROR* OF THE HUMAN RACE!

LOOK! HEIMDALL! CONQUEROR OF TIME AND SPACE! VOLSTAGG! CONQUEROR OF BEDTIMES!

A HUNDRED-FOOT-TALL *LIVING* COMPUTER!

A HUNDRED UNDEAD WARRIORS!

THAT'S OLD STUFF. MY PARENTS KNOW THOSE STORIES.

I SEE. WHEN I WAS YOUR AGE, I SPENT MANY HOURS WITH THE BOOKS IN OUR LIBRARY. IF YOU LOOK CAREFULLY, YOU WILL FIND SECRETS HIDDEN IN THE KNOWLEDGE UPON WHICH ASGARD IS BUILT.

MAYBE IF WE DIDN'T KEEP WRECKING IT, WE WOULDN'T HAVE TO KEEP BUILDING IT.

OUT OF THE MOUTHS OF BABES.

I AM SICK TO DEATH OF *LOSING*, GUDRUN. WE *SURVIVE* AN ATTACK, WE REBUILD, *AGAIN*, AND WE CALL IT *VICTORY*. AND I TELL YOU, IT IS *NOT*.

ALL I EVER WANTED IS TO SERVE ASGARD. TO HAVE FORCE ENOUGH TO WIN HER FIGHTS, BUT CAN WE NOT BE *STRONGER* STILL TO PREVENT THE FIGHT IN THE FIRST PLACE?

THAT IS WISDOM, MY LADY.

I SEEK IT NOT, HILDE. BUT THERE ARE ANCIENT WAYS WE HAVE LEFT BY THE ROAD ON OUR PATH TO IT, AND I DO NOT BELIEVE US STRONGER FOR IT.

I CANNOT IMAGINE A STRONGER SIF.

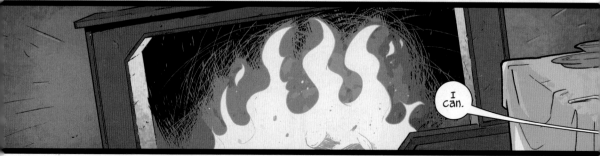

I CAN.

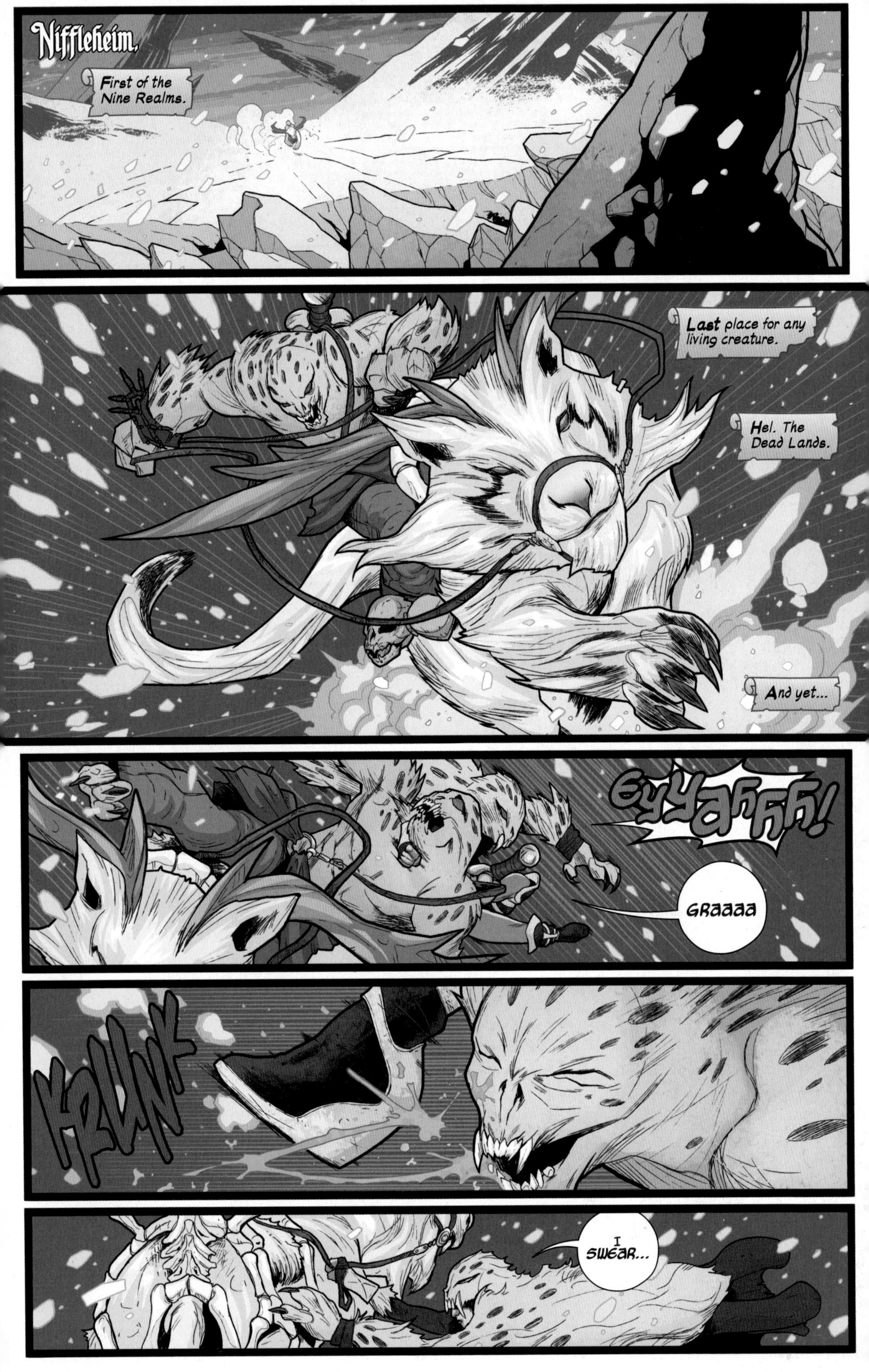
Niffleheim,
First of the Nine Realms.
Last place for any living creature.
Hel. The Dead Lands.
And yet...
EyYAHHH!
GRAAAAA
KRUNK
I SWEAR...

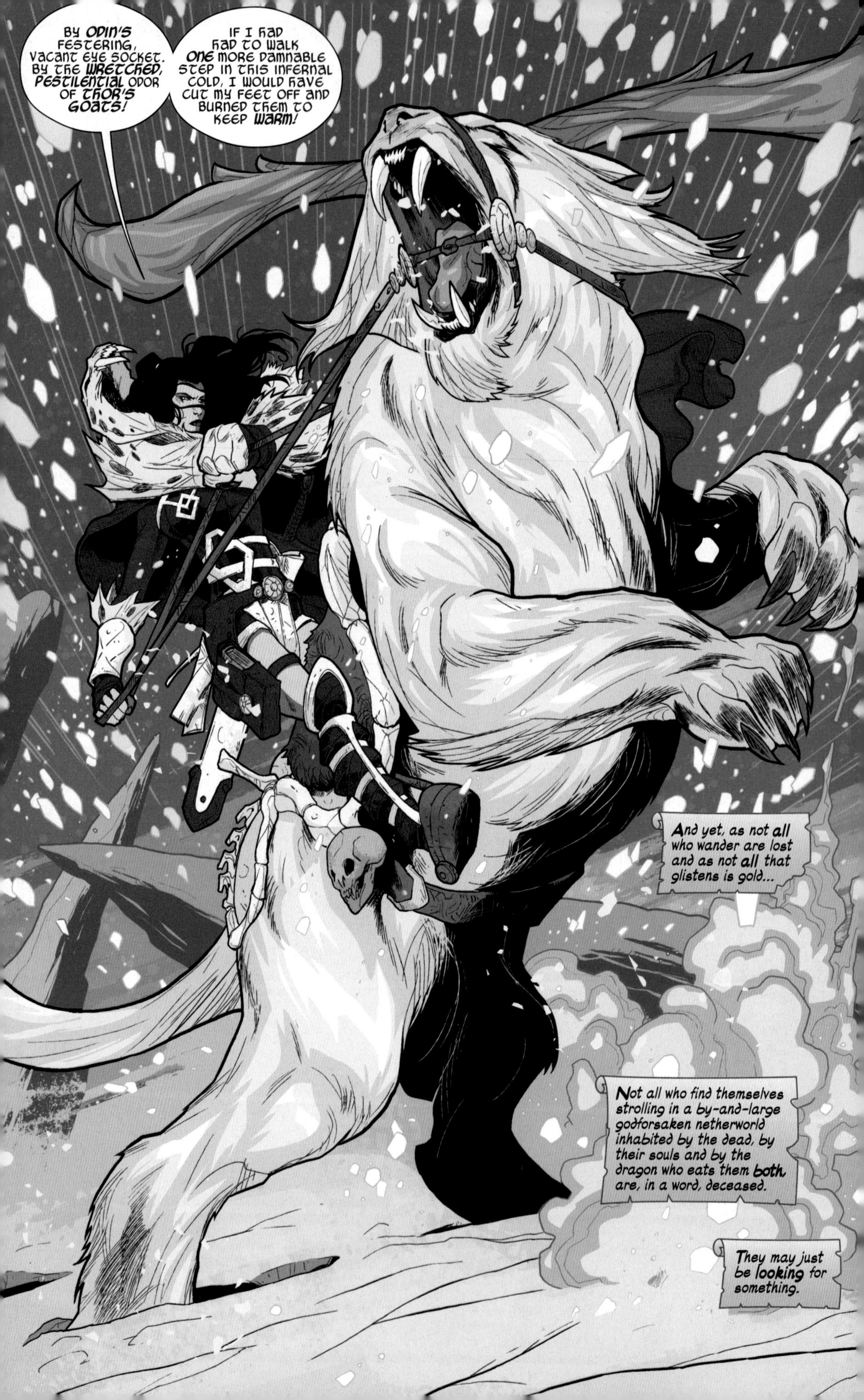

BY ODIN'S FESTERING, VACANT EYE SOCKET. BY THE WRETCHED, PESTILENTIAL ODOR OF THOR'S GOATS!
IF I HAD HAD TO WALK ONE MORE DAMNABLE STEP IN THIS INFERNAL COLD, I WOULD HAVE CUT MY FEET OFF AND BURNED THEM TO KEEP WARM!
And yet, as not all who wander are lost and as not all that glistens is gold...
Not all who find themselves strolling in a by-and-large godforsaken netherworld inhabited by the dead, by their souls and by the dragon who eats them both, are, in a word, deceased.
They may just be looking for something.

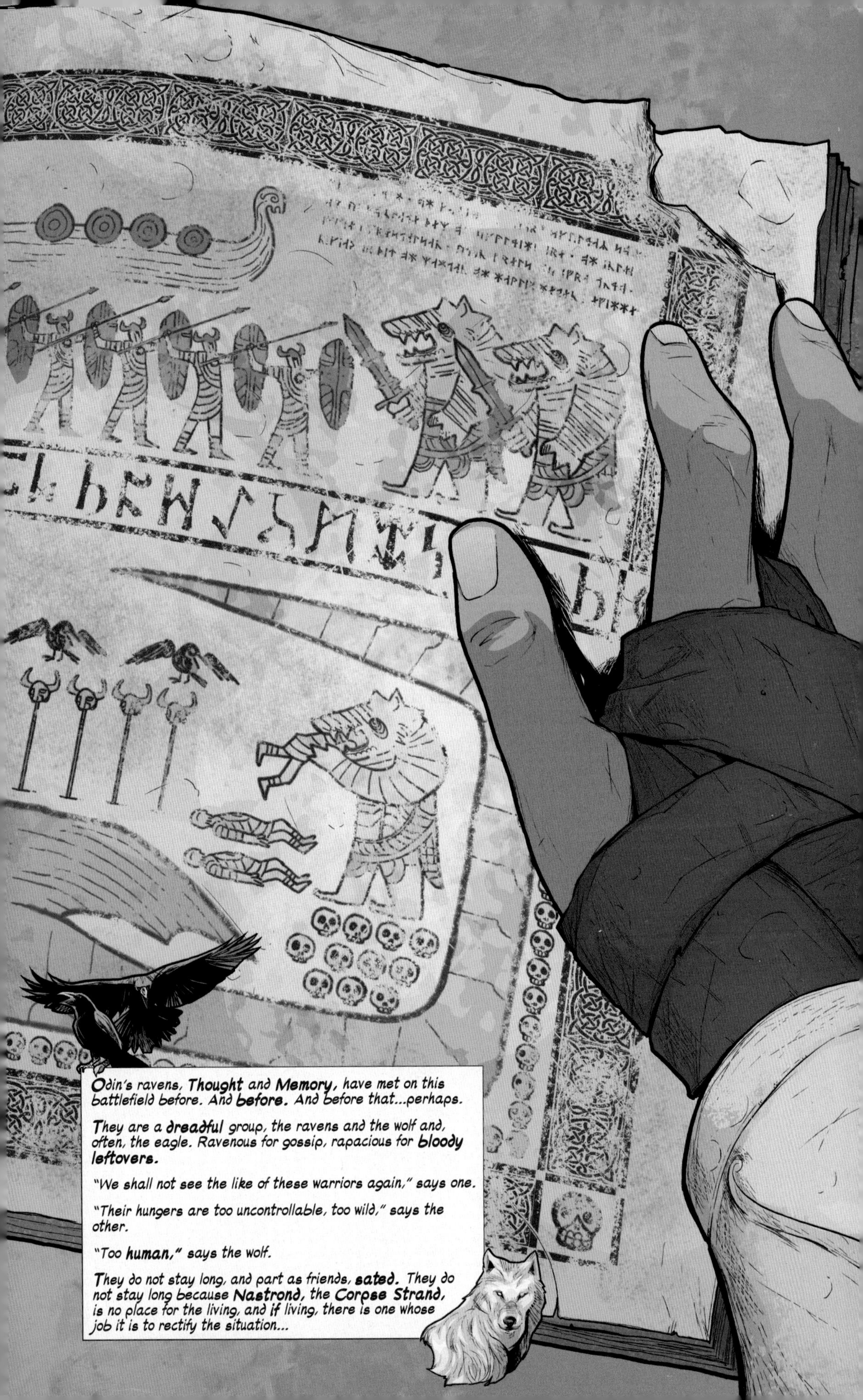
Odin's ravens, Thought and Memory, have met on this battlefield before. And before. And before that...perhaps.
They are a dreadful group, the ravens and the wolf and, often, the eagle. Ravenous for gossip, rapacious for bloody leftovers.
"We shall not see the like of these warriors again," says one.
"Their hungers are too uncontrollable, too wild," says the other.
"Too human," says the wolf.
They do not stay long, and part as friends, sated. They do not stay long because Nastrond, the Corpse Strand, is no place for the living, and if living, there is one whose job it is to rectify the situation...

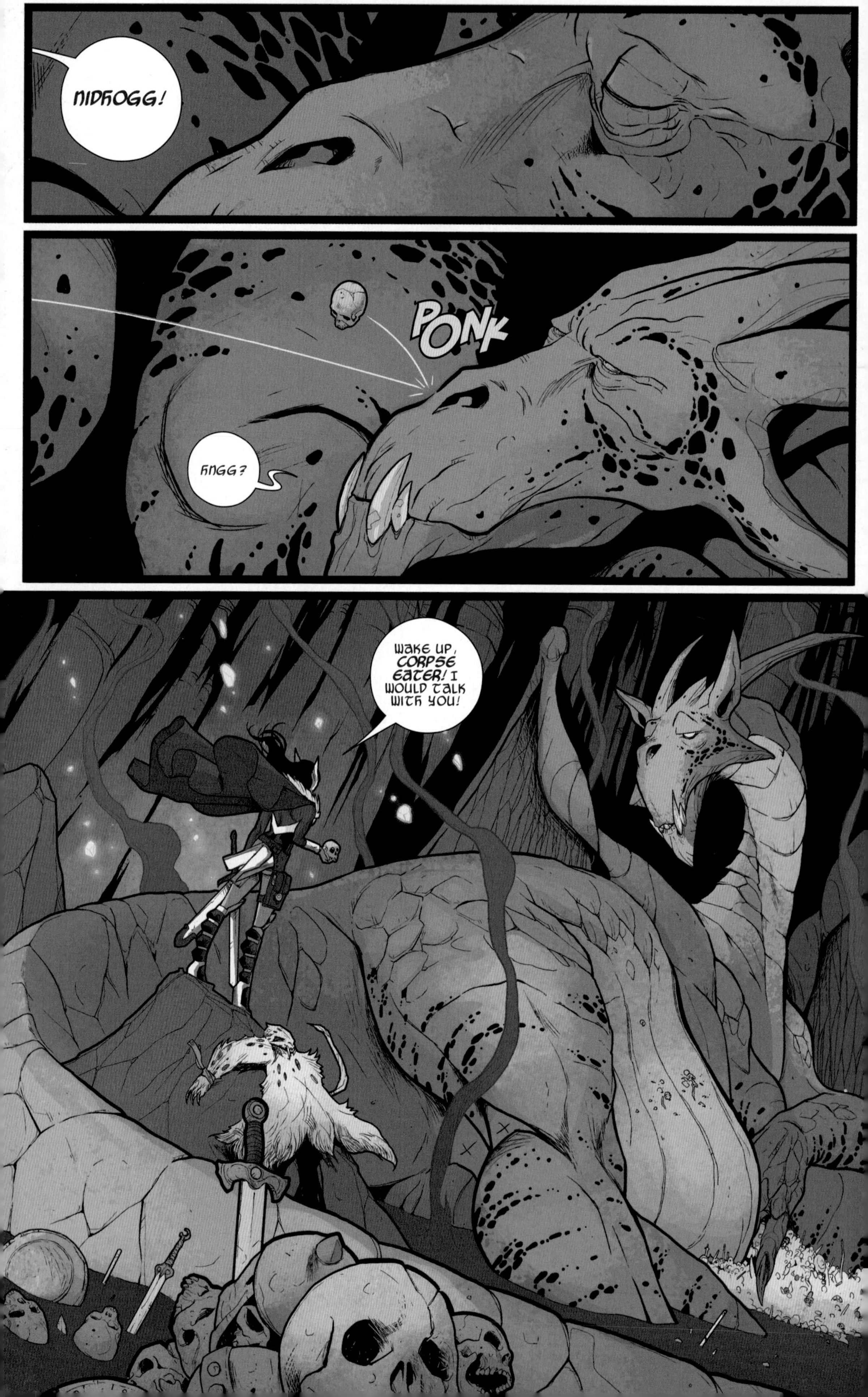
NIDHOGG!
PONK
HNGG?
WAKE UP, CORPSE EATER! I WOULD TALK WITH YOU!

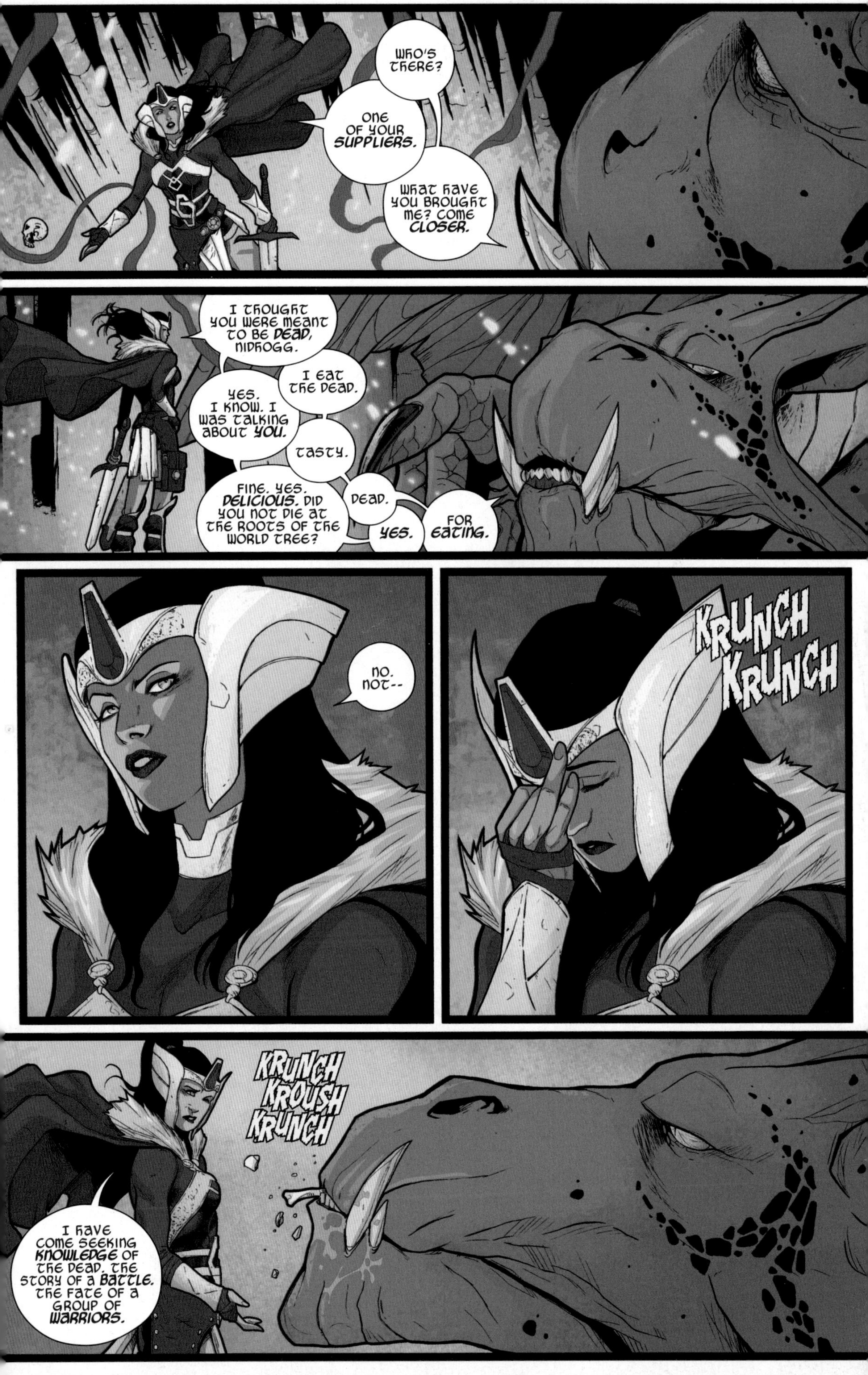

WHO'S THERE?
ONE OF YOUR SUPPLIERS.
WHAT HAVE YOU BROUGHT ME? COME CLOSER.
I THOUGHT YOU WERE MEANT TO BE DEAD, NIDHOGG.
I EAT THE DEAD.
YES. I KNOW. I WAS TALKING ABOUT YOU.
TASTY.
FINE. YES. DELICIOUS. DID YOU NOT DIE AT THE ROOTS OF THE WORLD TREE?
DEAD.
YES.
FOR EATING.
NO. NOT--
KRUNCH KRUNCH
KRUNCH KROUSH KRUNCH
I HAVE COME SEEKING KNOWLEDGE OF THE DEAD. THE STORY OF A BATTLE. THE FATE OF A GROUP OF WARRIORS.

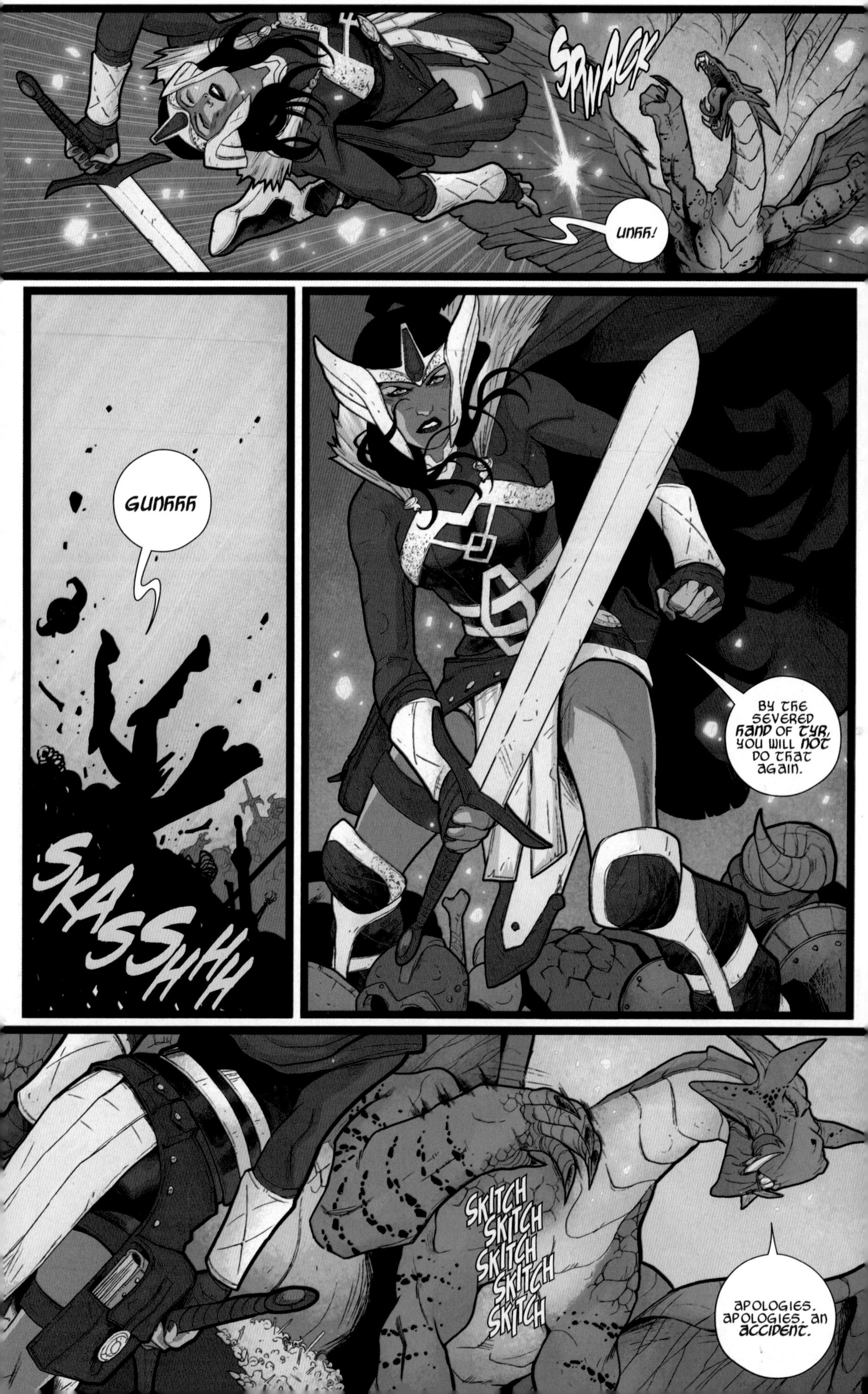
SPWACK
UNHH!
GUNHHH
SKASSHHH
BY THE SEVERED HAND OF TYR, YOU WILL NOT DO THAT AGAIN.
SKITCH SKITCH SKITCH SKITCH SKITCH SKITCH
APOLOGIES. APOLOGIES. AN ACCIDENT.

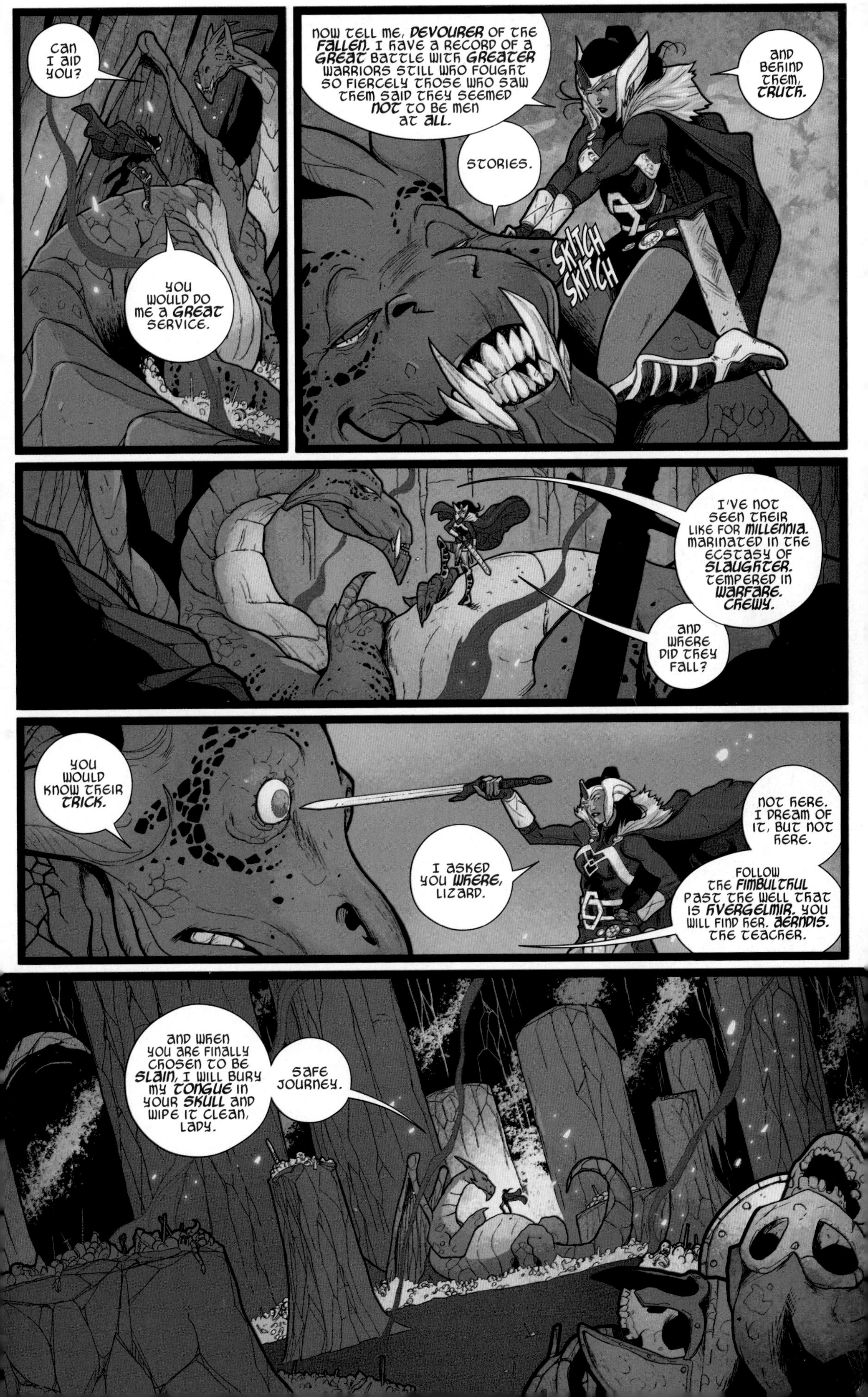
CAN I AID YOU?
YOU WOULD DO ME A GREAT SERVICE.
NOW TELL ME, DEVOURER OF THE FALLEN. I HAVE A RECORD OF A GREAT BATTLE WITH GREATER WARRIORS STILL WHO FOUGHT SO FIERCELY THOSE WHO SAW THEM SAID THEY SEEMED NOT TO BE MEN AT ALL.
STORIES.
AND BEHIND THEM, TRUTH.
SKITCH SKITCH
I'VE NOT SEEN THEIR LIKE FOR MILLENNIA. MARINATED IN THE ECSTASY OF SLAUGHTER. TEMPERED IN WARFARE. CHEWY.
AND WHERE DID THEY FALL?
YOU WOULD KNOW THEIR TRICK.
I ASKED YOU WHERE, LIZARD.
NOT HERE. I DREAM OF IT, BUT NOT HERE.
FOLLOW THE FIMBULTHUL PAST THE WELL THAT IS HVERGELMIR. YOU WILL FIND HER. AERNDIS. THE TEACHER.
AND WHEN YOU ARE FINALLY CHOSEN TO BE SLAIN, I WILL BURY MY TONGUE IN YOUR SKULL AND WIPE IT CLEAN, LADY.
SAFE JOURNEY.

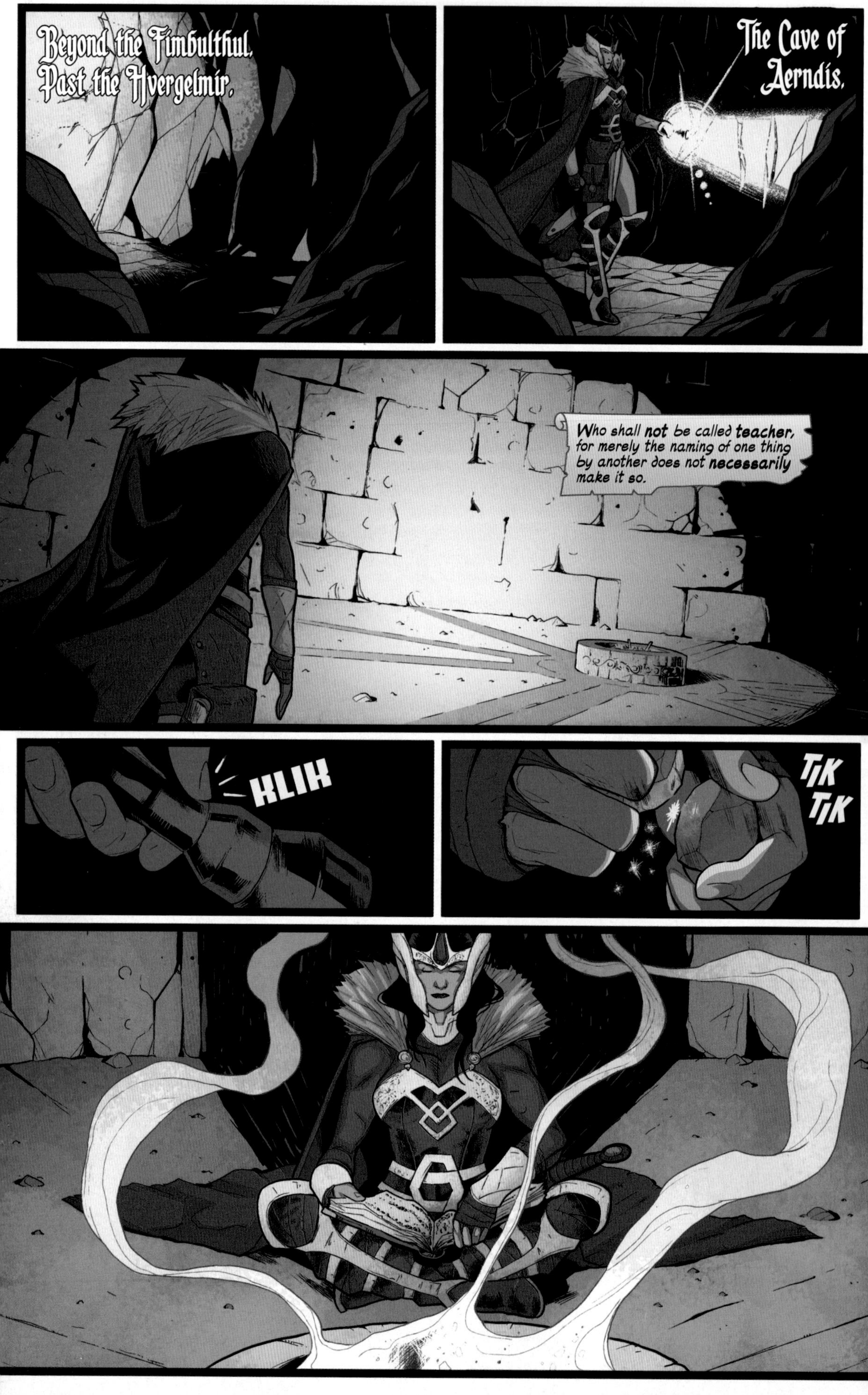
Beyond the Fimbulthul, Past the Hvergelmir,
The Cave of Aerndis.
Who shall not be called teacher, for merely the naming of one thing by another does not necessarily make it so.
KLIK
TIK TIK

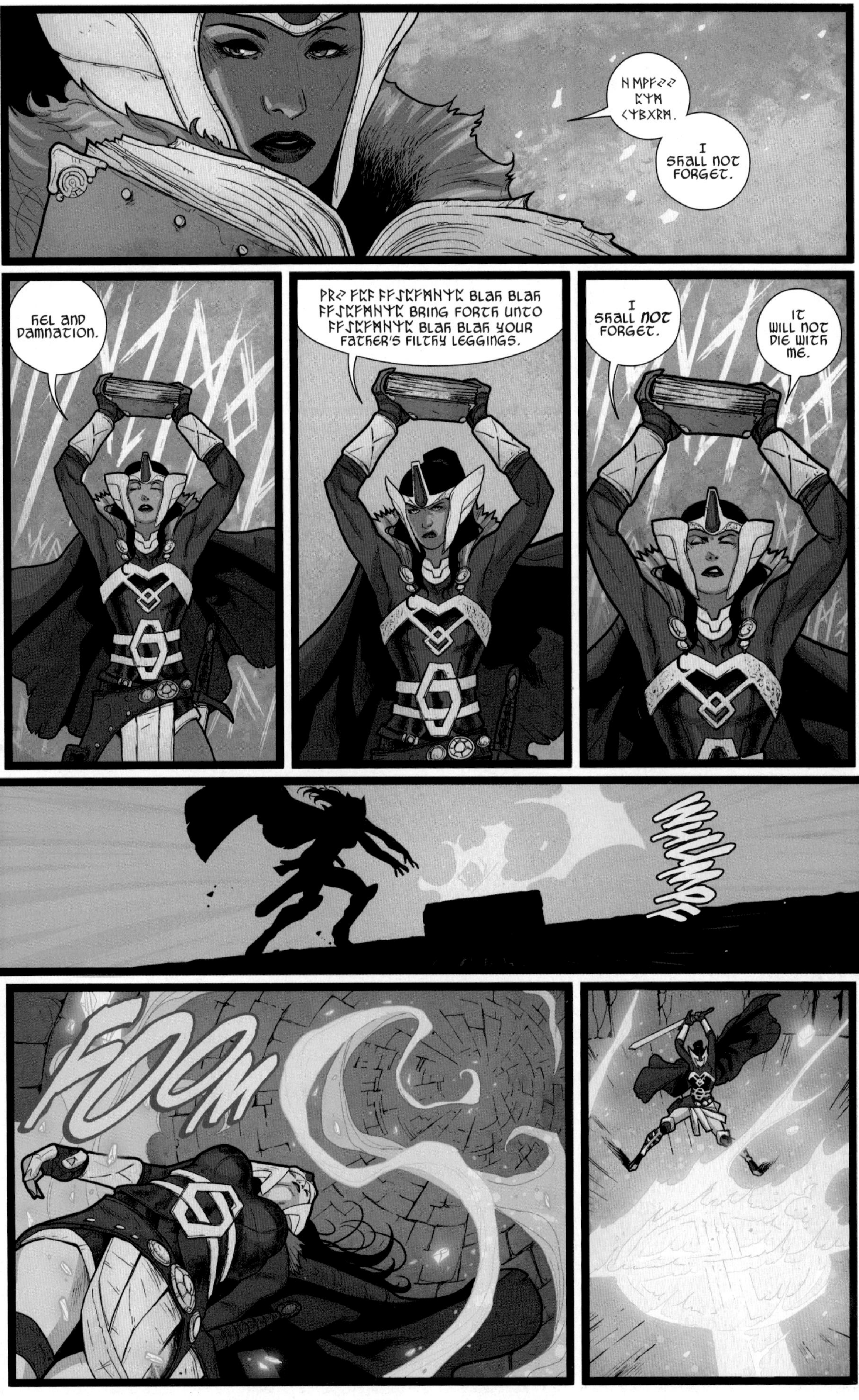

I SHALL NOT FORGET.
HEL AND DAMNATION.
BLAH BLAH BRING FORTH UNTO BLAH BLAH YOUR FATHER'S FILTHY LEGGINGS.
I SHALL NOT FORGET.
IT WILL NOT DIE WITH ME.
WHUMPF
FOOM

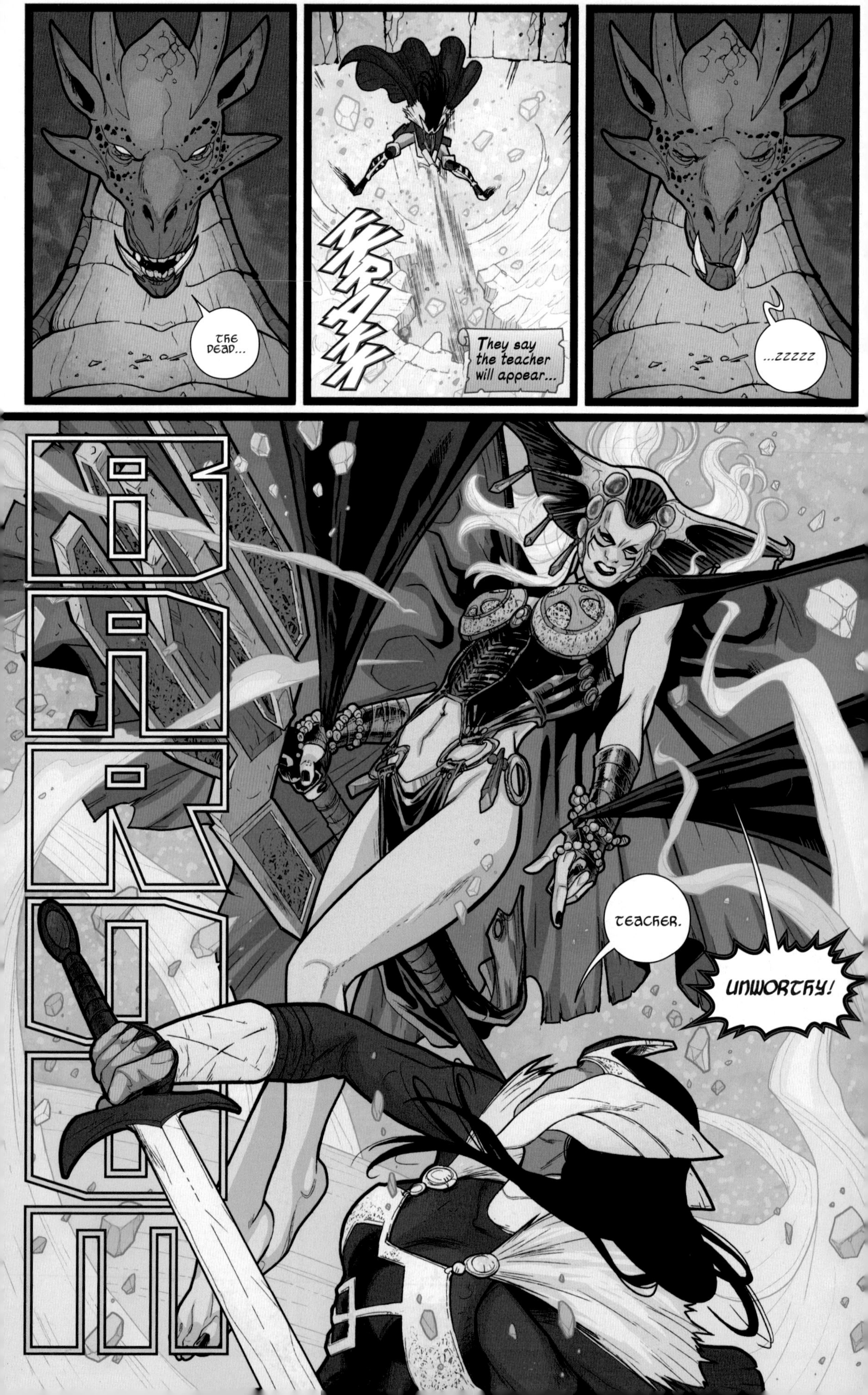
THE DEAD...
KKRAKK
They say the teacher will appear...
...zzzzz
TEACHER.
UNWORTHY!

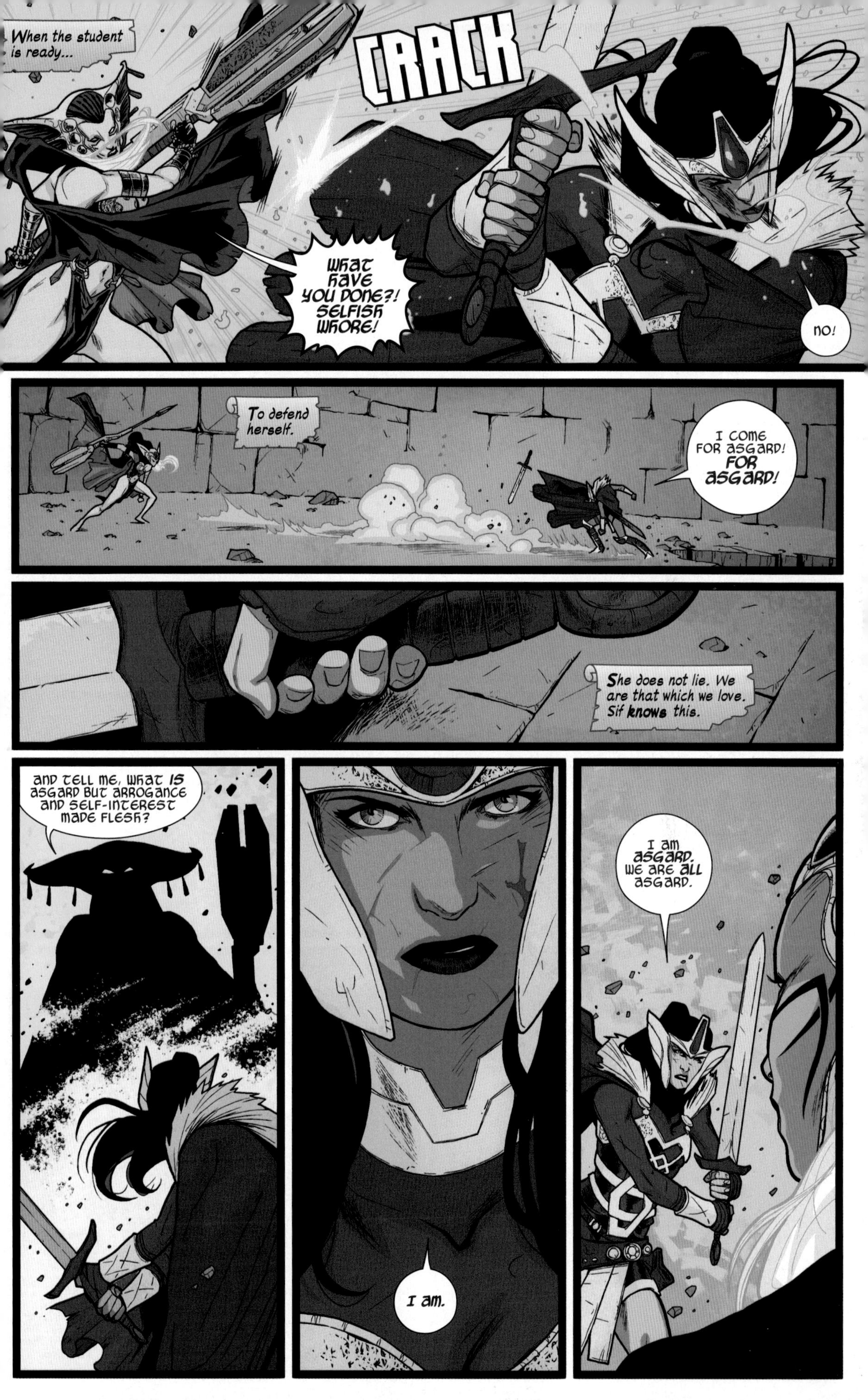
When the student is ready...
CRACK
WHAT HAVE YOU DONE?! SELFISH WHORE!
no!
To defend herself.
I COME FOR ASGARD! FOR ASGARD!
She does not lie. We are that which we love. Sif knows this.
AND TELL ME, WHAT IS ASGARD BUT ARROGANCE AND SELF-INTEREST MADE FLESH?
I am.
I AM ASGARD. WE ARE ALL ASGARD.

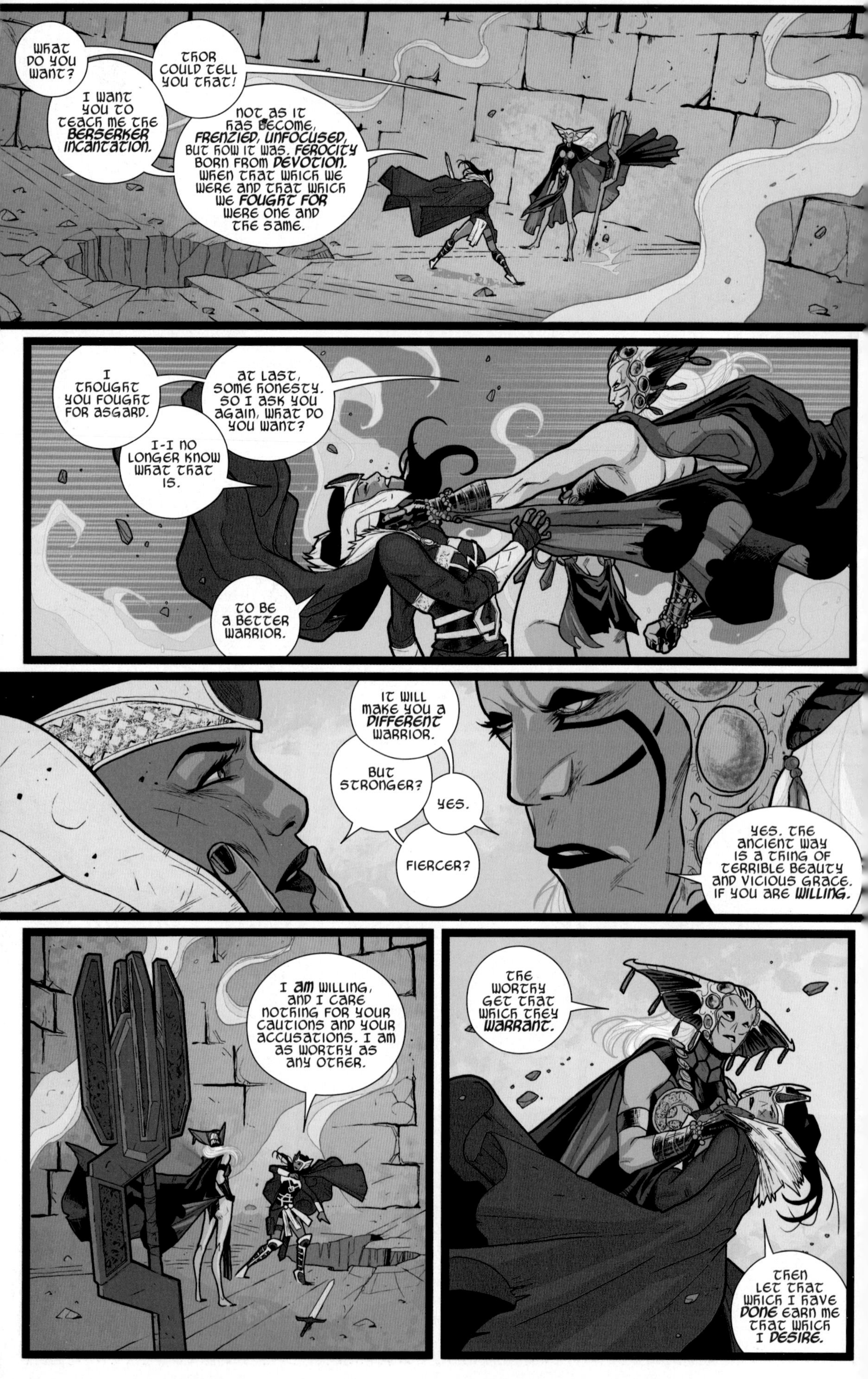
WHAT DO YOU WANT?
THOR COULD TELL YOU THAT!
I WANT YOU TO TEACH ME THE BERSERKER INCANTATION.
NOT AS IT HAS BECOME, FRENZIED, UNFOCUSED, BUT HOW IT WAS. FEROCITY BORN FROM DEVOTION. WHEN THAT WHICH WE WERE AND THAT WHICH WE FOUGHT FOR WERE ONE AND THE SAME.
I THOUGHT YOU FOUGHT FOR ASGARD.
AT LAST, SOME HONESTY. SO I ASK YOU AGAIN, WHAT DO YOU WANT?
I-I NO LONGER KNOW WHAT THAT IS.
TO BE A BETTER WARRIOR.
IT WILL MAKE YOU A DIFFERENT WARRIOR.
BUT STRONGER?
YES.
FIERCER?
YES. THE ANCIENT WAY IS A THING OF TERRIBLE BEAUTY AND VICIOUS GRACE. IF YOU ARE WILLING.
I AM WILLING, AND I CARE NOTHING FOR YOUR CAUTIONS AND YOUR ACCUSATIONS. I AM AS WORTHY AS ANY OTHER.
THE WORTHY GET THAT WHICH THEY WARRANT.
THEN LET THAT WHICH I HAVE DONE EARN ME THAT WHICH I DESIRE.

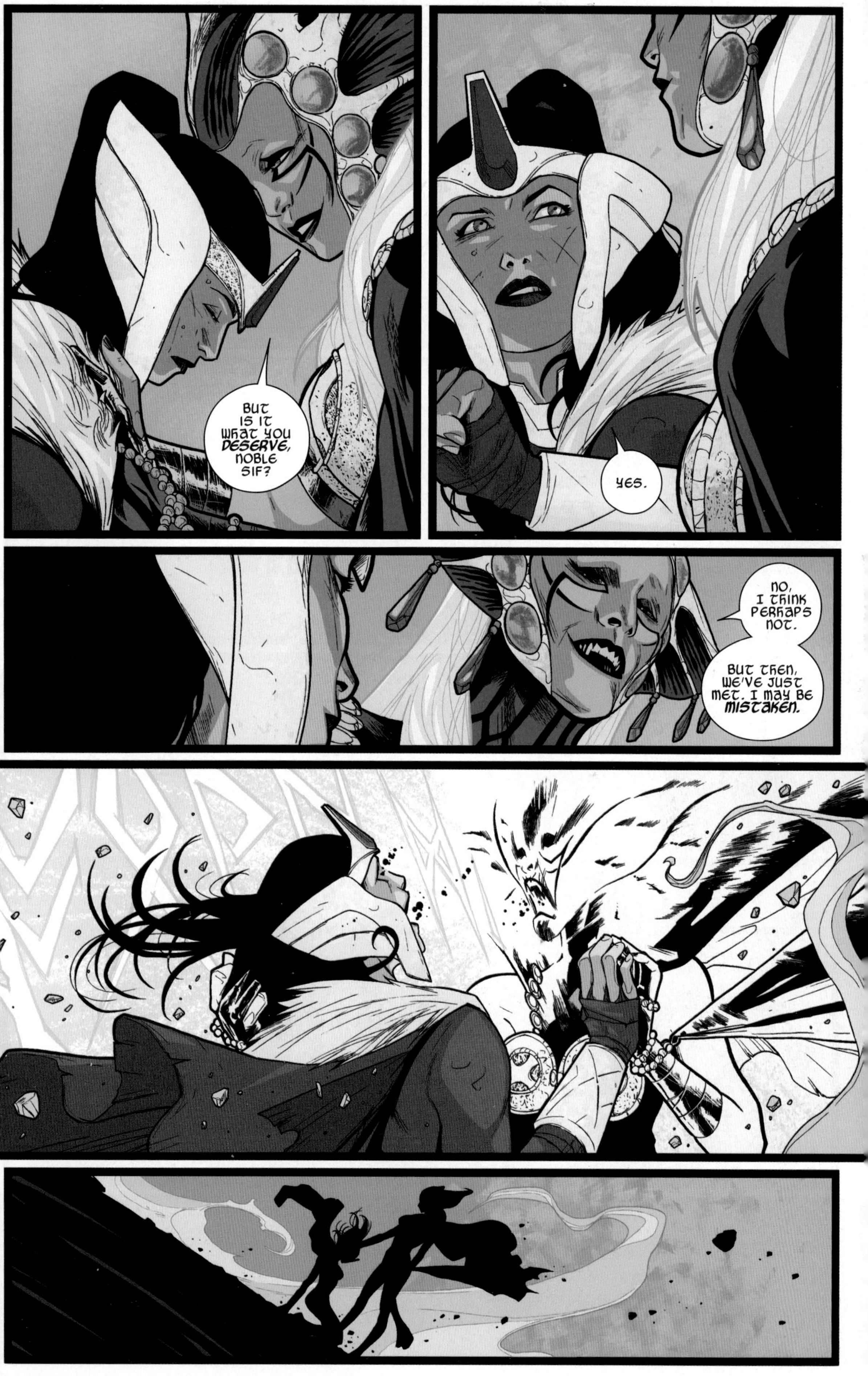

BUT IS IT WHAT YOU DESERVE, NOBLE SIF?
YES.
NO, I THINK PERHAPS NOT.
BUT THEN, WE'VE JUST MET. I MAY BE MISTAKEN.

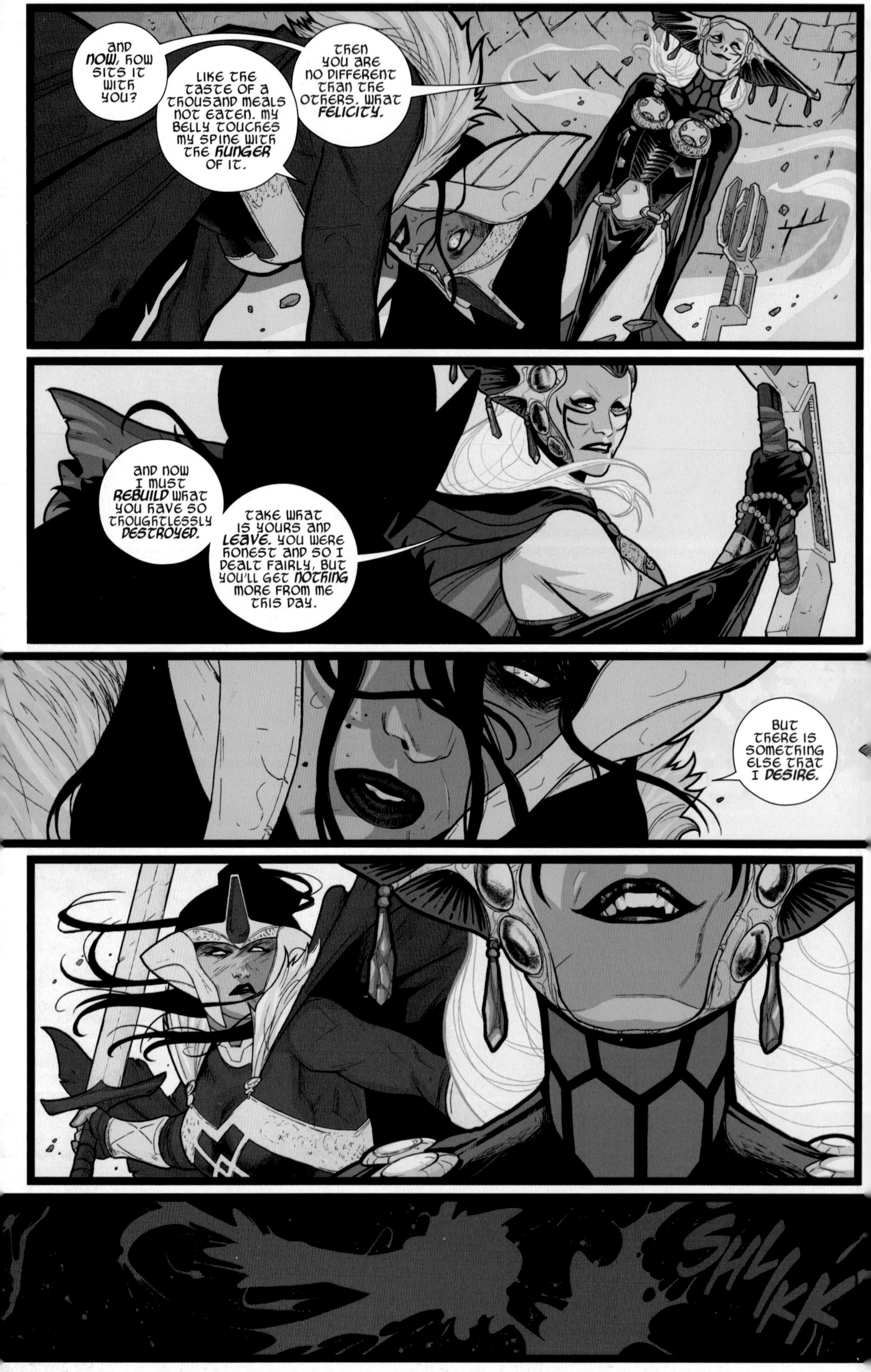

AND NOW, HOW SITS IT WITH YOU?
LIKE THE TASTE OF A THOUSAND MEALS NOT EATEN. MY BELLY TOUCHES MY SPINE WITH THE HUNGER OF IT.
THEN YOU ARE NO DIFFERENT THAN THE OTHERS. WHAT FELICITY.
AND NOW I MUST REBUILD WHAT YOU HAVE SO THOUGHTLESSLY DESTROYED.
TAKE WHAT IS YOURS AND LEAVE. YOU WERE HONEST AND SO I DEALT FAIRLY, BUT YOU'LL GET NOTHING MORE FROM ME THIS DAY.
BUT THERE IS SOMETHING ELSE THAT I DESIRE.
SHLIKK

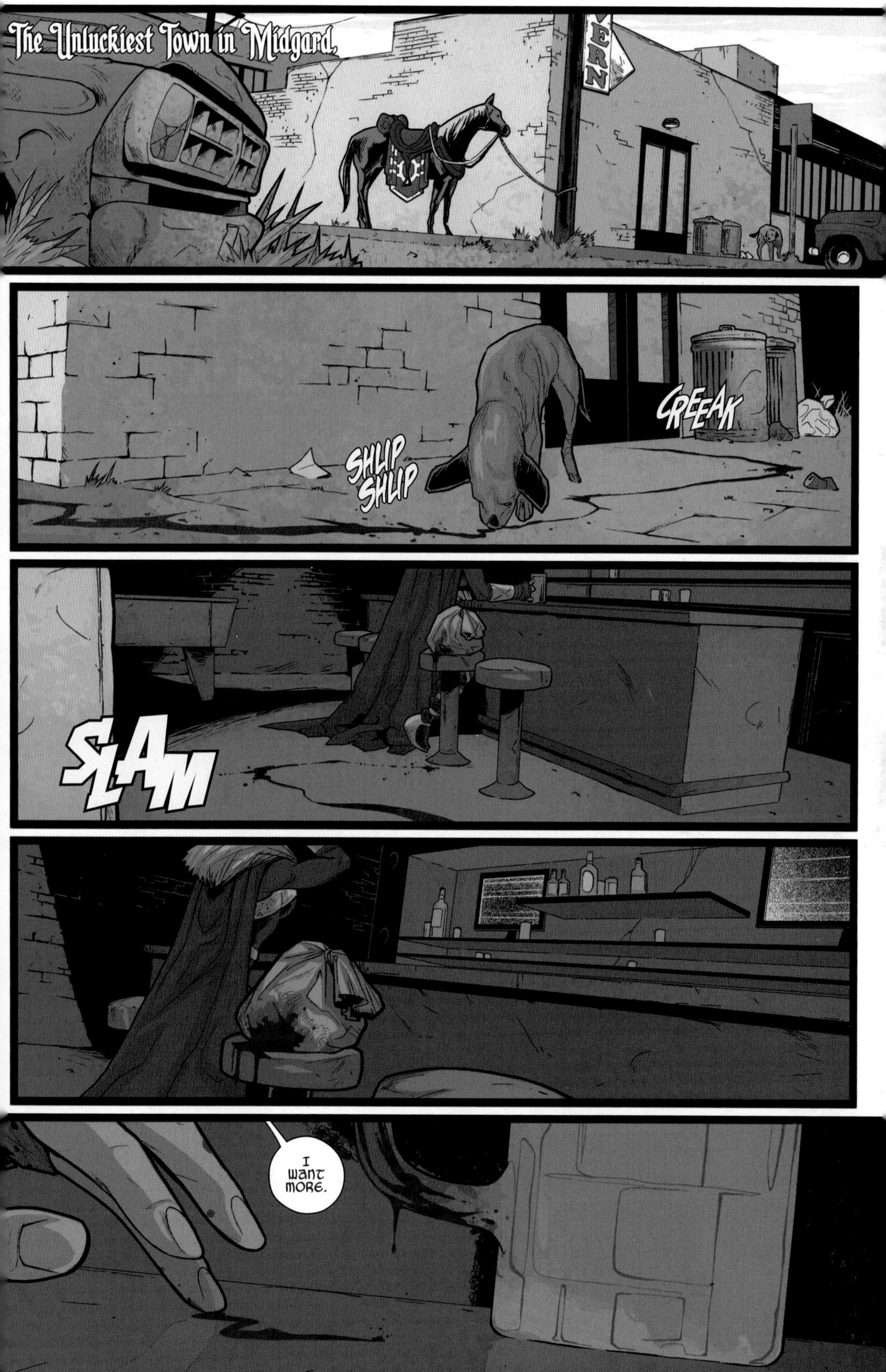
The Unluckiest Town in Midgard,
VERN
SHLIP SHLIP
CREEAK
SLAM
I WANT MORE.

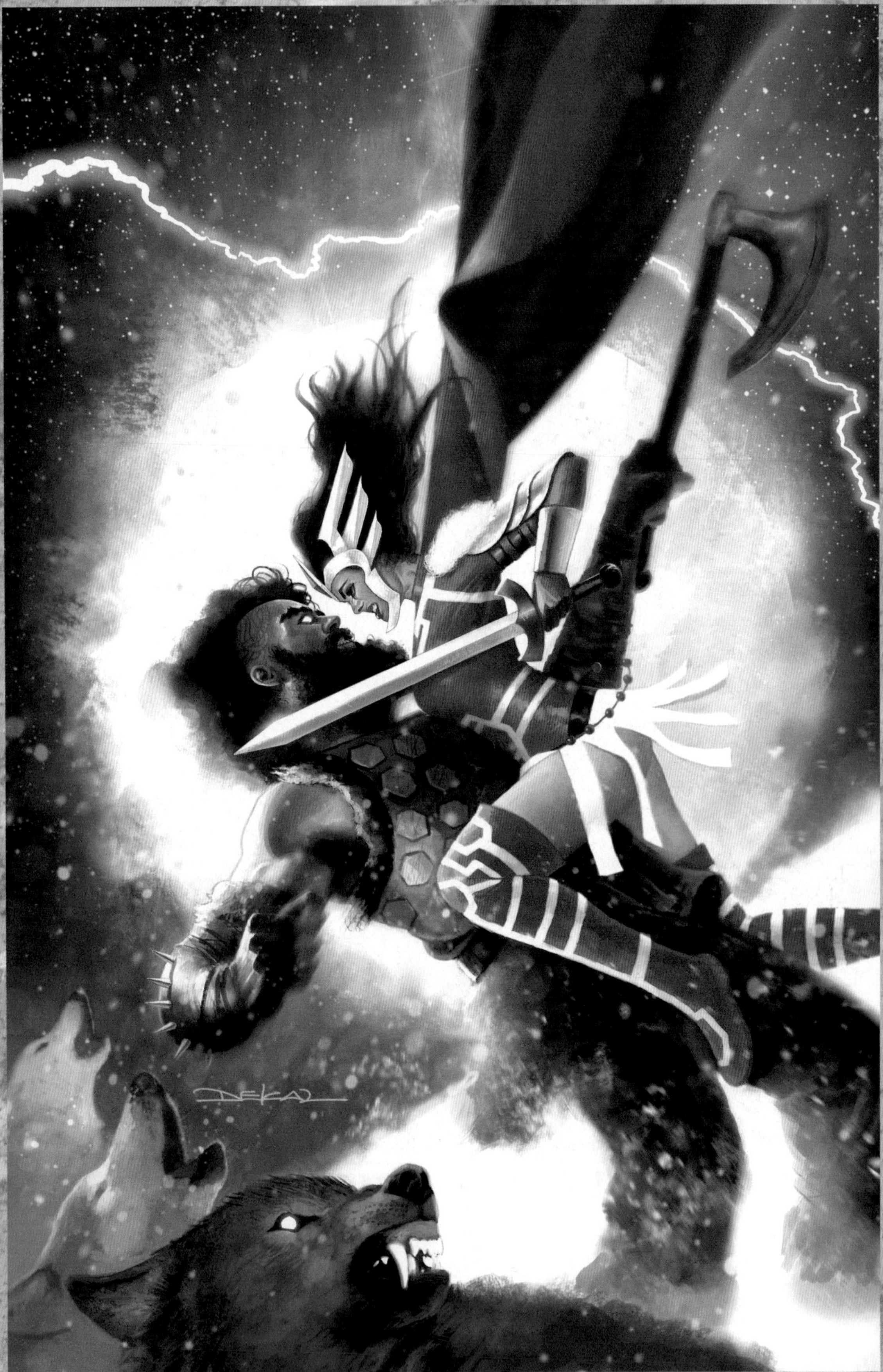

#647

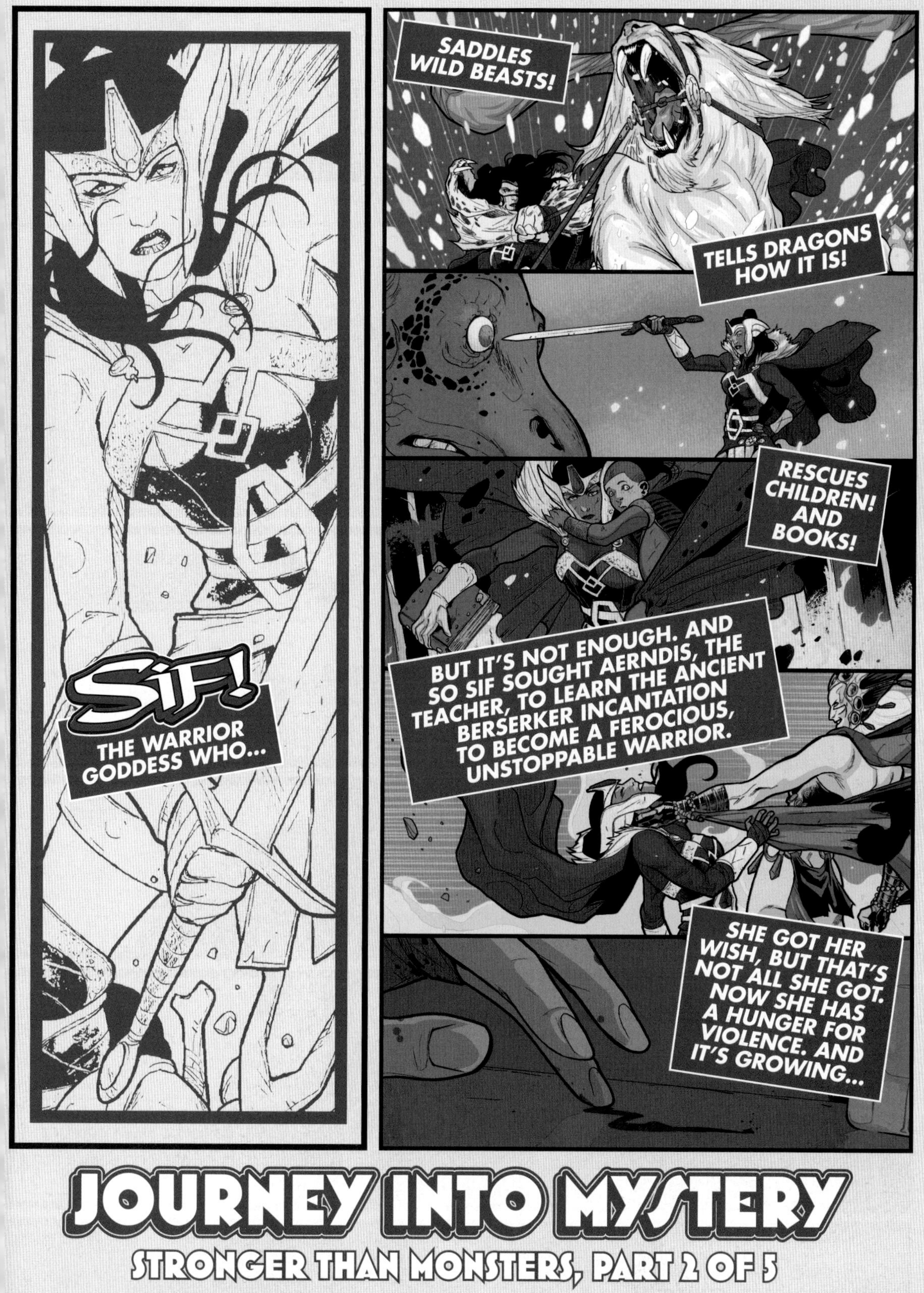
SIF!
THE WARRIOR GODDESS WHO...
SADDLES WILD BEASTS!
TELLS DRAGONS HOW IT IS!
RESCUES CHILDREN! AND BOOKS!
BUT IT'S NOT ENOUGH. AND SO SIF SOUGHT AERNDIS, THE TEACHER, TO LEARN THE ANCIENT BERSERKER INCANTATION TO BECOME A FEROCIOUS, UNSTOPPABLE WARRIOR.
SHE GOT HER WISH, BUT THAT'S NOT ALL SHE GOT. NOW SHE HAS A HUNGER FOR VIOLENCE. AND IT'S GROWING...

JOURNEY INTO MYSTERY

STRONGER THAN MONSTERS, PART 2 OF 5

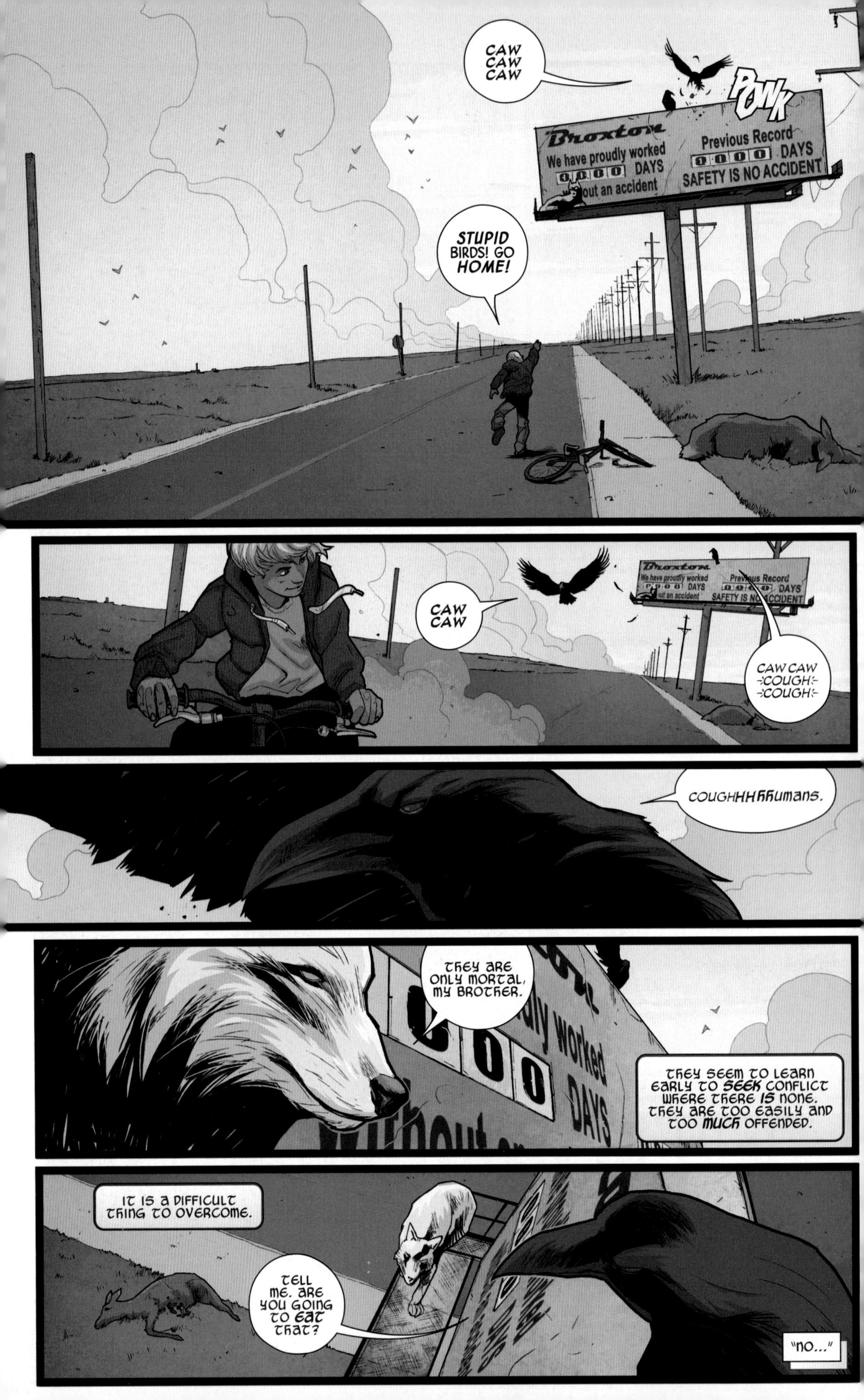
CAW
CAW
CAW
POWK
Broxton
We have proudly worked
DAYS
out an accident
Previous Record
DAYS
SAFETY IS NO ACCIDENT
STUPID BIRDS! GO HOME!
CAW
CAW
CAW CAW
-COUGH-
-COUGH-
COUGHHHHhumans.
THEY ARE ONLY MORTAL, MY BROTHER.
THEY SEEM TO LEARN EARLY TO SEEK CONFLICT WHERE THERE IS NONE. THEY ARE TOO EASILY AND TOO MUCH OFFENDED.
IT IS A DIFFICULT THING TO OVERCOME.
TELL ME. ARE YOU GOING TO EAT THAT?
"NO..."

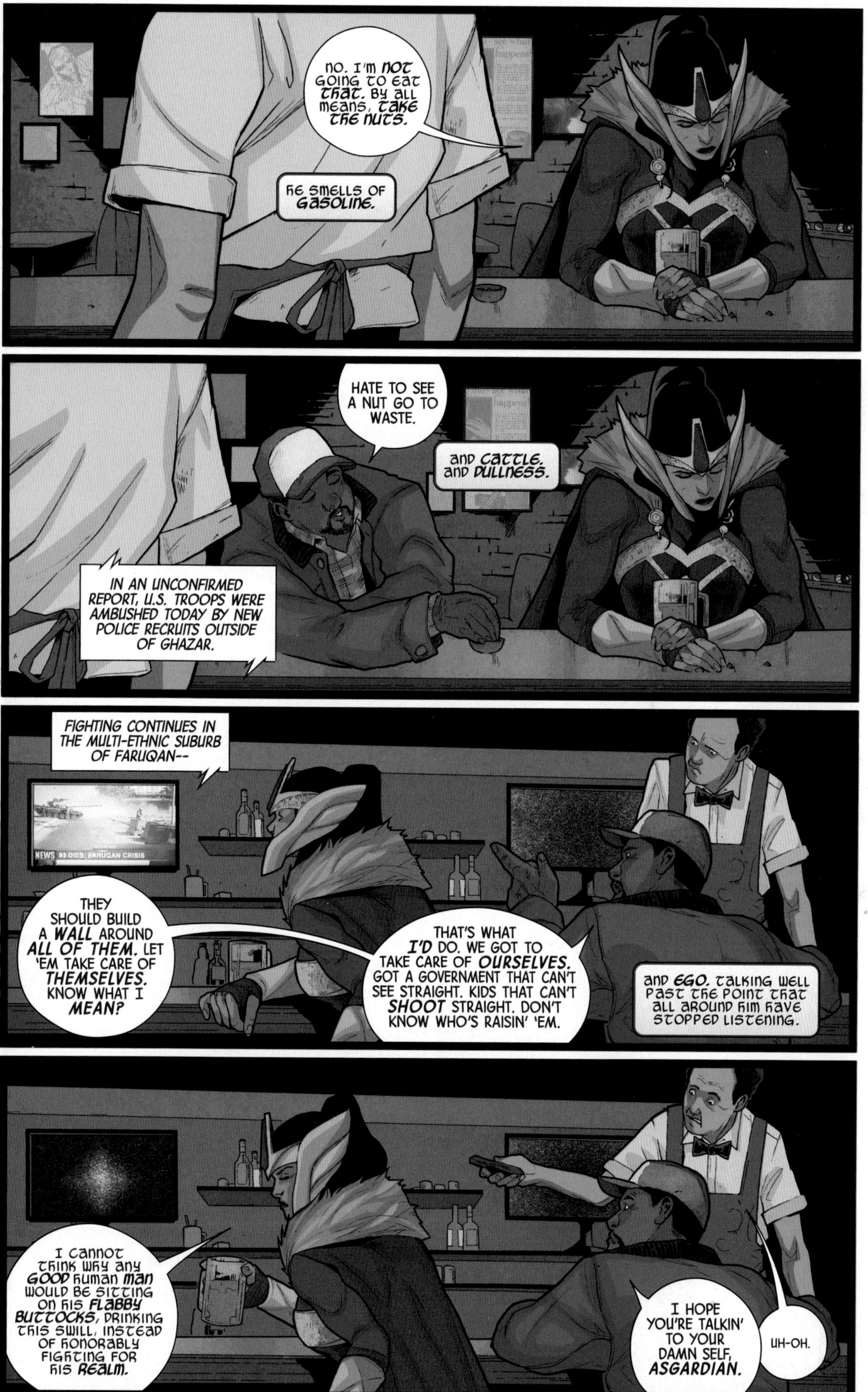
NO. I'M NOT GOING TO EAT THAT. BY ALL MEANS, TAKE THE NUTS.
HE SMELLS OF GASOLINE.
HATE TO SEE A NUT GO TO WASTE.
AND CATTLE. AND DULLNESS.
IN AN UNCONFIRMED REPORT, U.S. TROOPS WERE AMBUSHED TODAY BY NEW POLICE RECRUITS OUTSIDE OF GHAZAR.
FIGHTING CONTINUES IN THE MULTI-ETHNIC SUBURB OF FARUQAN--
NEWS 93 DIES: FARUQAN CRISIS
THEY SHOULD BUILD A WALL AROUND ALL OF THEM. LET 'EM TAKE CARE OF THEMSELVES. KNOW WHAT I MEAN?
THAT'S WHAT I'D DO. WE GOT TO TAKE CARE OF OURSELVES. GOT A GOVERNMENT THAT CAN'T SEE STRAIGHT. KIDS THAT CAN'T SHOOT STRAIGHT. DON'T KNOW WHO'S RAISIN' 'EM.
AND EGO. TALKING WELL PAST THE POINT THAT ALL AROUND HIM HAVE STOPPED LISTENING.
I CANNOT THINK WHY ANY GOOD HUMAN MAN WOULD BE SITTING ON HIS FLABBY BUTTOCKS, DRINKING THIS SWILL, INSTEAD OF HONORABLY FIGHTING FOR HIS REALM.
I HOPE YOU'RE TALKIN' TO YOUR DAMN SELF, ASGARDIAN.
UH-OH.

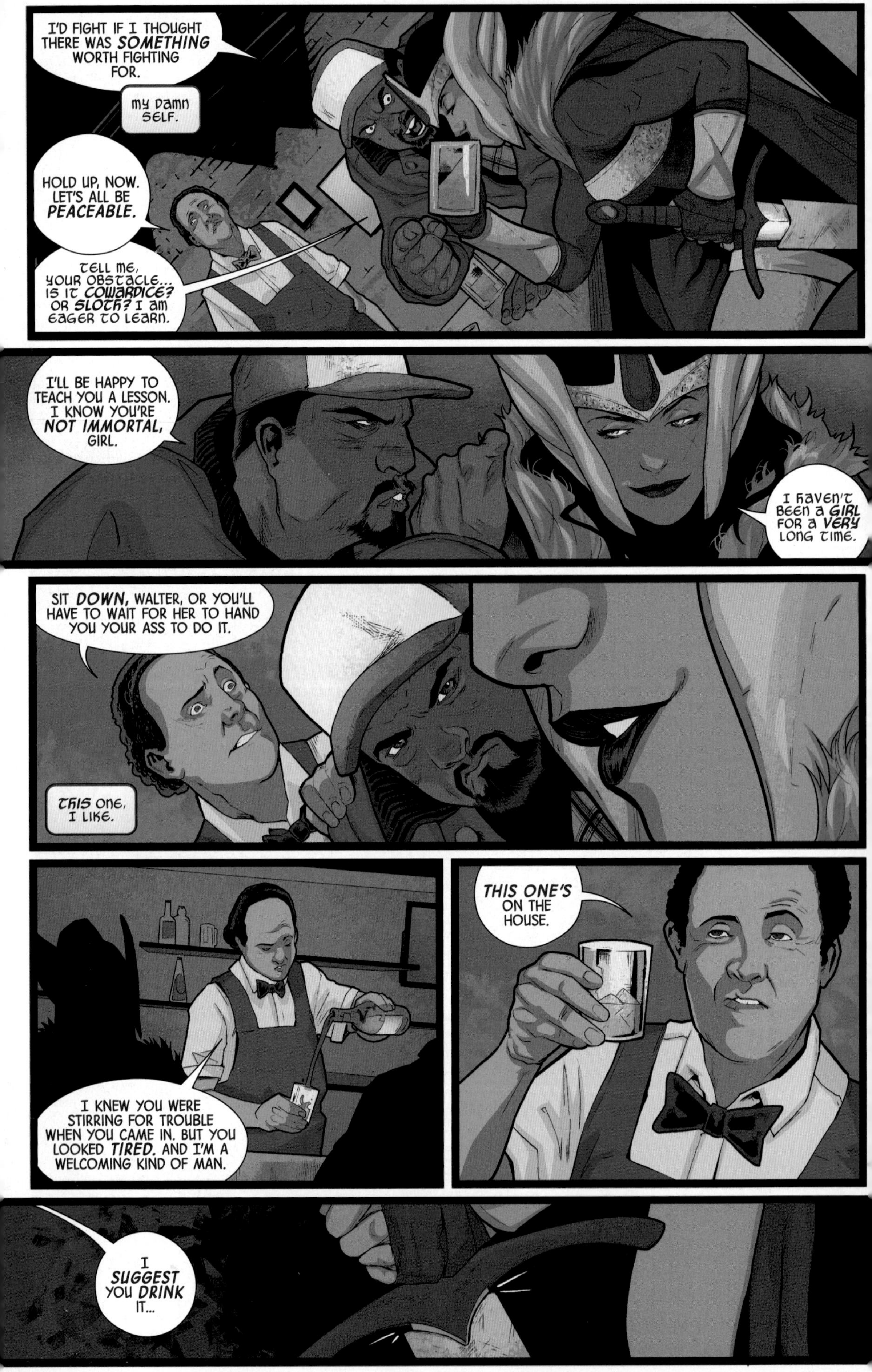

I'D FIGHT IF I THOUGHT THERE WAS SOMETHING WORTH FIGHTING FOR.
MY DAMN SELF.
HOLD UP, NOW. LET'S ALL BE PEACEABLE.
TELL ME, YOUR OBSTACLE... IS IT COWARDICE? OR SLOTH? I AM EAGER TO LEARN.
I'LL BE HAPPY TO TEACH YOU A LESSON. I KNOW YOU'RE NOT IMMORTAL, GIRL.
I HAVEN'T BEEN A GIRL FOR A VERY LONG TIME.
SIT DOWN, WALTER, OR YOU'LL HAVE TO WAIT FOR HER TO HAND YOU YOUR ASS TO DO IT.
THIS ONE, I LIKE.
I KNEW YOU WERE STIRRING FOR TROUBLE WHEN YOU CAME IN. BUT YOU LOOKED TIRED. AND I'M A WELCOMING KIND OF MAN.
THIS ONE'S ON THE HOUSE.
I SUGGEST YOU DRINK IT...

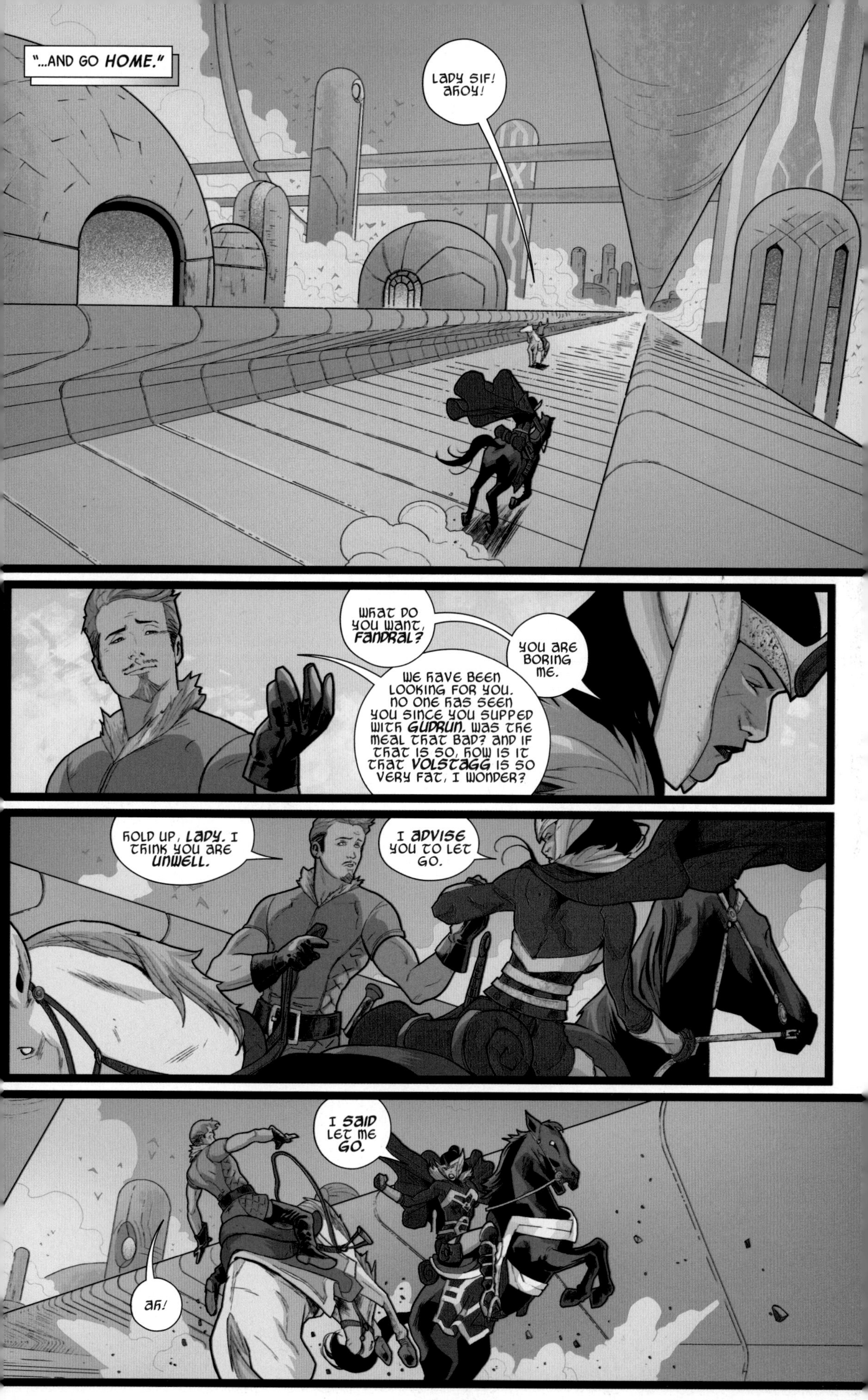
"...AND GO HOME."
LADY SIF! AHOY!
WHAT DO YOU WANT, FANDRAL?
YOU ARE BORING ME.
WE HAVE BEEN LOOKING FOR YOU. NO ONE HAS SEEN YOU SINCE YOU SUPPED WITH GUDRUN. WAS THE MEAL THAT BAD? AND IF THAT IS SO, HOW IS IT THAT VOLSTAGG IS SO VERY FAT, I WONDER?
HOLD UP, LADY. I THINK YOU ARE UNWELL.
I ADVISE YOU TO LET GO.
I SAID LET ME GO.
AH!

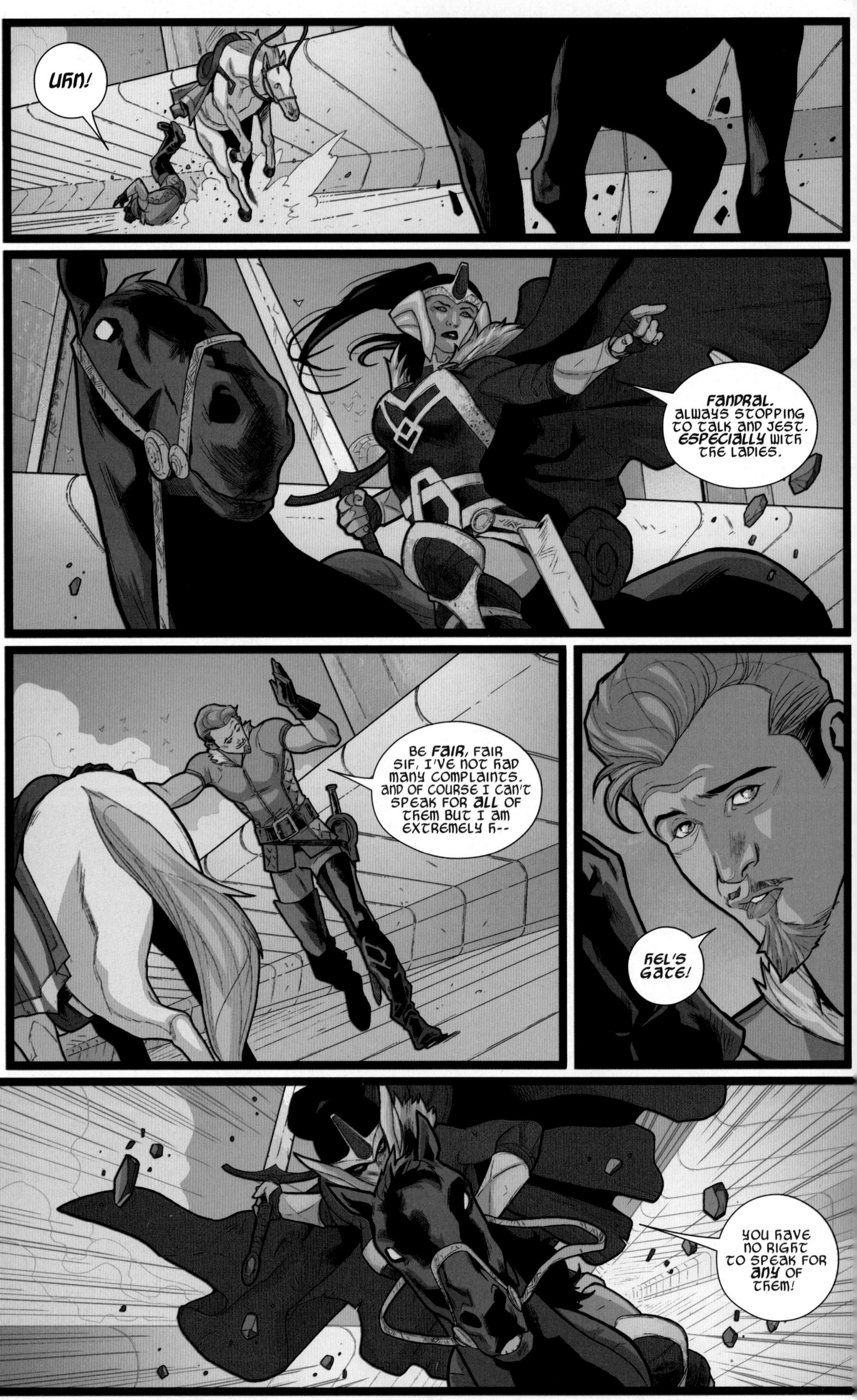
UHN!
FANDRAL. ALWAYS STOPPING TO TALK AND JEST. ESPECIALLY WITH THE LADIES.
BE FAIR, FAIR SIF, I'VE NOT HAD MANY COMPLAINTS. AND OF COURSE I CAN'T SPEAK FOR ALL OF THEM BUT I AM EXTREMELY H--
HEL'S GATE!
YOU HAVE NO RIGHT TO SPEAK FOR ANY OF THEM!

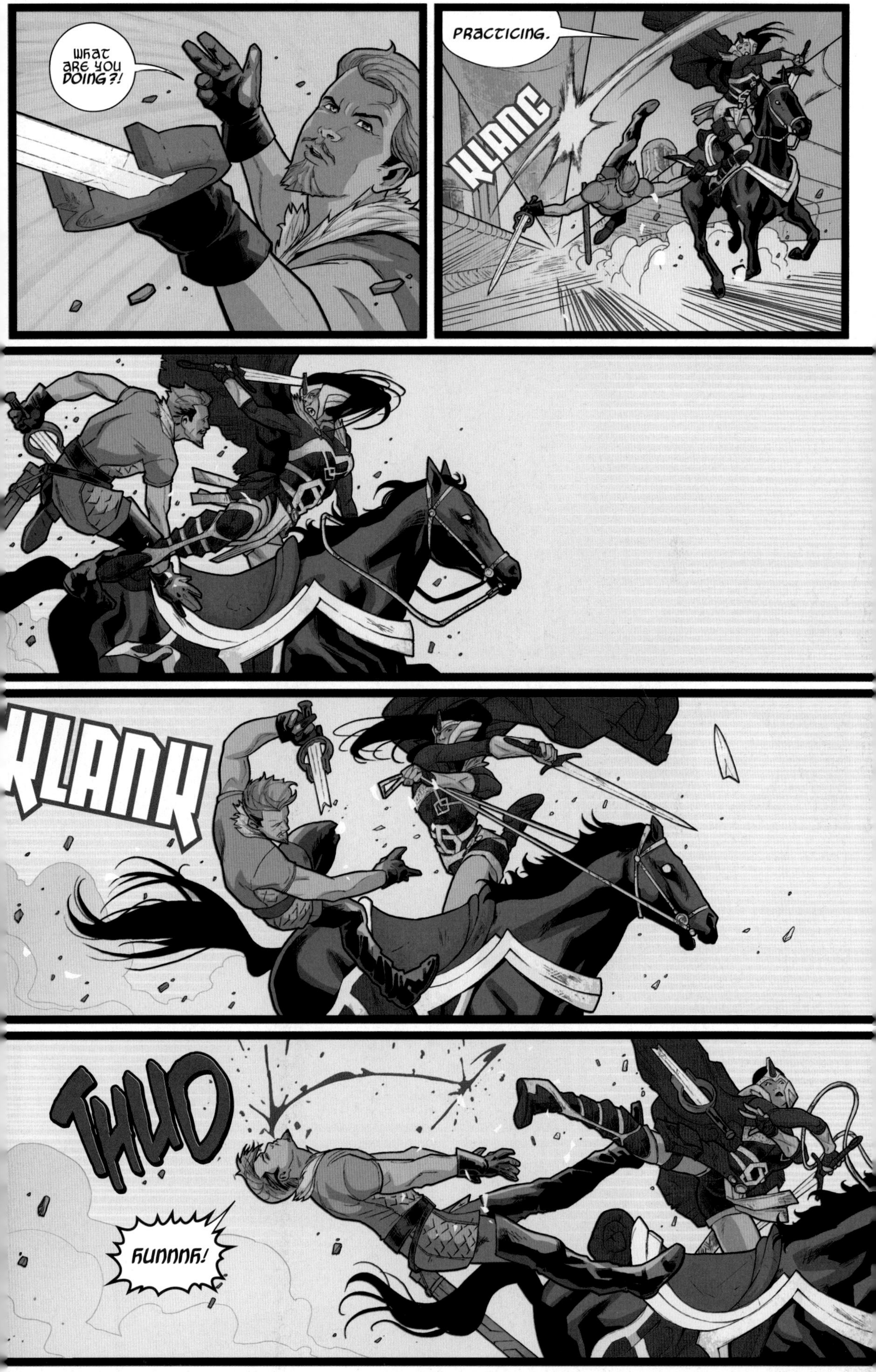
WHAT ARE YOU DOING?!
PRACTICING.
KLANG
KLANK
THUD
HUNNNH!

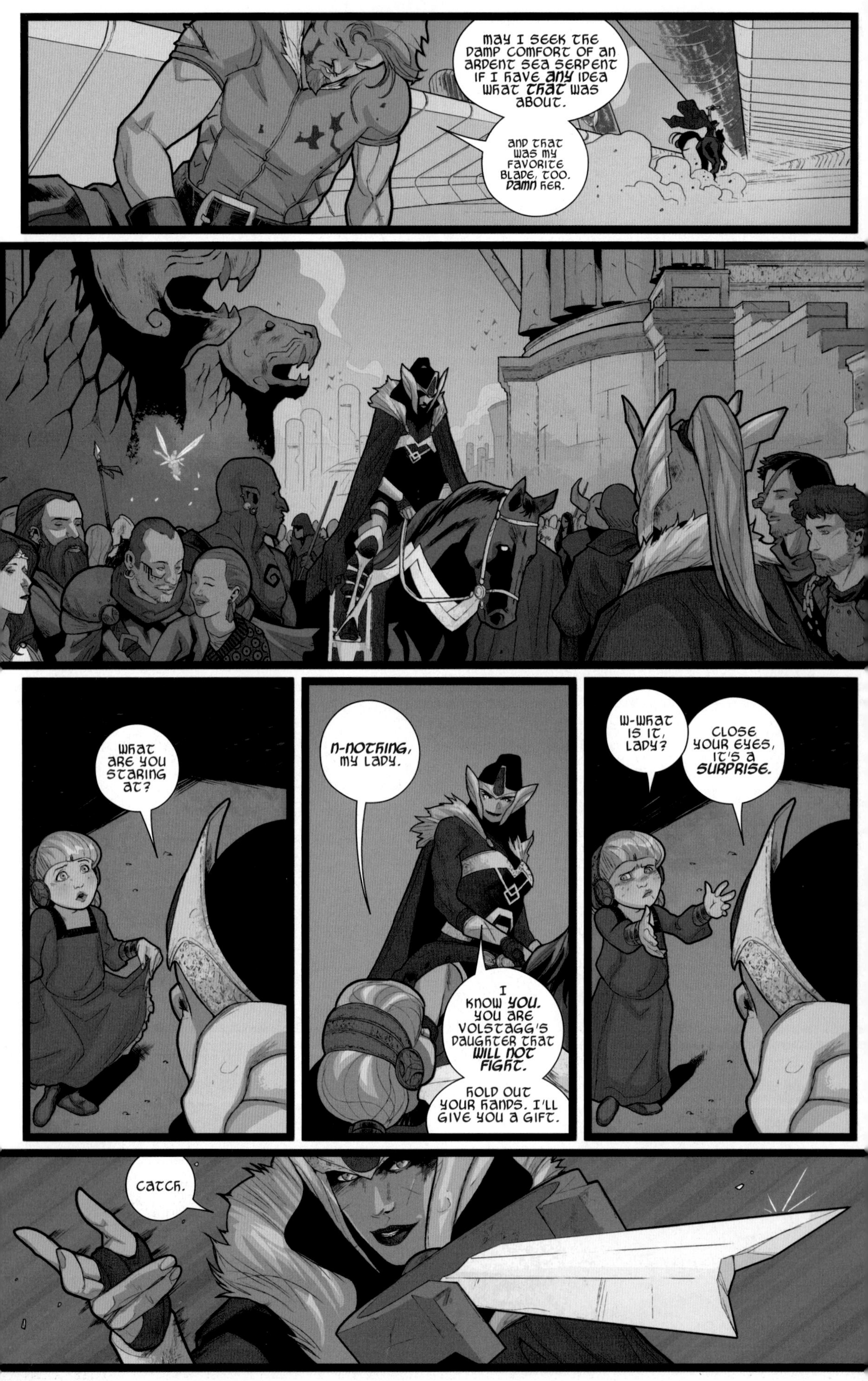
MAY I SEEK THE DAMP COMFORT OF AN ARDENT SEA SERPENT IF I HAVE ANY IDEA WHAT THAT WAS ABOUT.
AND THAT WAS MY FAVORITE BLADE, TOO. DAMN HER.
WHAT ARE YOU STARING AT?
N-NOTHING, MY LADY.
I KNOW YOU. YOU ARE VOLSTAGG'S DAUGHTER THAT WILL NOT FIGHT.
HOLD OUT YOUR HANDS. I'LL GIVE YOU A GIFT.
W-WHAT IS IT, LADY?
CLOSE YOUR EYES, IT'S A SURPRISE.
CATCH.

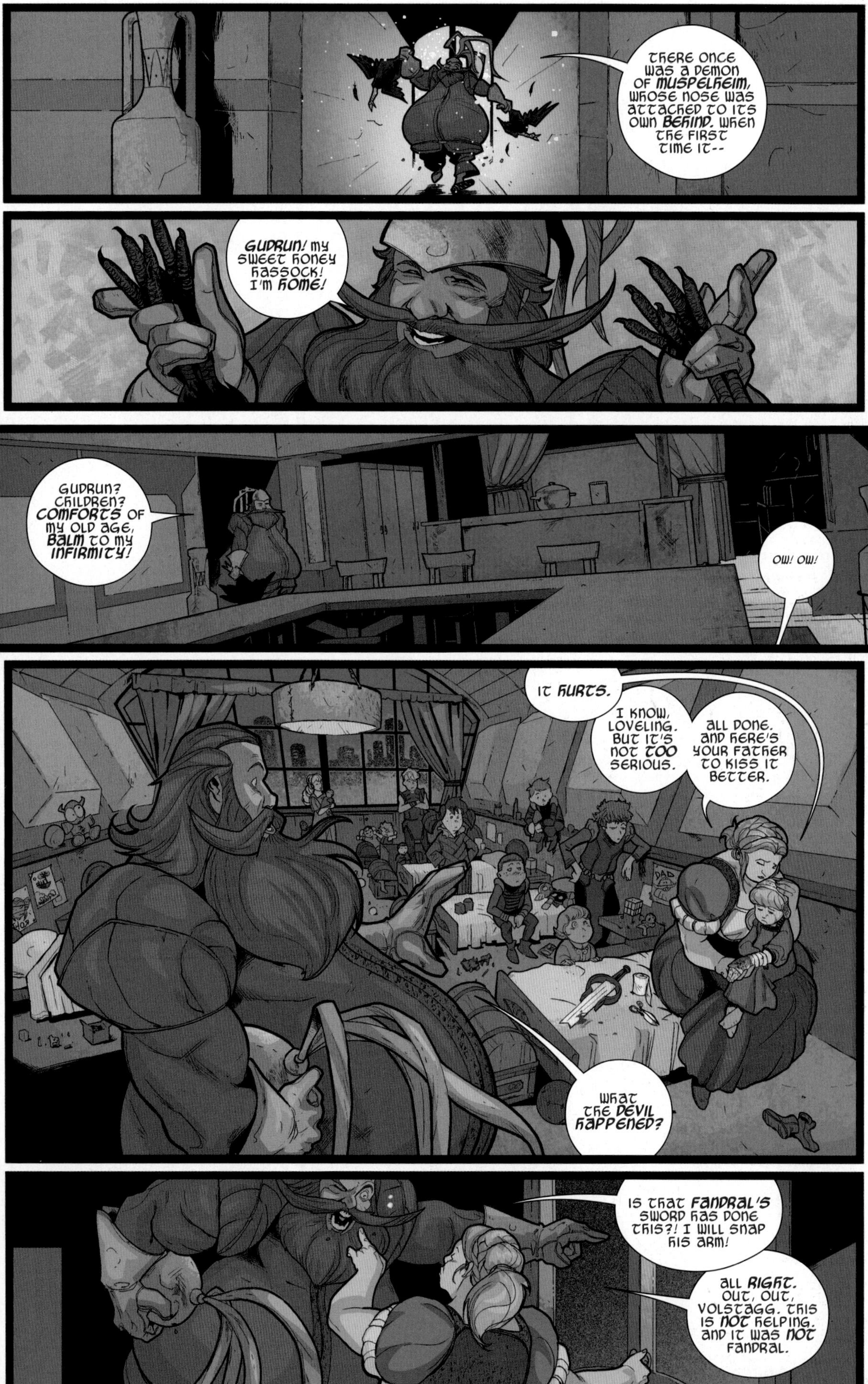
THERE ONCE WAS A DEMON OF MUSPELHEIM, WHOSE NOSE WAS ATTACHED TO ITS OWN BEHIND. WHEN THE FIRST TIME IT--
GUDRUN! MY SWEET HONEY HASSOCK! I'M HOME!
GUDRUN? CHILDREN? COMFORTS OF MY OLD AGE, BALM TO MY INFIRMITY!
OW! OW!
IT HURTS.
I KNOW, LOVELING. BUT IT'S NOT TOO SERIOUS.
ALL DONE. AND HERE'S YOUR FATHER TO KISS IT BETTER.
DAD
WHAT THE DEVIL HAPPENED?
IS THAT FANDRAL'S SWORD HAS DONE THIS?! I WILL SNAP HIS ARM!
ALL RIGHT. OUT, OUT, VOLSTAGG. THIS IS NOT HELPING. AND IT WAS NOT FANDRAL.

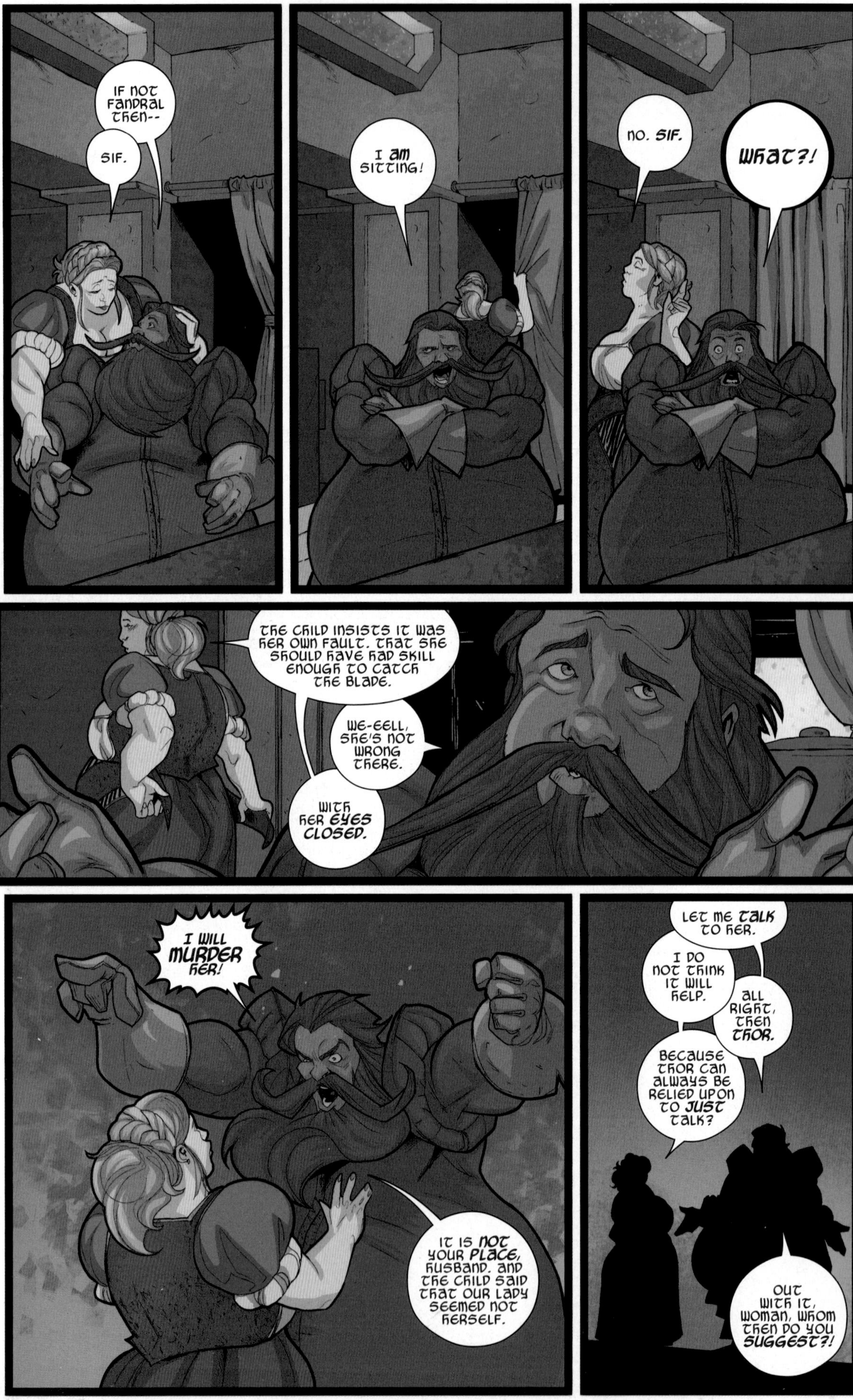
IF NOT FANDRAL THEN--
SIF.
I AM SITTING!
NO. SIF.
WHAT?!
THE CHILD INSISTS IT WAS HER OWN FAULT. THAT SHE SHOULD HAVE HAD SKILL ENOUGH TO CATCH THE BLADE.
WE-EELL, SHE'S NOT WRONG THERE.
WITH HER EYES CLOSED.
I WILL MURDER HER!
IT IS NOT YOUR PLACE, HUSBAND. AND THE CHILD SAID THAT OUR LADY SEEMED NOT HERSELF.
LET ME TALK TO HER.
I DO NOT THINK IT WILL HELP.
ALL RIGHT, THEN THOR.
BECAUSE THOR CAN ALWAYS BE RELIED UPON TO JUST TALK?
OUT WITH IT, WOMAN, WHOM THEN DO YOU SUGGEST?!

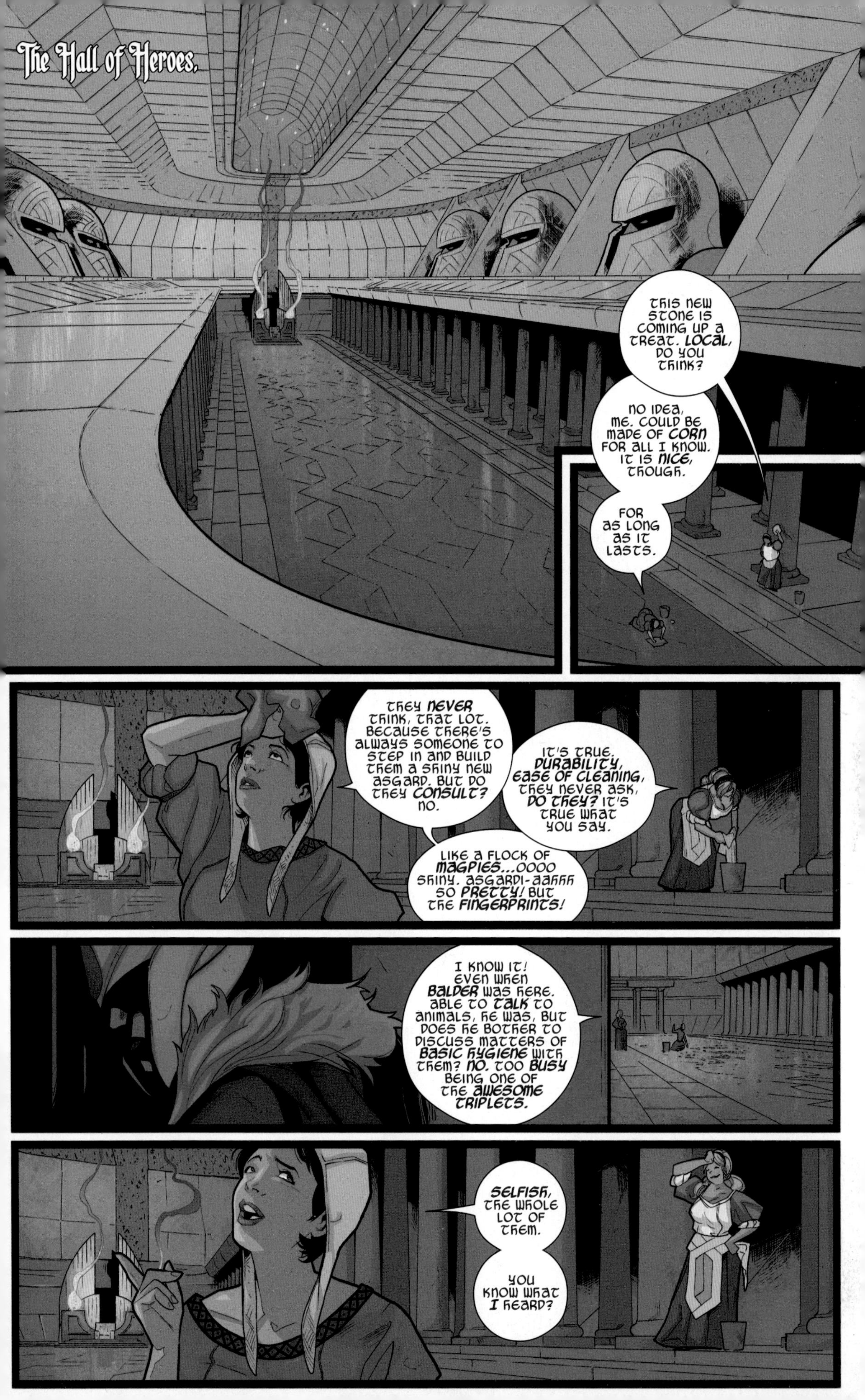
The Hall of Heroes.
THIS NEW STONE IS COMING UP A TREAT. LOCAL, DO YOU THINK?
NO IDEA, ME. COULD BE MADE OF CORN FOR ALL I KNOW. IT IS NICE, THOUGH.
FOR AS LONG AS IT LASTS.
THEY NEVER THINK, THAT LOT. BECAUSE THERE'S ALWAYS SOMEONE TO STEP IN AND BUILD THEM A SHINY NEW ASGARD. BUT DO THEY CONSULT? NO.
IT'S TRUE. DURABILITY, EASE OF CLEANING, THEY NEVER ASK, DO THEY? IT'S TRUE WHAT YOU SAY.
LIKE A FLOCK OF MAGPIES...OOOO SHINY. ASGARDI-AAHHH SO PRETTY! BUT THE FINGERPRINTS!
I KNOW IT! EVEN WHEN BALDER WAS HERE. ABLE TO TALK TO ANIMALS, HE WAS, BUT DOES HE BOTHER TO DISCUSS MATTERS OF BASIC HYGIENE WITH THEM? NO. TOO BUSY BEING ONE OF THE AWESOME TRIPLETS.
SELFISH, THE WHOLE LOT OF THEM.
YOU KNOW WHAT I HEARD?

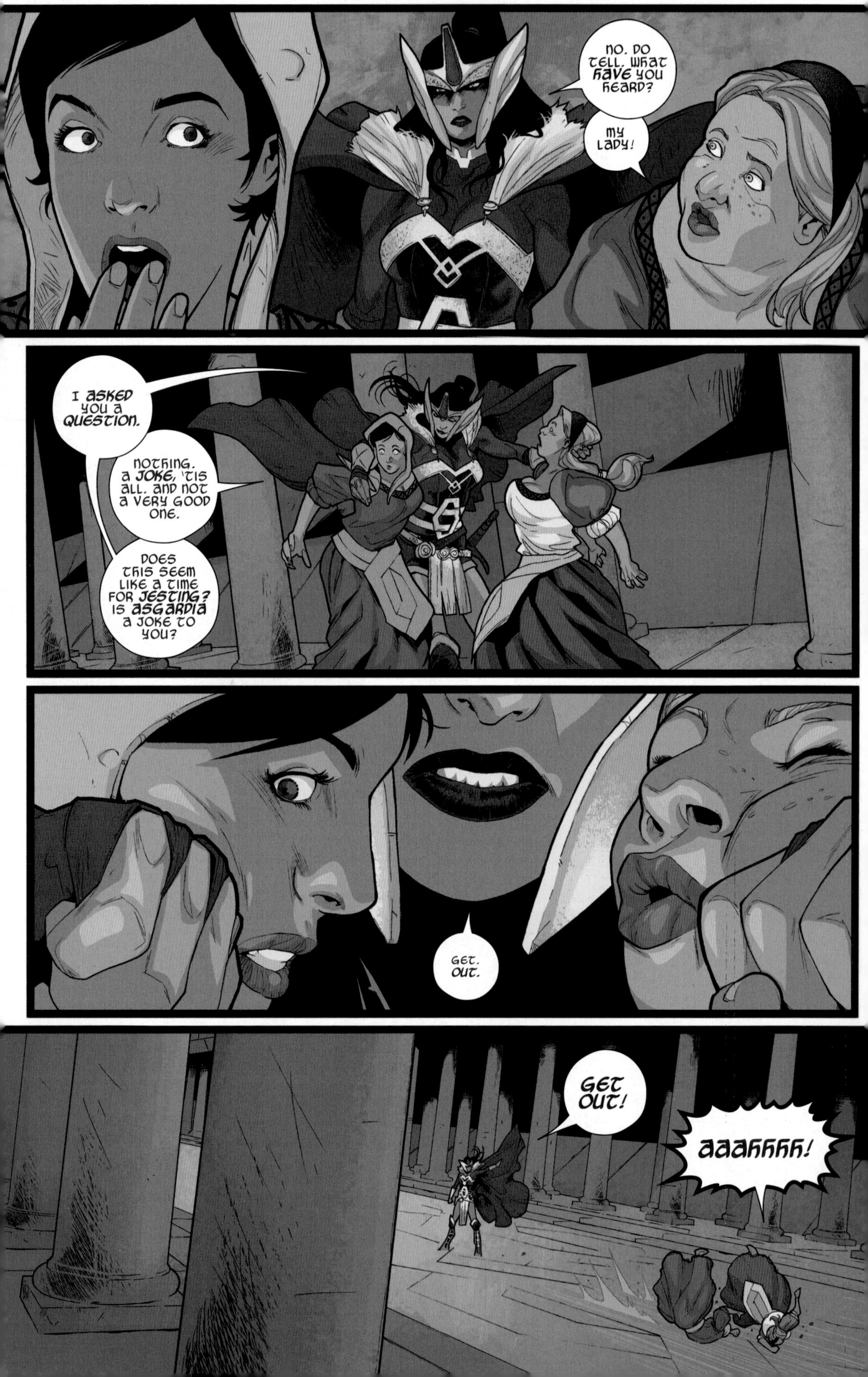
NO. DO TELL. WHAT HAVE YOU HEARD?
MY LADY!
I ASKED YOU A QUESTION.
NOTHING. A JOKE, 'TIS ALL. AND NOT A VERY GOOD ONE.
DOES THIS SEEM LIKE A TIME FOR JESTING? IS ASGARDIA A JOKE TO YOU?
GET. OUT.
GET OUT!
AAAHHHH!

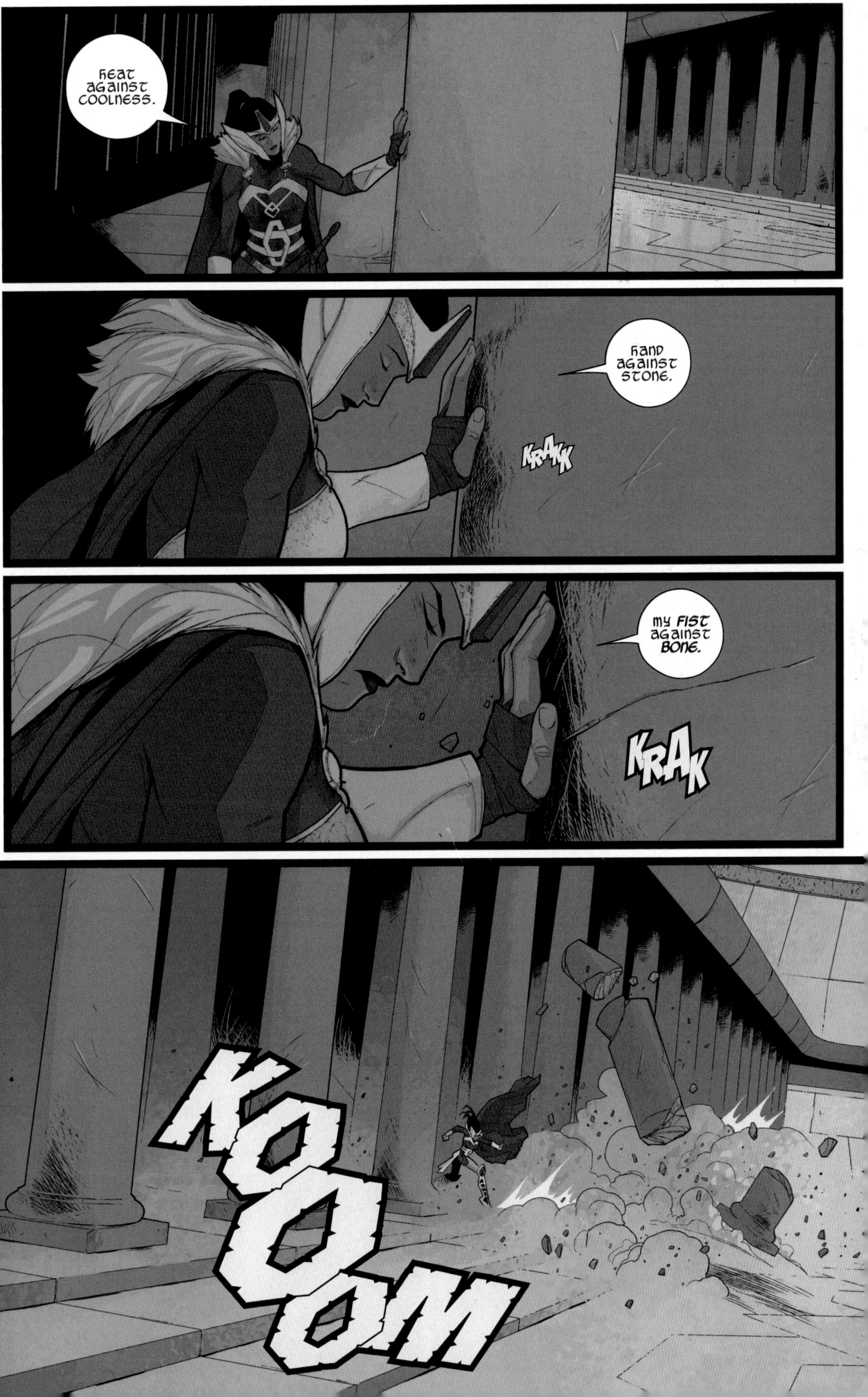
HEAT AGAINST COOLNESS.
HAND AGAINST STONE.
KRAKK
MY FIST AGAINST BONE.
KRAK
KOOOM

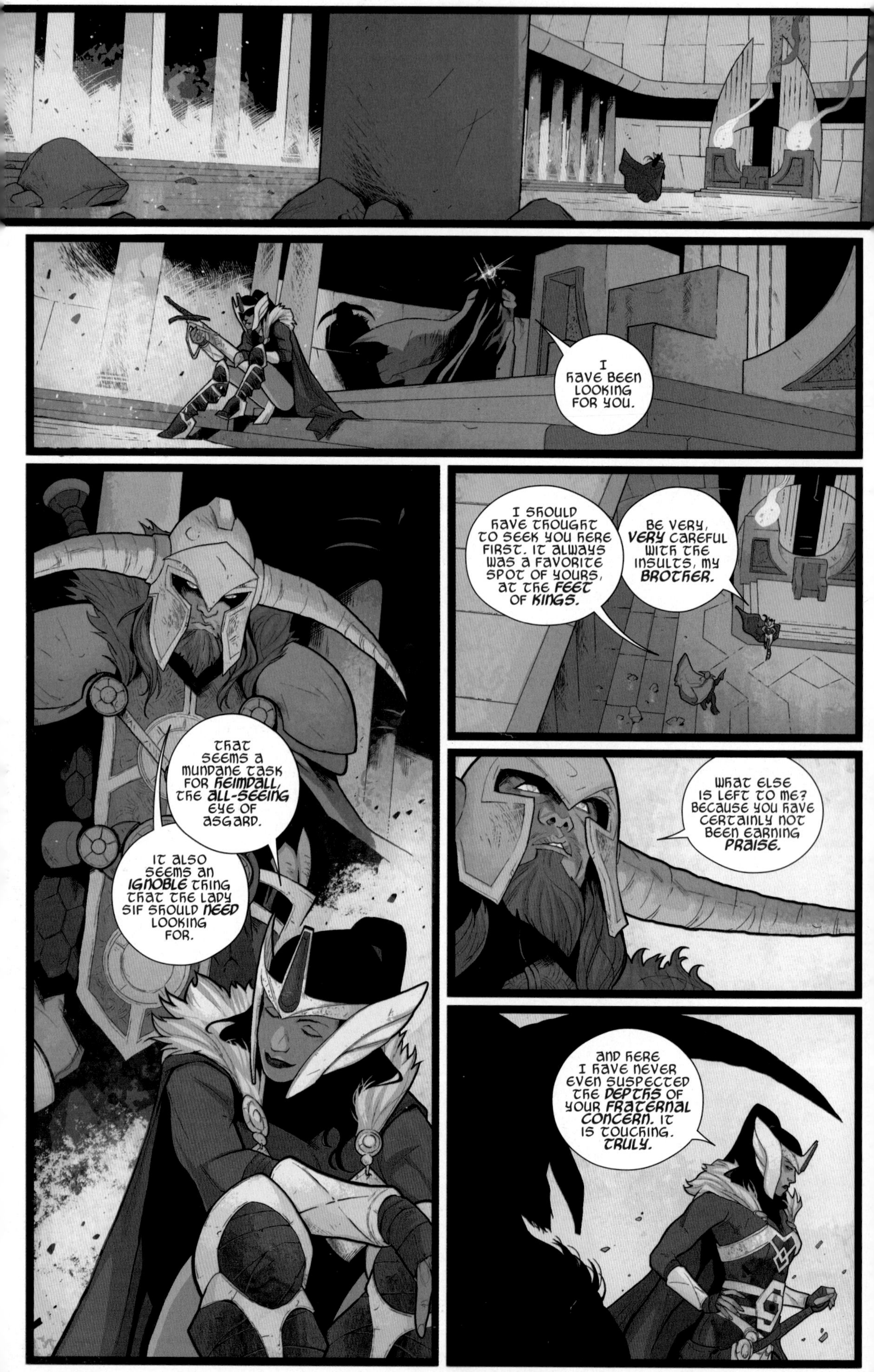
I HAVE BEEN LOOKING FOR YOU.
THAT SEEMS A MUNDANE TASK FOR HEIMDALL, THE ALL-SEEING EYE OF ASGARD.
IT ALSO SEEMS AN IGNOBLE THING THAT THE LADY SIF SHOULD NEED LOOKING FOR.
I SHOULD HAVE THOUGHT TO SEEK YOU HERE FIRST. IT ALWAYS WAS A FAVORITE SPOT OF YOURS, AT THE FEET OF KINGS.
BE VERY, VERY CAREFUL WITH THE INSULTS, MY BROTHER.
WHAT ELSE IS LEFT TO ME? BECAUSE YOU HAVE CERTAINLY NOT BEEN EARNING PRAISE.
AND HERE I HAVE NEVER EVEN SUSPECTED THE DEPTHS OF YOUR FRATERNAL CONCERN. IT IS TOUCHING. TRULY.

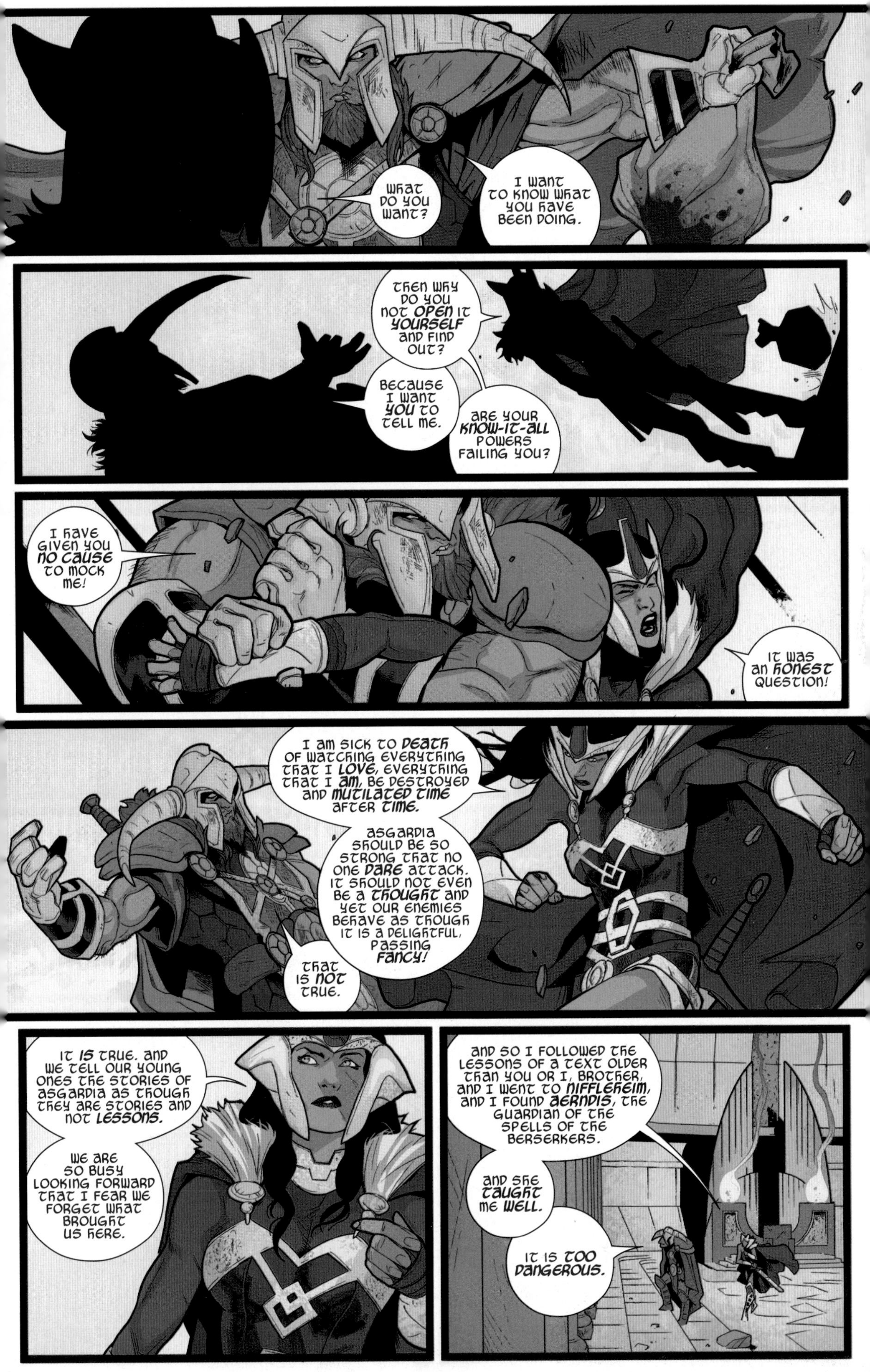
WHAT DO YOU WANT?
I WANT TO KNOW WHAT YOU HAVE BEEN DOING.
THEN WHY DO YOU NOT OPEN IT YOURSELF AND FIND OUT?
BECAUSE I WANT YOU TO TELL ME.
ARE YOUR KNOW-IT-ALL POWERS FAILING YOU?
I HAVE GIVEN YOU NO CAUSE TO MOCK ME!
IT WAS AN HONEST QUESTION!
I AM SICK TO DEATH OF WATCHING EVERYTHING THAT I LOVE, EVERYTHING THAT I AM, BE DESTROYED AND MUTILATED TIME AFTER TIME.
ASGARDIA SHOULD BE SO STRONG THAT NO ONE DARE ATTACK. IT SHOULD NOT EVEN BE A THOUGHT AND YET OUR ENEMIES BEHAVE AS THOUGH IT IS A DELIGHTFUL, PASSING FANCY!
THAT IS NOT TRUE.
IT IS TRUE. AND WE TELL OUR YOUNG ONES THE STORIES OF ASGARDIA AS THOUGH THEY ARE STORIES AND NOT LESSONS.
WE ARE SO BUSY LOOKING FORWARD THAT I FEAR WE FORGET WHAT BROUGHT US HERE.
AND SO I FOLLOWED THE LESSONS OF A TEXT OLDER THAN YOU OR I, BROTHER, AND I WENT TO NIFFLEHEIM, AND I FOUND AERNDIS, THE GUARDIAN OF THE SPELLS OF THE BERSERKERS.
AND SHE TAUGHT ME WELL.
IT IS TOO DANGEROUS.

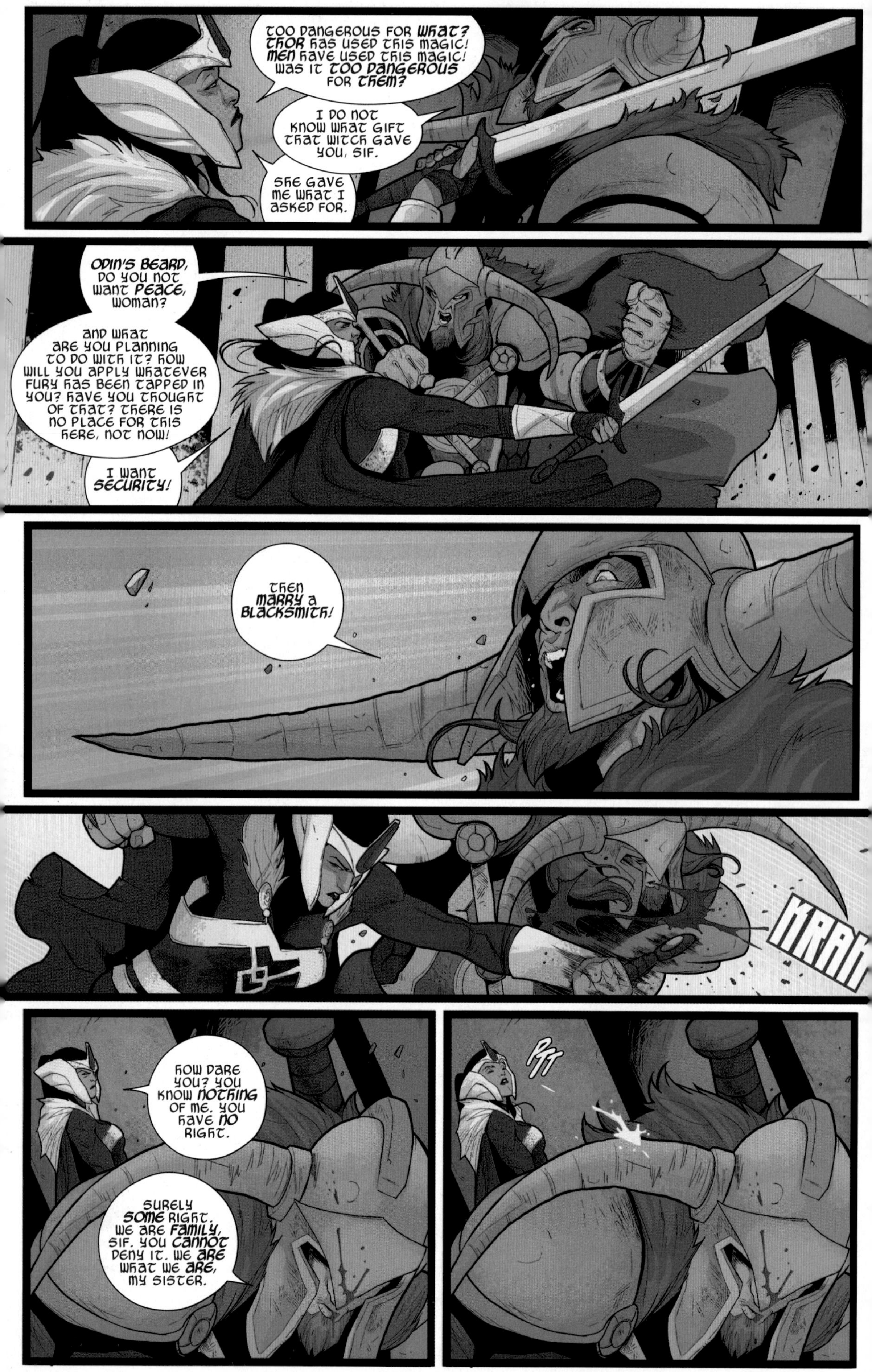

TOO DANGEROUS FOR WHAT? THOR HAS USED THIS MAGIC! MEN HAVE USED THIS MAGIC! WAS IT TOO DANGEROUS FOR THEM?
I DO NOT KNOW WHAT GIFT THAT WITCH GAVE YOU, SIF.
SHE GAVE ME WHAT I ASKED FOR.
ODIN'S BEARD, DO YOU NOT WANT PEACE, WOMAN?
AND WHAT ARE YOU PLANNING TO DO WITH IT? HOW WILL YOU APPLY WHATEVER FURY HAS BEEN TAPPED IN YOU? HAVE YOU THOUGHT OF THAT? THERE IS NO PLACE FOR THIS HERE, NOT NOW!
I WANT SECURITY!
THEN MARRY A BLACKSMITH!
KRAK
HOW DARE YOU? YOU KNOW NOTHING OF ME. YOU HAVE NO RIGHT.
SURELY SOME RIGHT. WE ARE FAMILY, SIF. YOU CANNOT DENY IT. WE ARE WHAT WE ARE, MY SISTER.
PTT

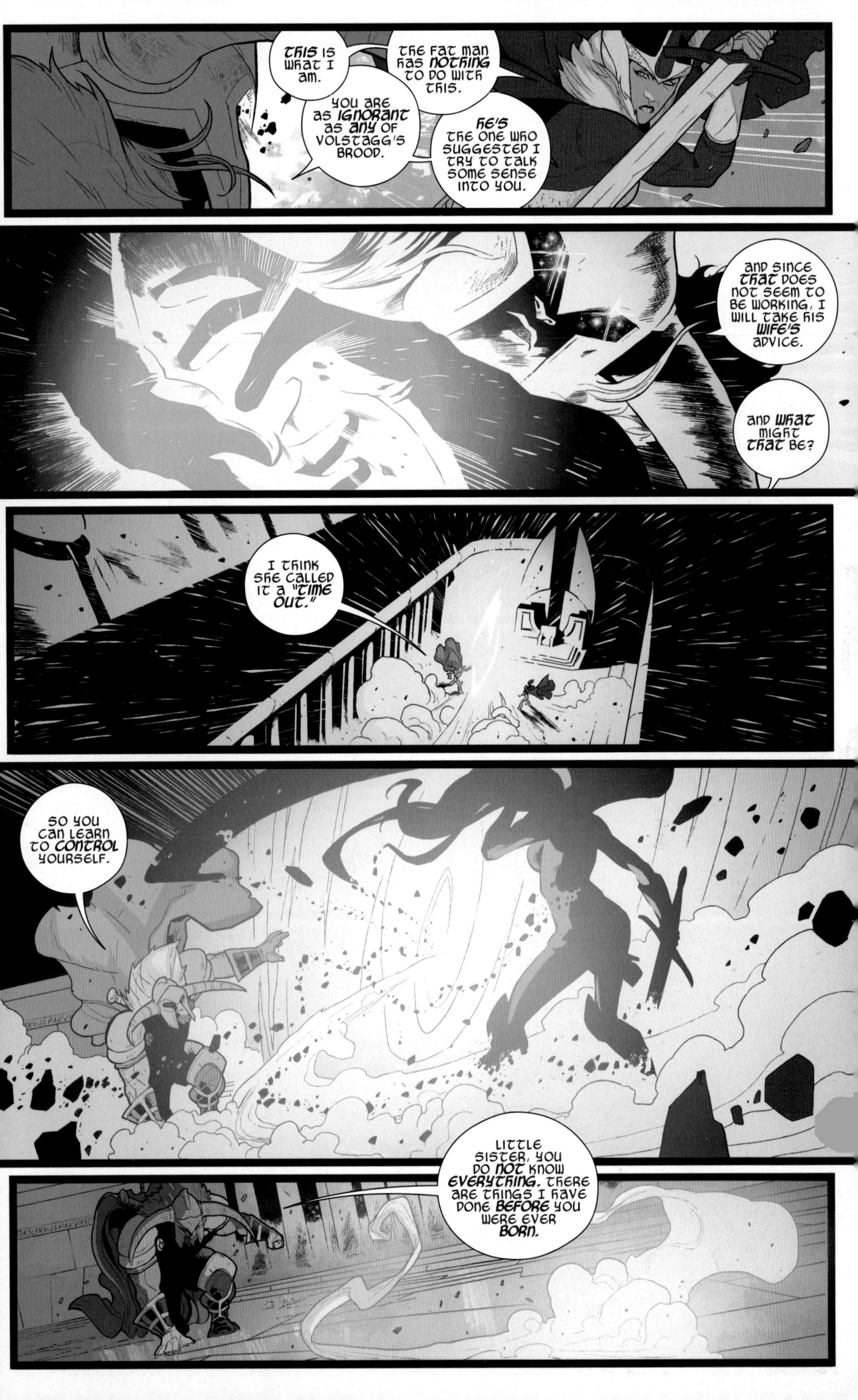
THIS IS WHAT I AM.
THE FAT MAN HAS NOTHING TO DO WITH THIS.
YOU ARE AS IGNORANT AS ANY OF VOLSTAGG'S BROOD.
HE'S THE ONE WHO SUGGESTED I TRY TO TALK SOME SENSE INTO YOU.
AND SINCE THAT DOES NOT SEEM TO BE WORKING, I WILL TAKE HIS WIFE'S ADVICE.
AND WHAT MIGHT THAT BE?
I THINK SHE CALLED IT A "TIME OUT."
SO YOU CAN LEARN TO CONTROL YOURSELF.
LITTLE SISTER, YOU DO NOT KNOW EVERYTHING. THERE ARE THINGS I HAVE DONE BEFORE YOU WERE EVER BORN.

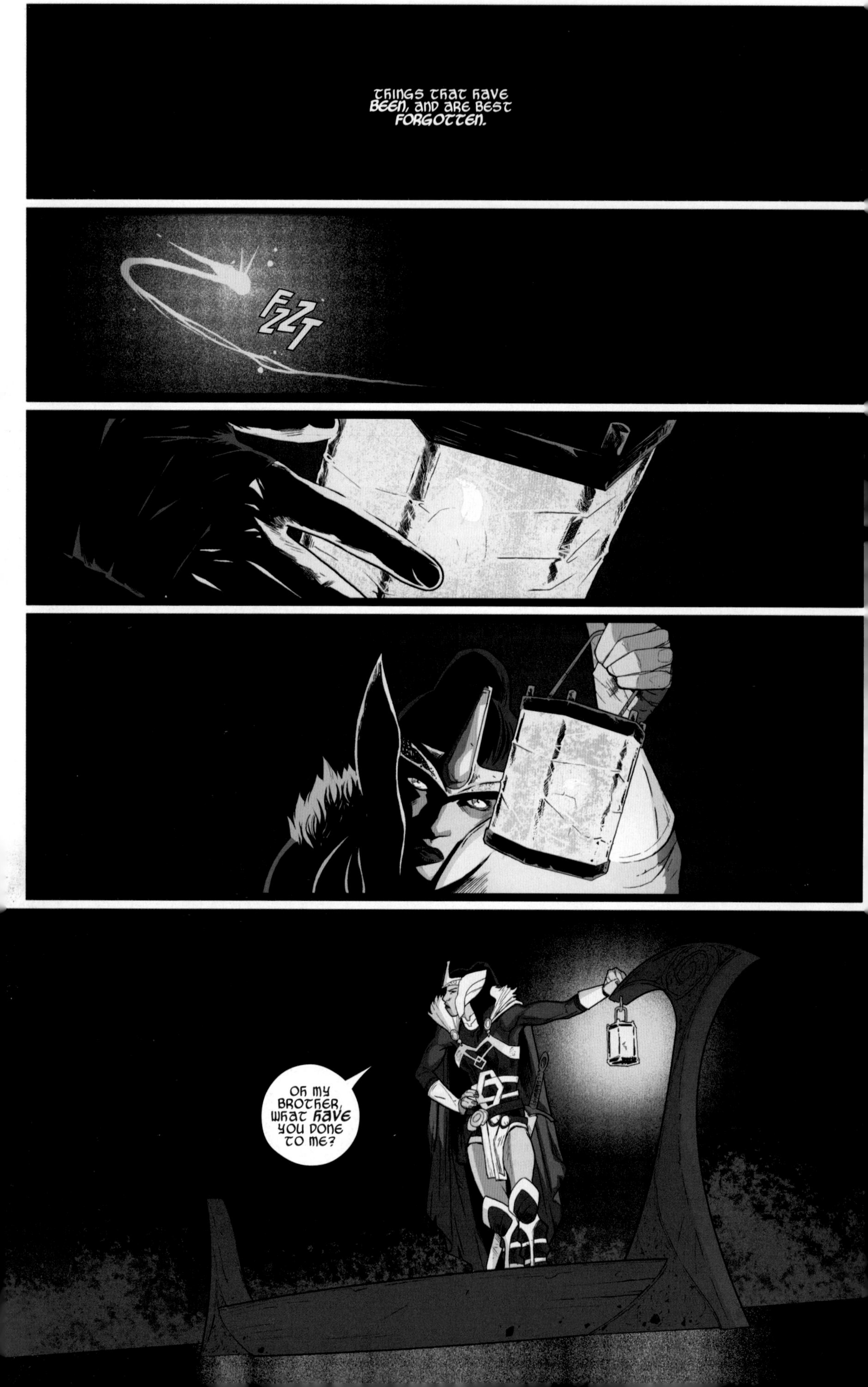
THINGS THAT HAVE BEEN, AND ARE BEST FORGOTTEN.
FZZT
OH MY BROTHER, WHAT HAVE YOU DONE TO ME?

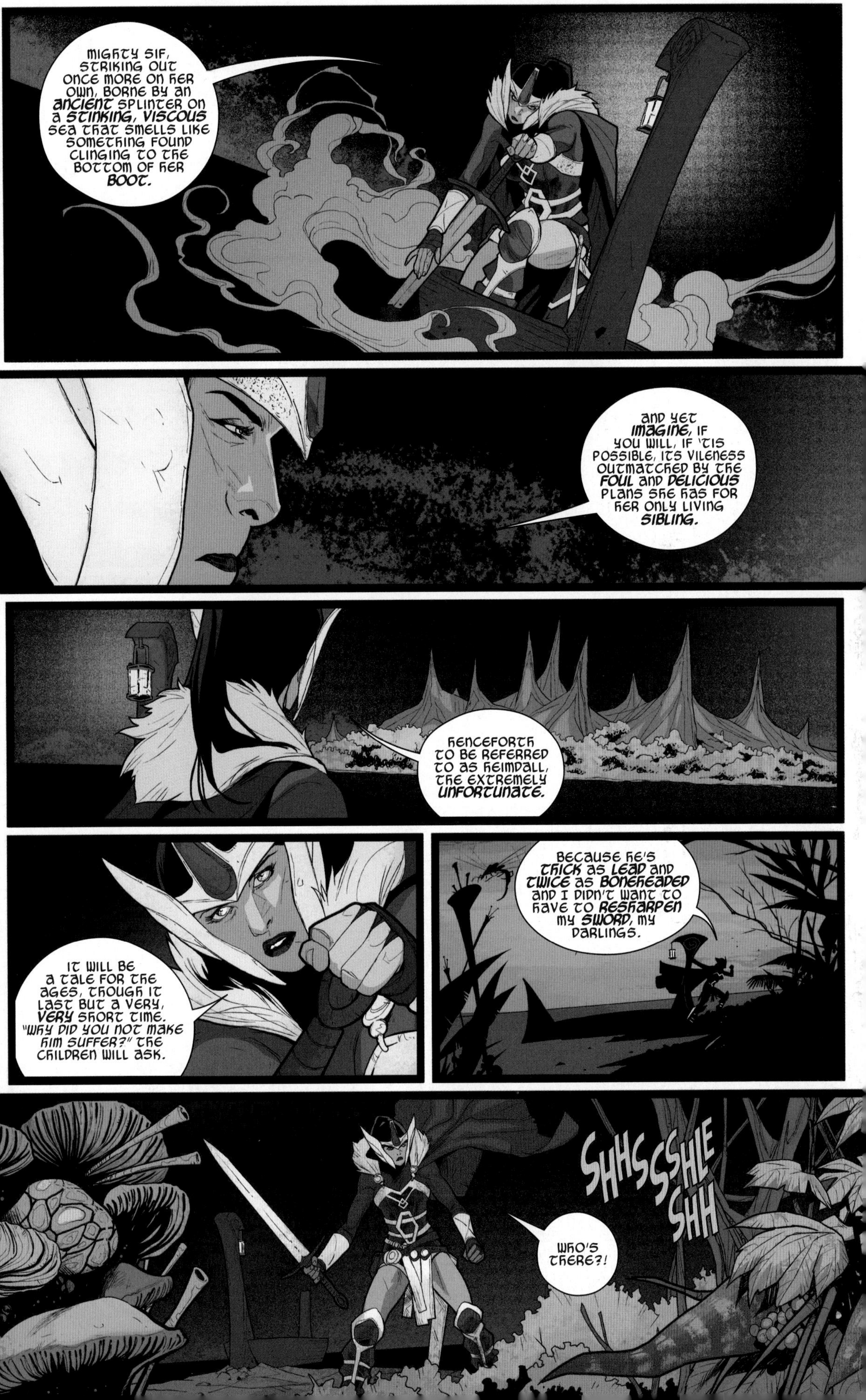
MIGHTY SIF, STRIKING OUT ONCE MORE ON HER OWN, BORNE BY AN ANCIENT SPLINTER ON A STINKING, VISCOUS SEA THAT SMELLS LIKE SOMETHING FOUND CLINGING TO THE BOTTOM OF HER BOOT.
AND YET IMAGINE, IF YOU WILL, IF 'TIS POSSIBLE, ITS VILENESS OUTMATCHED BY THE FOUL AND DELICIOUS PLANS SHE HAS FOR HER ONLY LIVING SIBLING.
HENCEFORTH TO BE REFERRED TO AS HEIMDALL, THE EXTREMELY UNFORTUNATE.
IT WILL BE A TALE FOR THE AGES, THOUGH IT LAST BUT A VERY, VERY SHORT TIME. "WHY DID YOU NOT MAKE HIM SUFFER?" THE CHILDREN WILL ASK.
BECAUSE HE'S THICK AS LEAD AND TWICE AS BONEHEADED AND I DIDN'T WANT TO HAVE TO RESHARPEN MY SWORD, MY DARLINGS.
SHHSSSHLE SHH
WHO'S THERE?!

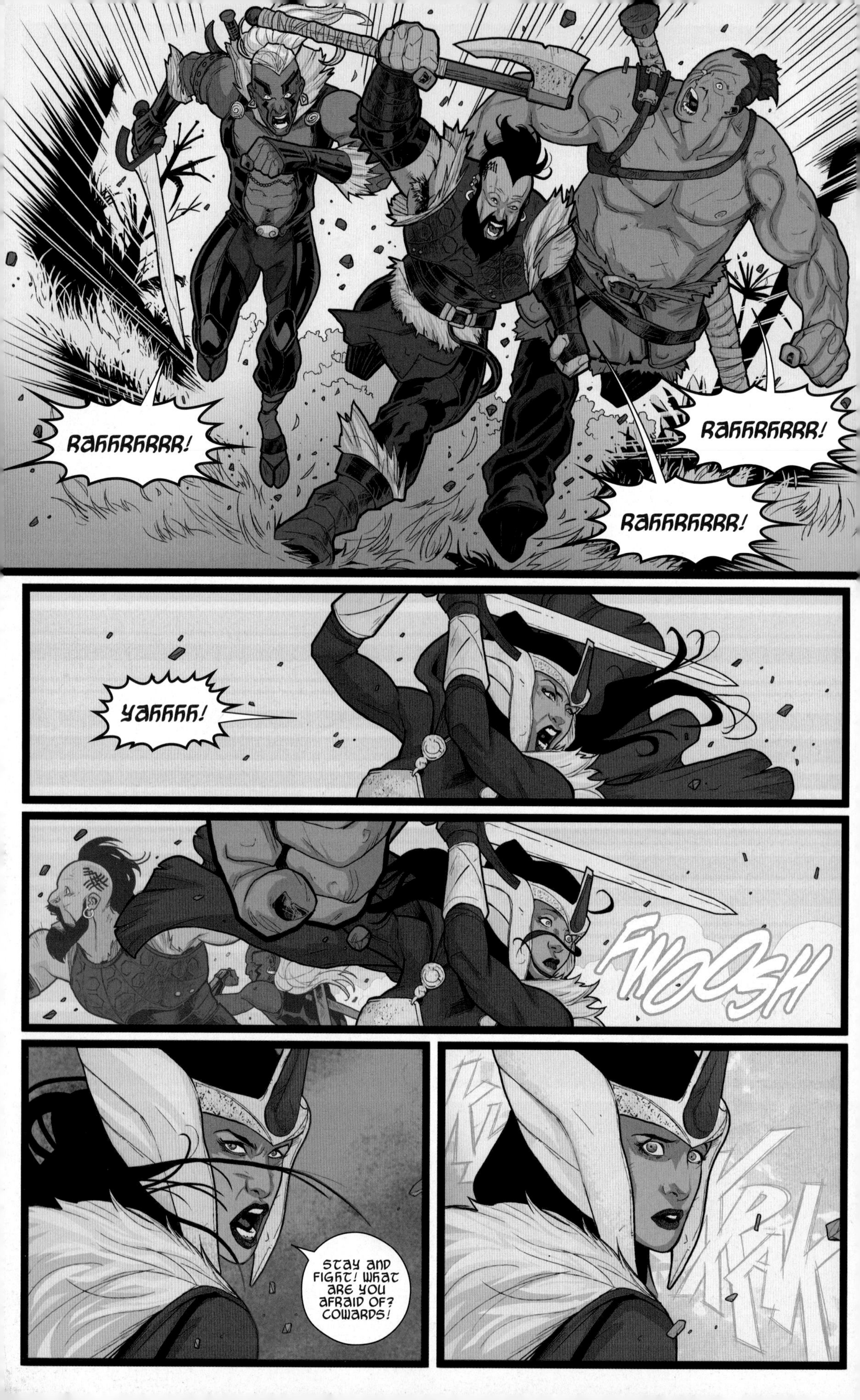
RAHHRHRRR!
RAHHRHRRR!
RAHHRHRRR!
YAHHHH!
FWOOSH
STAY AND FIGHT! WHAT ARE YOU AFRAID OF? COWARDS!

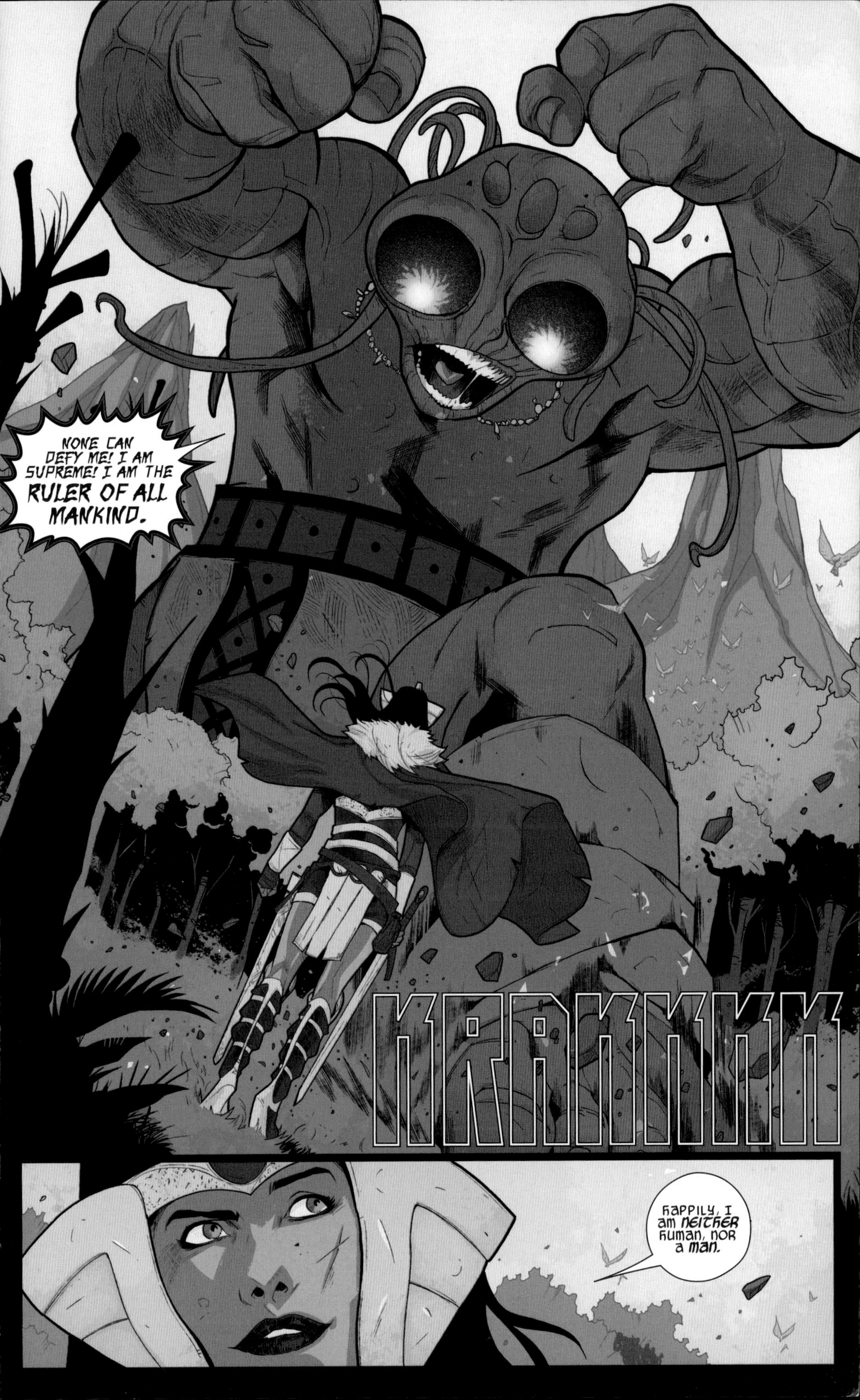
NONE CAN DEFY ME! I AM SUPREME! I AM THE RULER OF ALL MANKIND.
KRAKKKKK
HAPPILY, I AM NEITHER HUMAN, NOR A MAN.

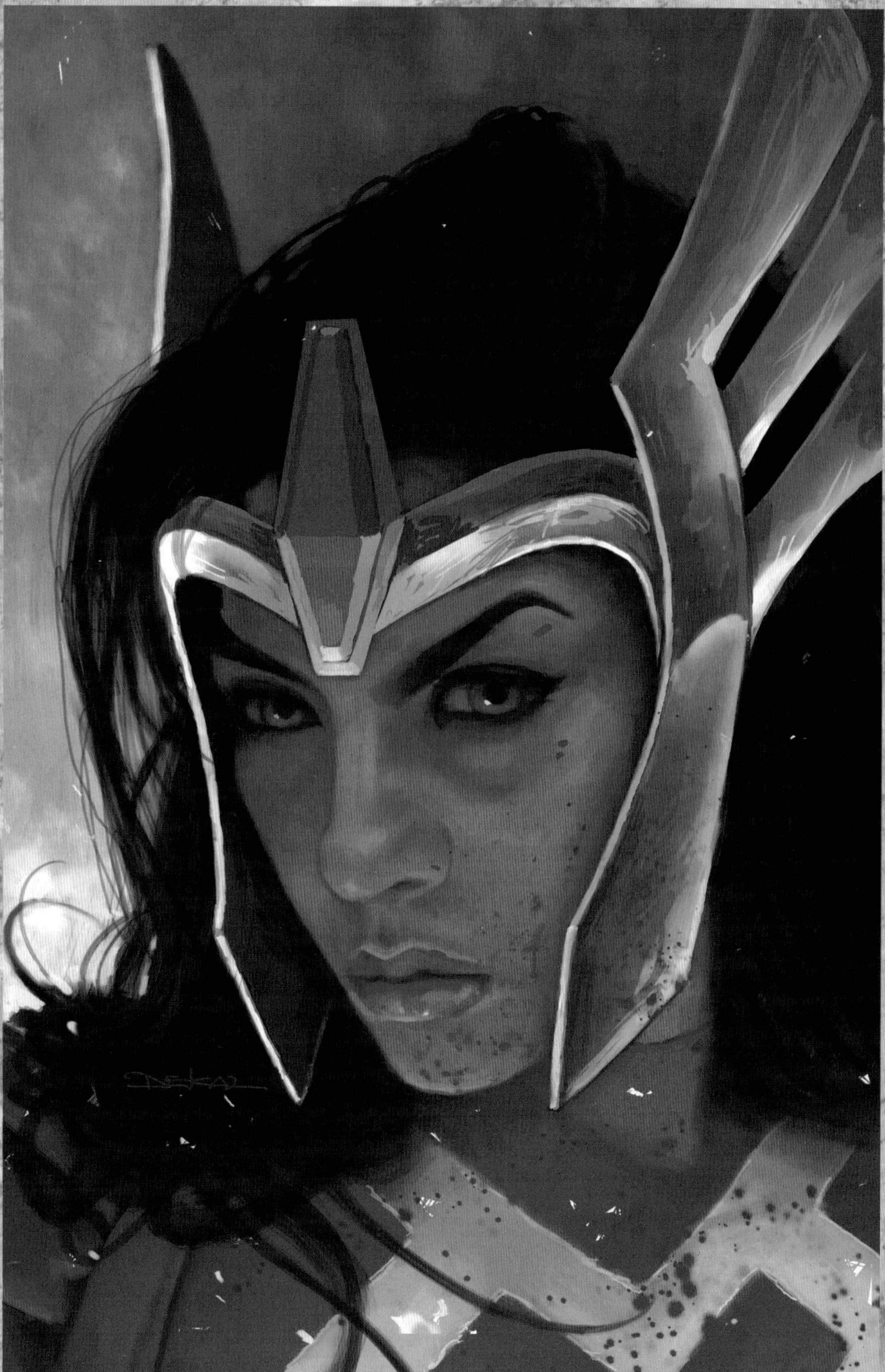

#648

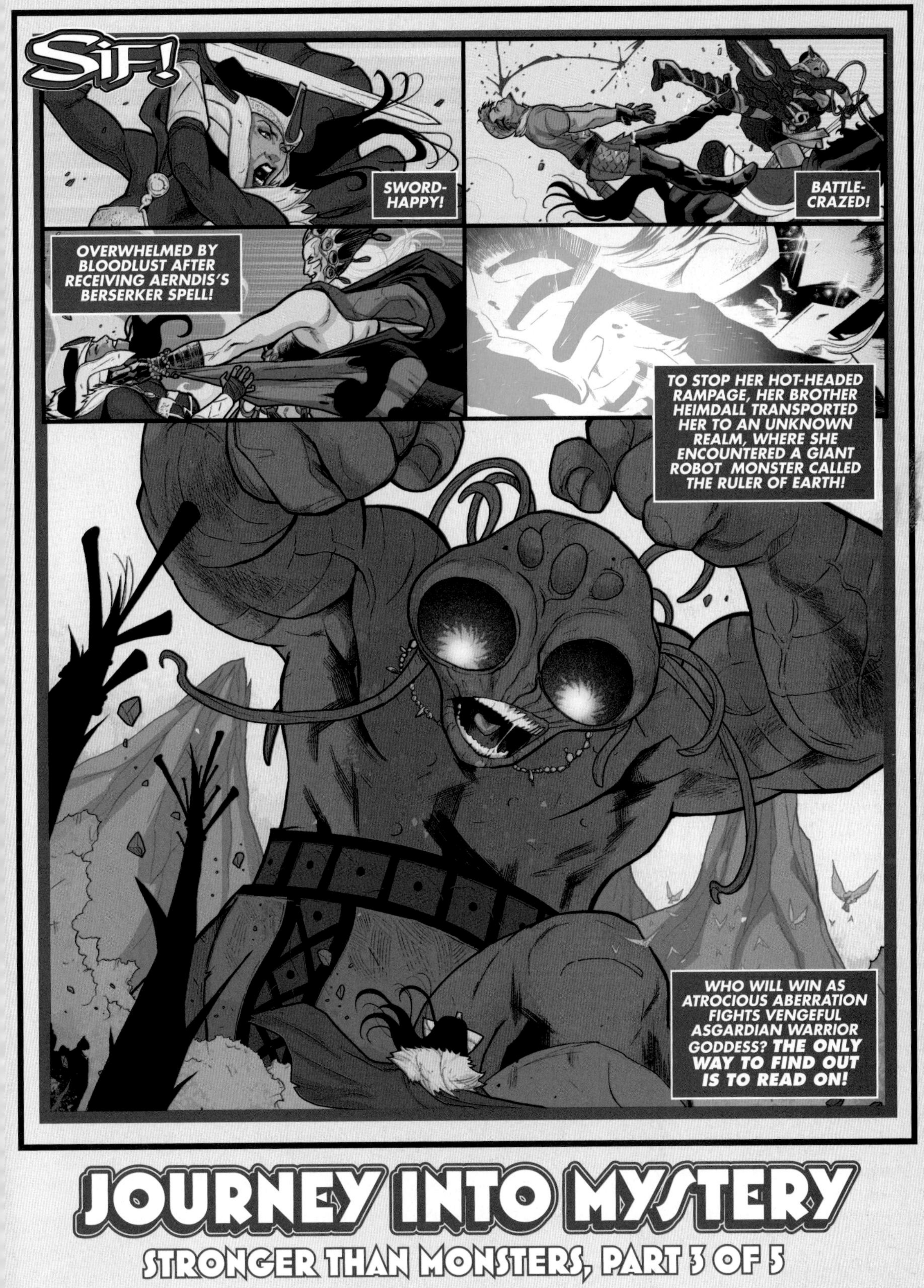
SIF!
SWORD-HAPPY!
BATTLE-CRAZED!
OVERWHELMED BY BLOODLUST AFTER RECEIVING AERNDIS'S BERSERKER SPELL!
TO STOP HER HOT-HEADED RAMPAGE, HER BROTHER HEIMDALL TRANSPORTED HER TO AN UNKNOWN REALM, WHERE SHE ENCOUNTERED A GIANT ROBOT MONSTER CALLED THE RULER OF EARTH!
WHO WILL WIN AS ATROCIOUS ABERRATION FIGHTS VENGEFUL ASGARDIAN WARRIOR GODDESS? THE ONLY WAY TO FIND OUT IS TO READ ON!

JOURNEY INTO MYSTERY

STRONGER THAN MONSTERS, PART 3 OF 5

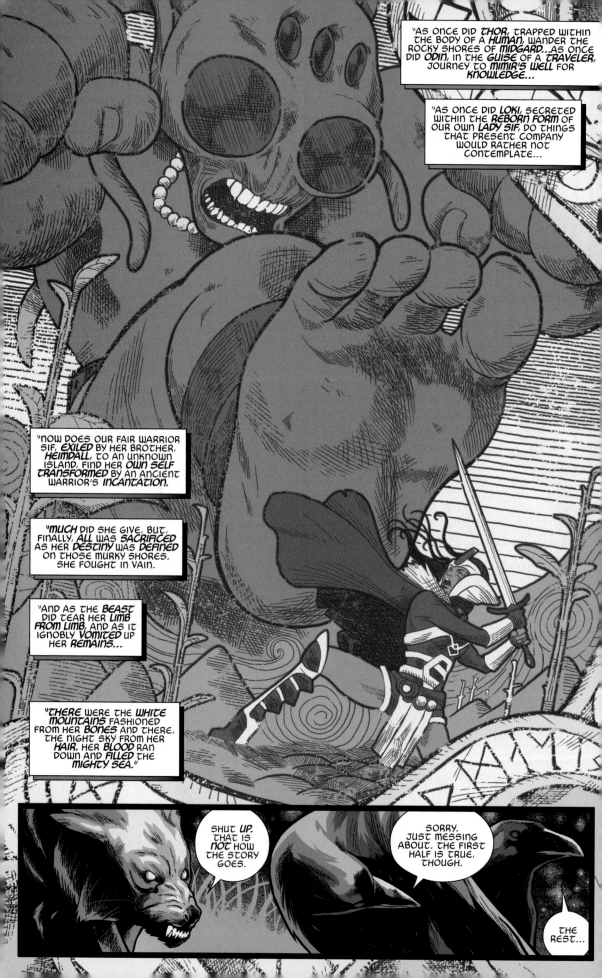

"AS ONCE DID *THOR*, TRAPPED WITHIN THE BODY OF A *HUMAN*, WANDER THE ROCKY SHORES OF *MIDGARD*...AS ONCE DID *ODIN*, IN THE *GUISE* OF A *TRAVELER*, JOURNEY TO *MIMIR'S WELL* FOR *KNOWLEDGE*...

"AS ONCE DID *LOKI*, SECRETED WITHIN THE *REBORN FORM* OF OUR OWN *LADY SIF*, DO THINGS THAT PRESENT COMPANY WOULD RATHER NOT CONTEMPLATE...

"NOW DOES OUR FAIR WARRIOR SIF, *EXILED* BY HER BROTHER, *HEIMDALL*, TO AN UNKNOWN ISLAND, FIND HER *OWN SELF* *TRANSFORMED* BY AN ANCIENT WARRIOR'S *INCANTATION*.

"*MUCH* DID SHE GIVE, BUT, FINALLY, *ALL* WAS *SACRIFICED* AS HER *DESTINY* WAS *DEFINED* ON THOSE MURKY SHORES. SHE FOUGHT IN VAIN.

"AND AS THE *BEAST* DID TEAR HER *LIMB FROM LIMB*, AND AS IT IGNOBLY *VOMITED* UP HER *REMAINS*...

"*THERE* WERE THE *WHITE MOUNTAINS* FASHIONED FROM HER *BONES* AND THERE, THE *NIGHT SKY* FROM HER *HAIR*. HER *BLOOD* RAN DOWN AND *FILLED* THE *MIGHTY SEA*."

SHUT *UP*. THAT IS *NOT* HOW THE STORY GOES.

SORRY. JUST MESSING ABOUT. THE FIRST HALF IS TRUE, THOUGH.

THE REST...

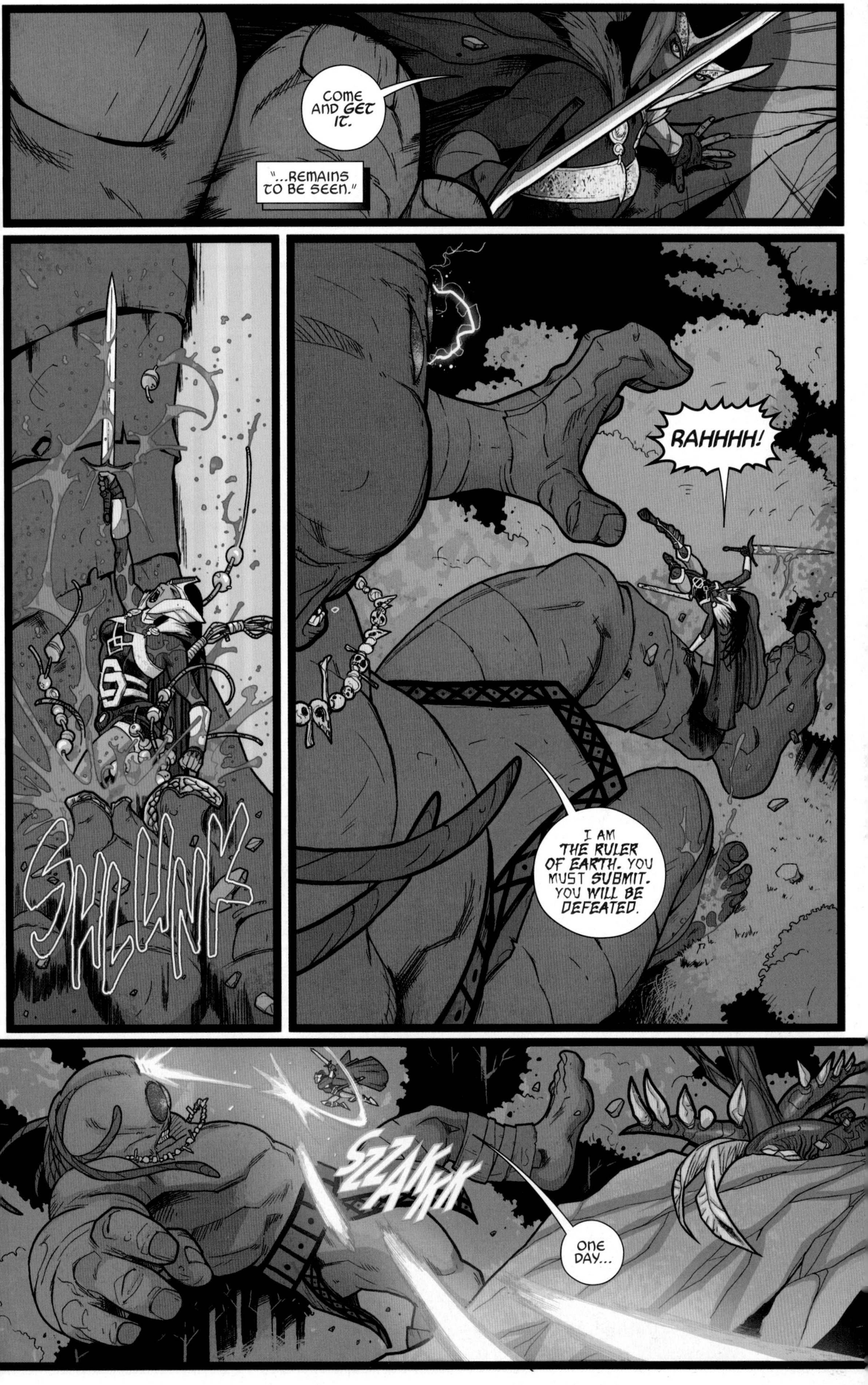
COME AND GET IT.
"...REMAINS TO BE SEEN."
SHLUNK
RAHHHH!
I AM THE RULER OF EARTH. YOU MUST SUBMIT. YOU WILL BE DEFEATED.
SZZAKKK
ONE DAY...

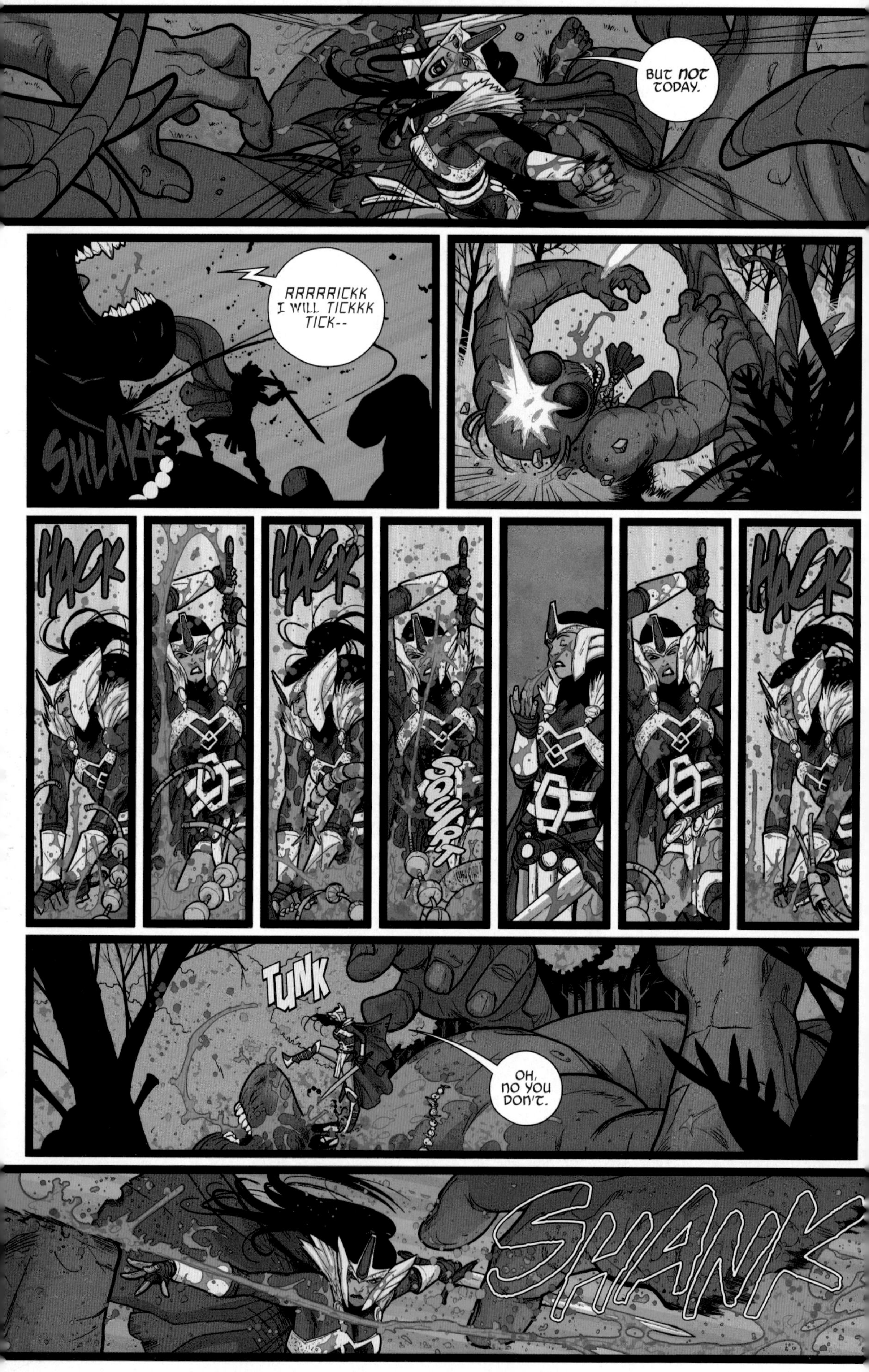
BUT NOT TODAY.
RRRRRICKK I WILL TICKKK TICK--
SHLAKK
HACK
HACK
SQUIRT
HACK
TUNK
OH, NO YOU DON'T.
SHANK

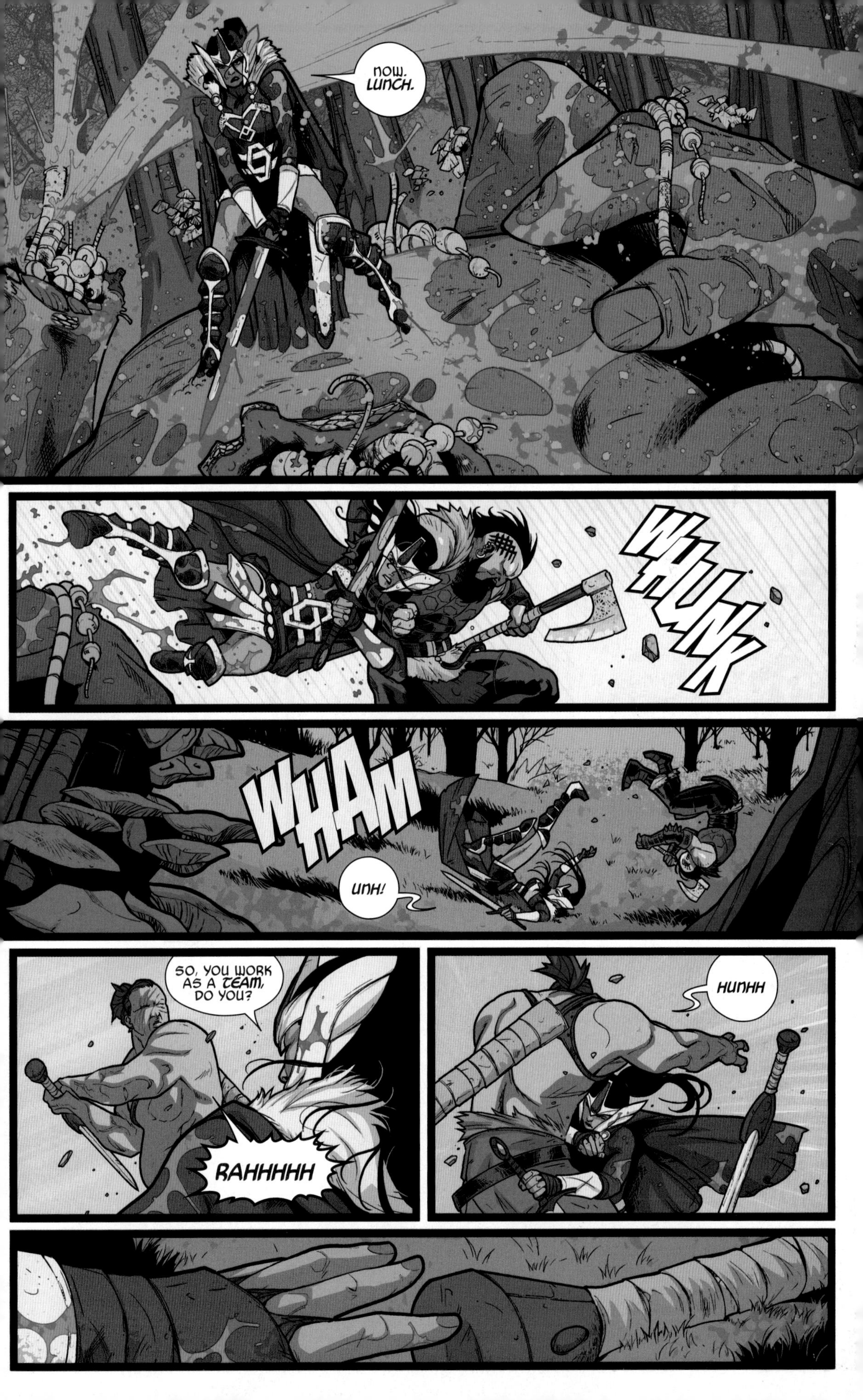
NOW. LUNCH.
WHUNK
WHAM
UNH!
SO, YOU WORK AS A TEAM, DO YOU?
RAHHHHH
HUNHH

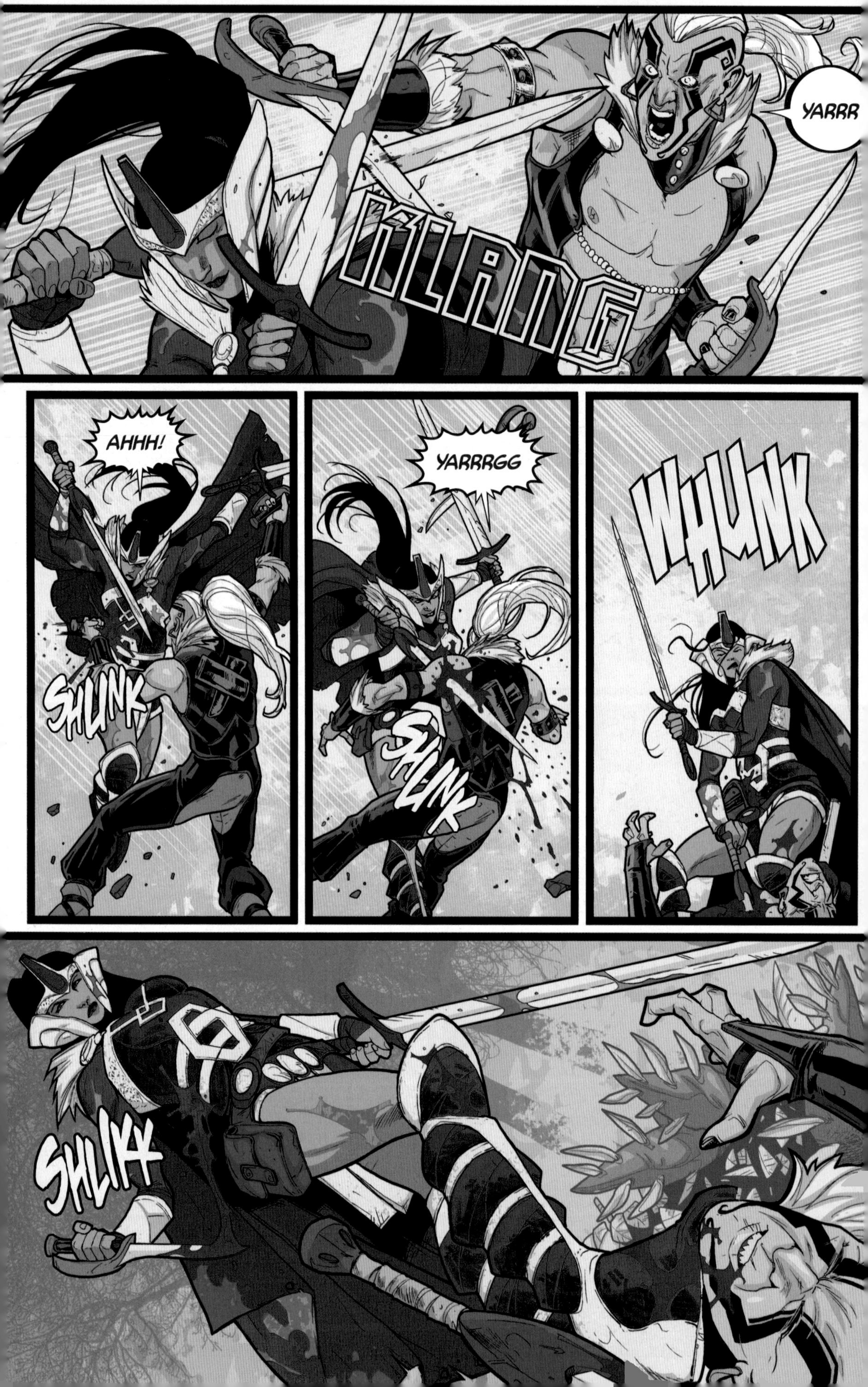

YARRR
KLANG
AHHH!
SHLINK
YARRRGG
SHLINK
WHUNK
SHLIKK

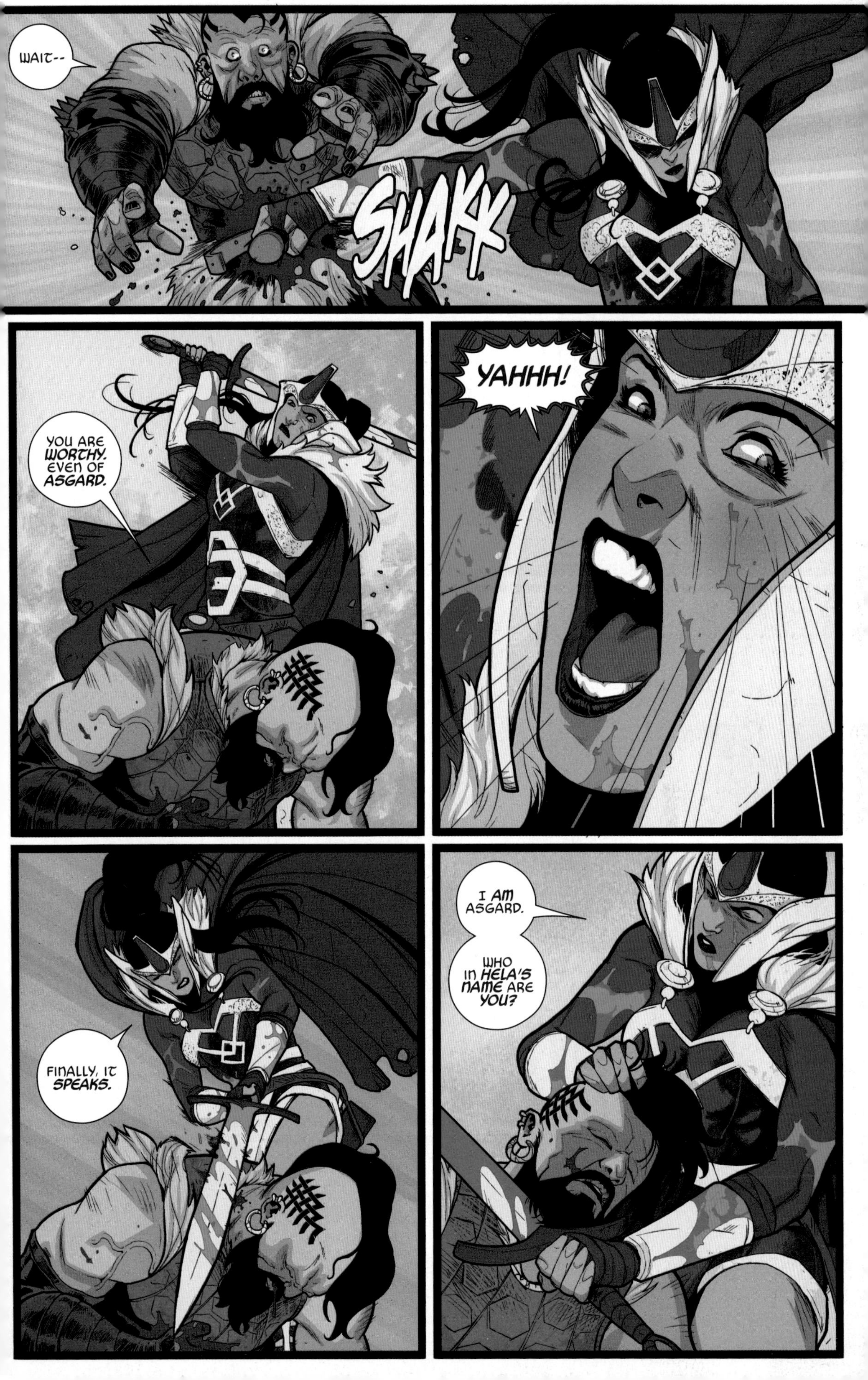
WAIT--
SHAKK
YOU ARE WORTHY. EVEN OF ASGARD.
YAHHH!
FINALLY, IT SPEAKS.
I AM ASGARD.
WHO IN HELA'S NAME ARE YOU?

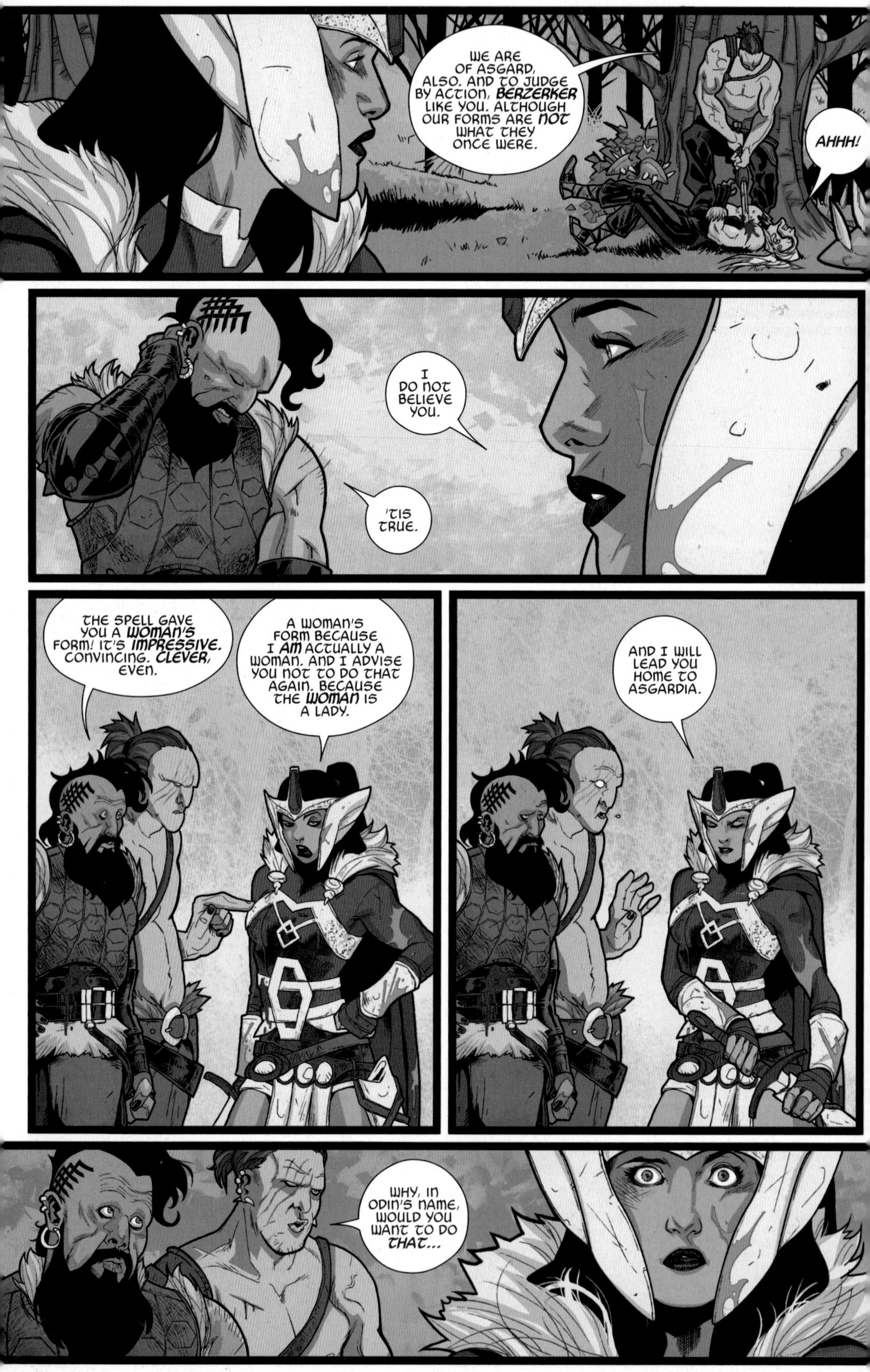
WE ARE OF ASGARD, ALSO. AND TO JUDGE BY ACTION, BERZERKER LIKE YOU. ALTHOUGH OUR FORMS ARE NOT WHAT THEY ONCE WERE.
AHHH!
I DO NOT BELIEVE YOU.
'TIS TRUE.
THE SPELL GAVE YOU A WOMAN'S FORM! IT'S IMPRESSIVE. CONVINCING. CLEVER, EVEN.
A WOMAN'S FORM BECAUSE I AM ACTUALLY A WOMAN. AND I ADVISE YOU NOT TO DO THAT AGAIN. BECAUSE THE WOMAN IS A LADY.
AND I WILL LEAD YOU HOME TO ASGARDIA.
WHY, IN ODIN'S NAME, WOULD YOU WANT TO DO THAT...

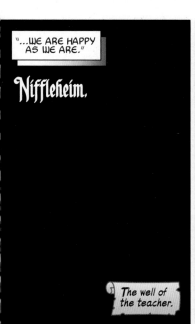

"...WE ARE HAPPY AS WE ARE."

Niffleheim.

The well of the teacher.

PAT PAT PAT

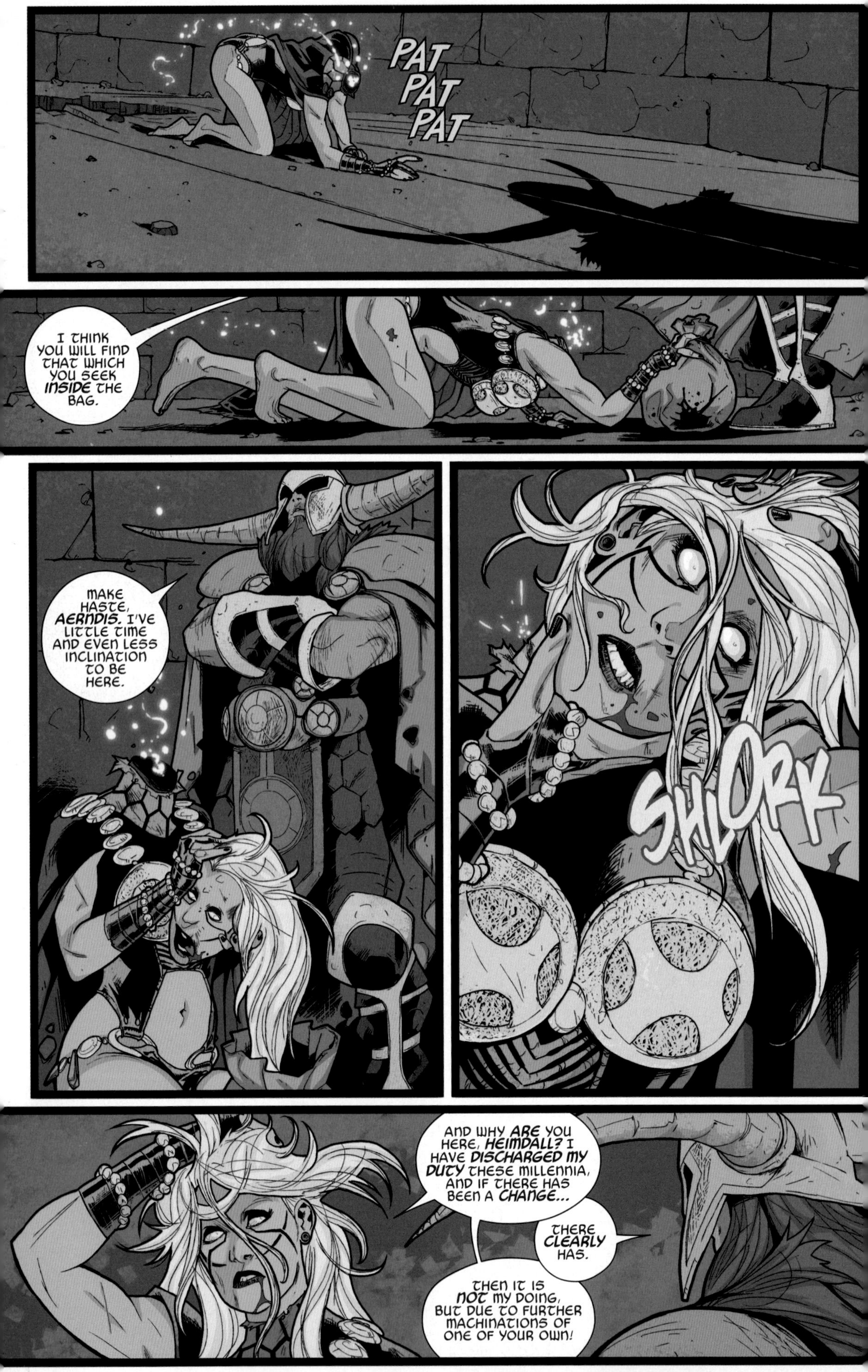
PAT
PAT
PAT
I THINK YOU WILL FIND THAT WHICH YOU SEEK INSIDE THE BAG.
MAKE HASTE, AERNDIS. I'VE LITTLE TIME AND EVEN LESS INCLINATION TO BE HERE.
SHLORK
AND WHY ARE YOU HERE, HEIMDALL? I HAVE DISCHARGED MY DUTY THESE MILLENNIA, AND IF THERE HAS BEEN A CHANGE...
THERE CLEARLY HAS.
THEN IT IS NOT MY DOING, BUT DUE TO FURTHER MACHINATIONS OF ONE OF YOUR OWN!

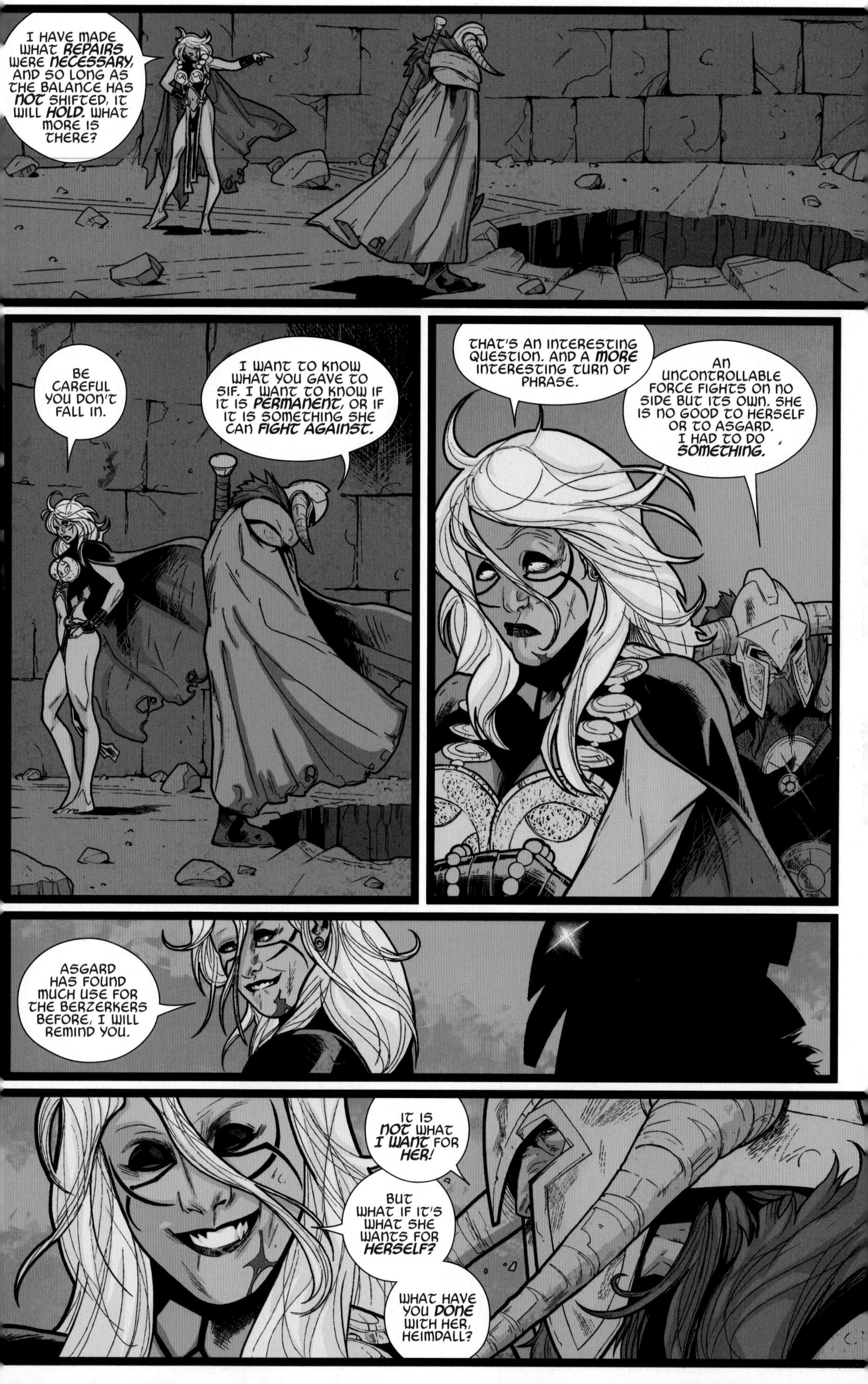
I HAVE MADE WHAT REPAIRS WERE NECESSARY, AND SO LONG AS THE BALANCE HAS NOT SHIFTED, IT WILL HOLD. WHAT MORE IS THERE?
BE CAREFUL YOU DON'T FALL IN.
I WANT TO KNOW WHAT YOU GAVE TO SIF. I WANT TO KNOW IF IT IS PERMANENT, OR IF IT IS SOMETHING SHE CAN FIGHT AGAINST.
THAT'S AN INTERESTING QUESTION. AND A MORE INTERESTING TURN OF PHRASE.
AN UNCONTROLLABLE FORCE FIGHTS ON NO SIDE BUT ITS OWN. SHE IS NO GOOD TO HERSELF OR TO ASGARD. I HAD TO DO SOMETHING.
ASGARD HAS FOUND MUCH USE FOR THE BERZERKERS BEFORE, I WILL REMIND YOU.
IT IS NOT WHAT I WANT FOR HER!
BUT WHAT IF IT'S WHAT SHE WANTS FOR HERSELF?
WHAT HAVE YOU DONE WITH HER, HEIMDALL?

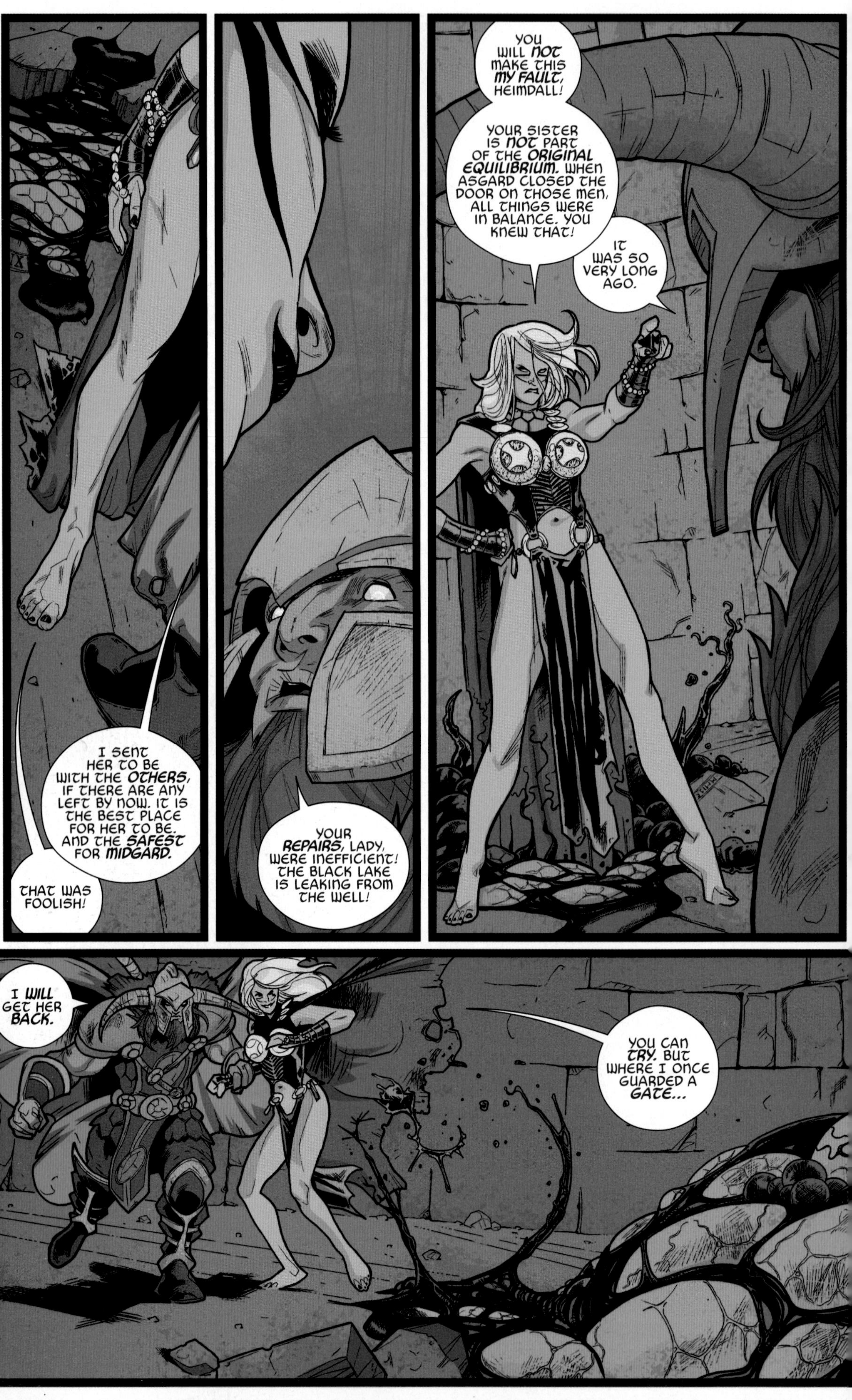
I SENT HER TO BE WITH THE OTHERS, IF THERE ARE ANY LEFT BY NOW. IT IS THE BEST PLACE FOR HER TO BE. AND THE SAFEST FOR MIDGARD.
THAT WAS FOOLISH!
YOUR REPAIRS, LADY, WERE INEFFICIENT! THE BLACK LAKE IS LEAKING FROM THE WELL!
YOU WILL NOT MAKE THIS MY FAULT, HEIMDALL!
YOUR SISTER IS NOT PART OF THE ORIGINAL EQUILIBRIUM. WHEN ASGARD CLOSED THE DOOR ON THOSE MEN, ALL THINGS WERE IN BALANCE. YOU KNEW THAT!
IT WAS SO VERY LONG AGO.
I WILL GET HER BACK.
YOU CAN TRY. BUT WHERE I ONCE GUARDED A GATE...

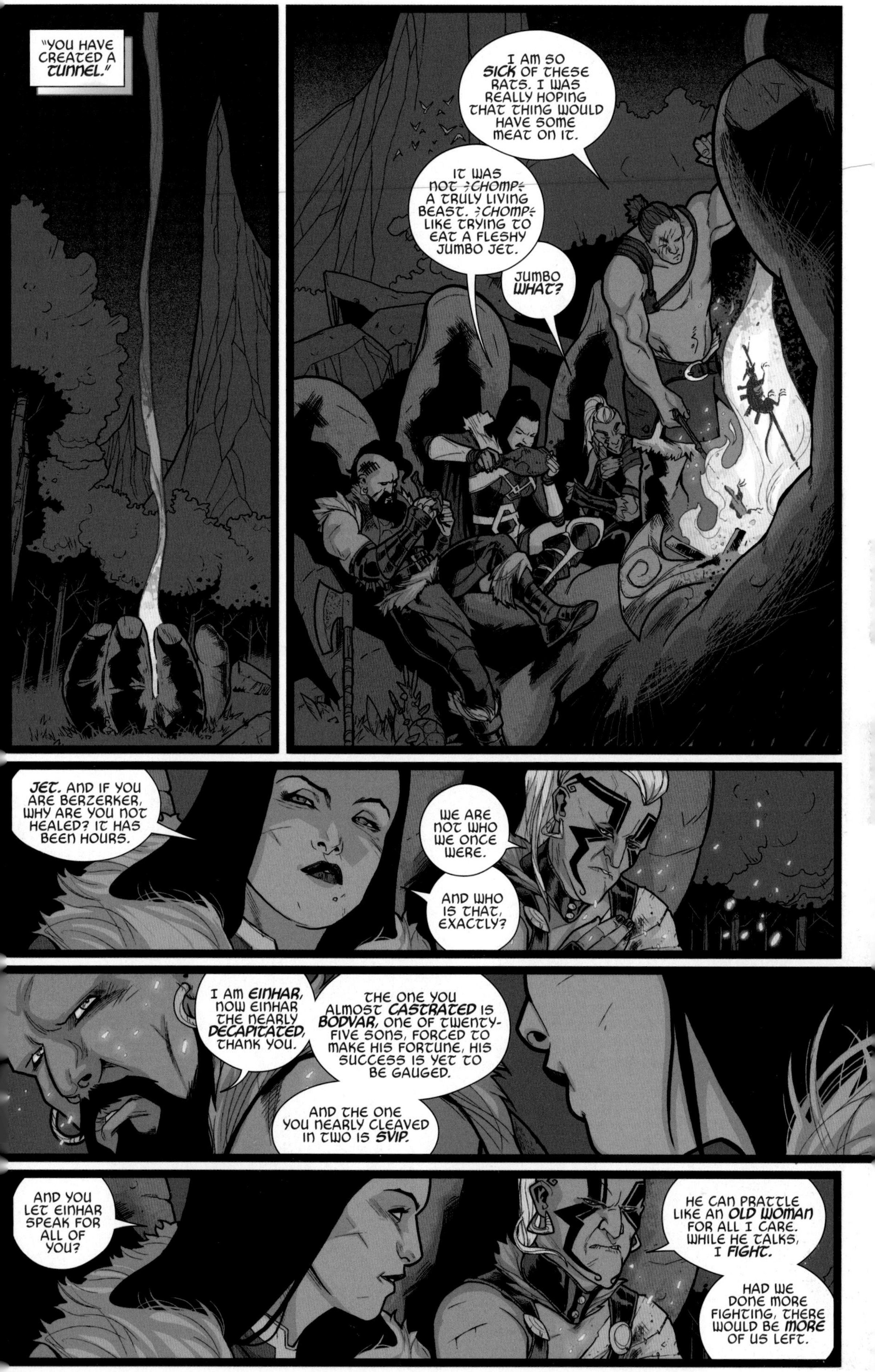
"YOU HAVE CREATED A TUNNEL."
I AM SO SICK OF THESE RATS. I WAS REALLY HOPING THAT THING WOULD HAVE SOME MEAT ON IT.
IT WAS NOT ~CHOMP~ A TRULY LIVING BEAST. ~CHOMP~ LIKE TRYING TO EAT A FLESHY JUMBO JET.
JUMBO WHAT?
JET. AND IF YOU ARE BERZERKER, WHY ARE YOU NOT HEALED? IT HAS BEEN HOURS.
WE ARE NOT WHO WE ONCE WERE.
AND WHO IS THAT, EXACTLY?
I AM EINHAR, NOW EINHAR THE NEARLY DECAPITATED, THANK YOU.
THE ONE YOU ALMOST CASTRATED IS BODVAR, ONE OF TWENTY-FIVE SONS, FORCED TO MAKE HIS FORTUNE, HIS SUCCESS IS YET TO BE GAUGED.
AND THE ONE YOU NEARLY CLEAVED IN TWO IS SVIP.
AND YOU LET EINHAR SPEAK FOR ALL OF YOU?
HE CAN PRATTLE LIKE AN OLD WOMAN FOR ALL I CARE. WHILE HE TALKS, I FIGHT.
HAD WE DONE MORE FIGHTING, THERE WOULD BE MORE OF US LEFT.

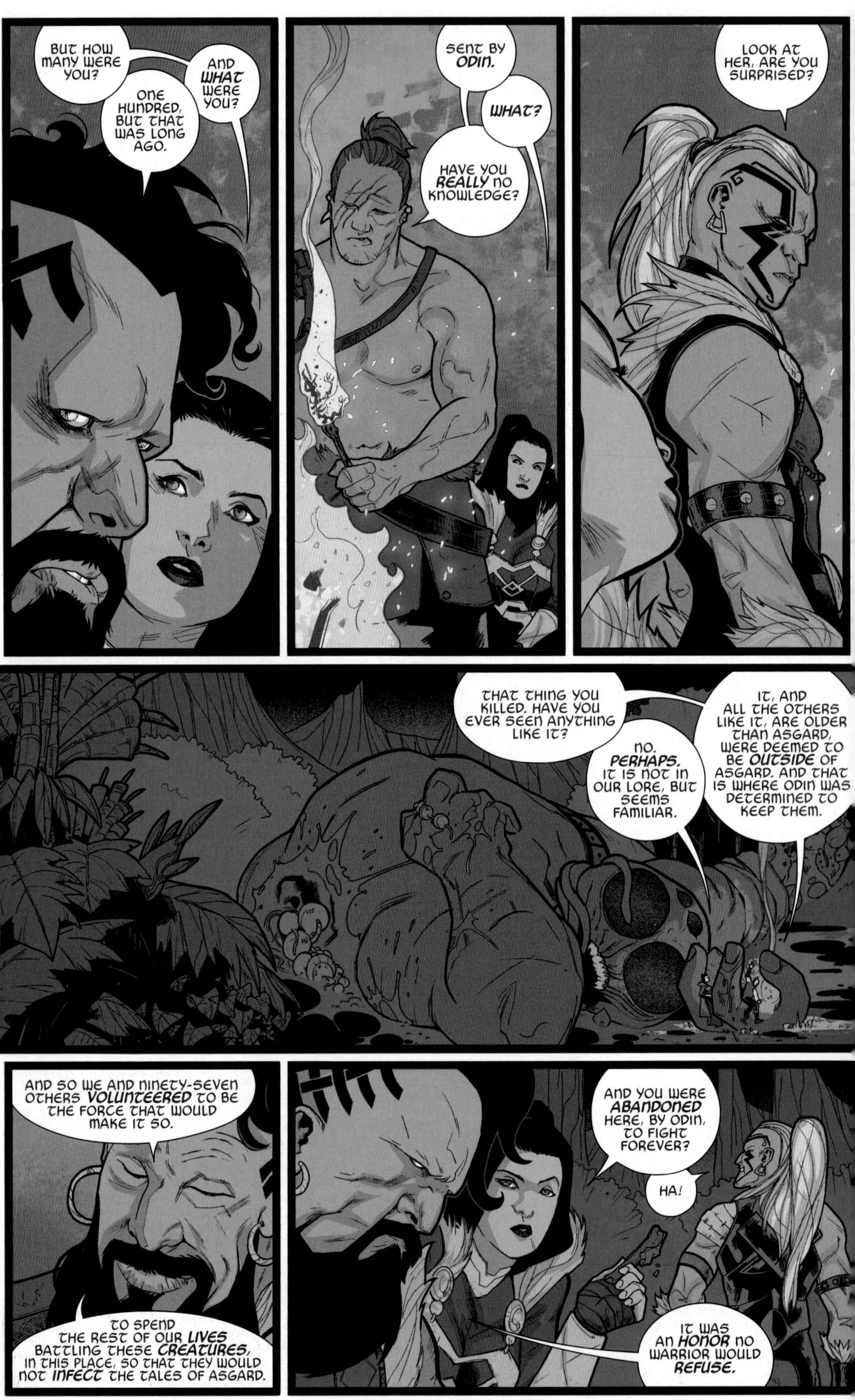

BUT HOW MANY WERE YOU?
AND WHAT WERE YOU?
ONE HUNDRED, BUT THAT WAS LONG AGO.
SENT BY ODIN.
WHAT?
HAVE YOU REALLY NO KNOWLEDGE?
LOOK AT HER, ARE YOU SURPRISED?
THAT THING YOU KILLED. HAVE YOU EVER SEEN ANYTHING LIKE IT?
NO. PERHAPS. IT IS NOT IN OUR LORE, BUT SEEMS FAMILIAR.
IT, AND ALL THE OTHERS LIKE IT, ARE OLDER THAN ASGARD, WERE DEEMED TO BE OUTSIDE OF ASGARD. AND THAT IS WHERE ODIN WAS DETERMINED TO KEEP THEM.
AND SO WE AND NINETY-SEVEN OTHERS VOLUNTEERED TO BE THE FORCE THAT WOULD MAKE IT SO.
TO SPEND THE REST OF OUR LIVES BATTLING THESE CREATURES, IN THIS PLACE, SO THAT THEY WOULD NOT INFECT THE TALES OF ASGARD.
AND YOU WERE ABANDONED HERE, BY ODIN, TO FIGHT FOREVER?
HA!
IT WAS AN HONOR NO WARRIOR WOULD REFUSE.

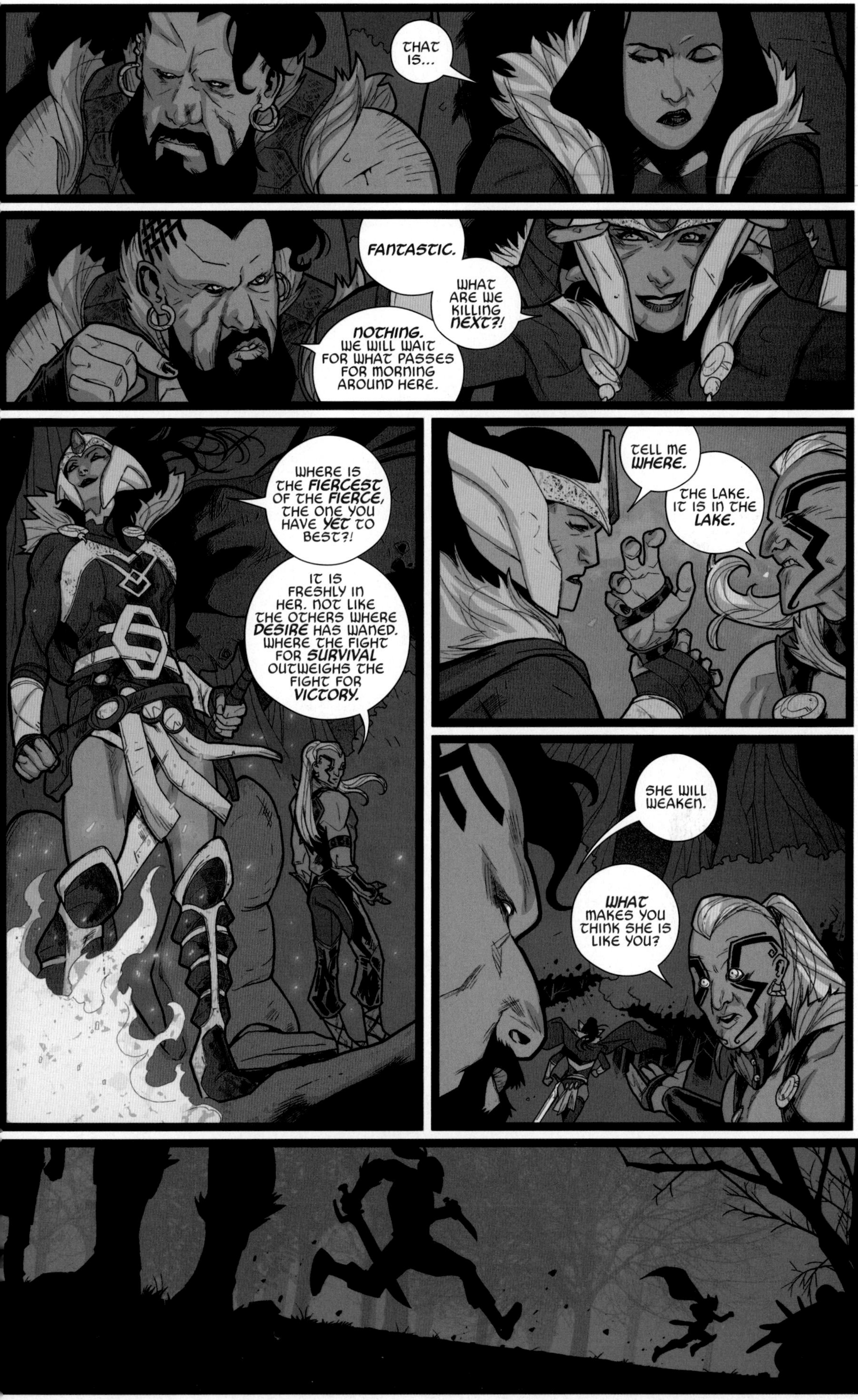
THAT IS...
FANTASTIC.
WHAT ARE WE KILLING NEXT?!
NOTHING. WE WILL WAIT FOR WHAT PASSES FOR MORNING AROUND HERE.
WHERE IS THE FIERCEST OF THE FIERCE, THE ONE YOU HAVE YET TO BEST?!
IT IS FRESHLY IN HER. NOT LIKE THE OTHERS WHERE DESIRE HAS WANED. WHERE THE FIGHT FOR SURVIVAL OUTWEIGHS THE FIGHT FOR VICTORY.
TELL ME WHERE.
THE LAKE. IT IS IN THE LAKE.
SHE WILL WEAKEN.
WHAT MAKES YOU THINK SHE IS LIKE YOU?

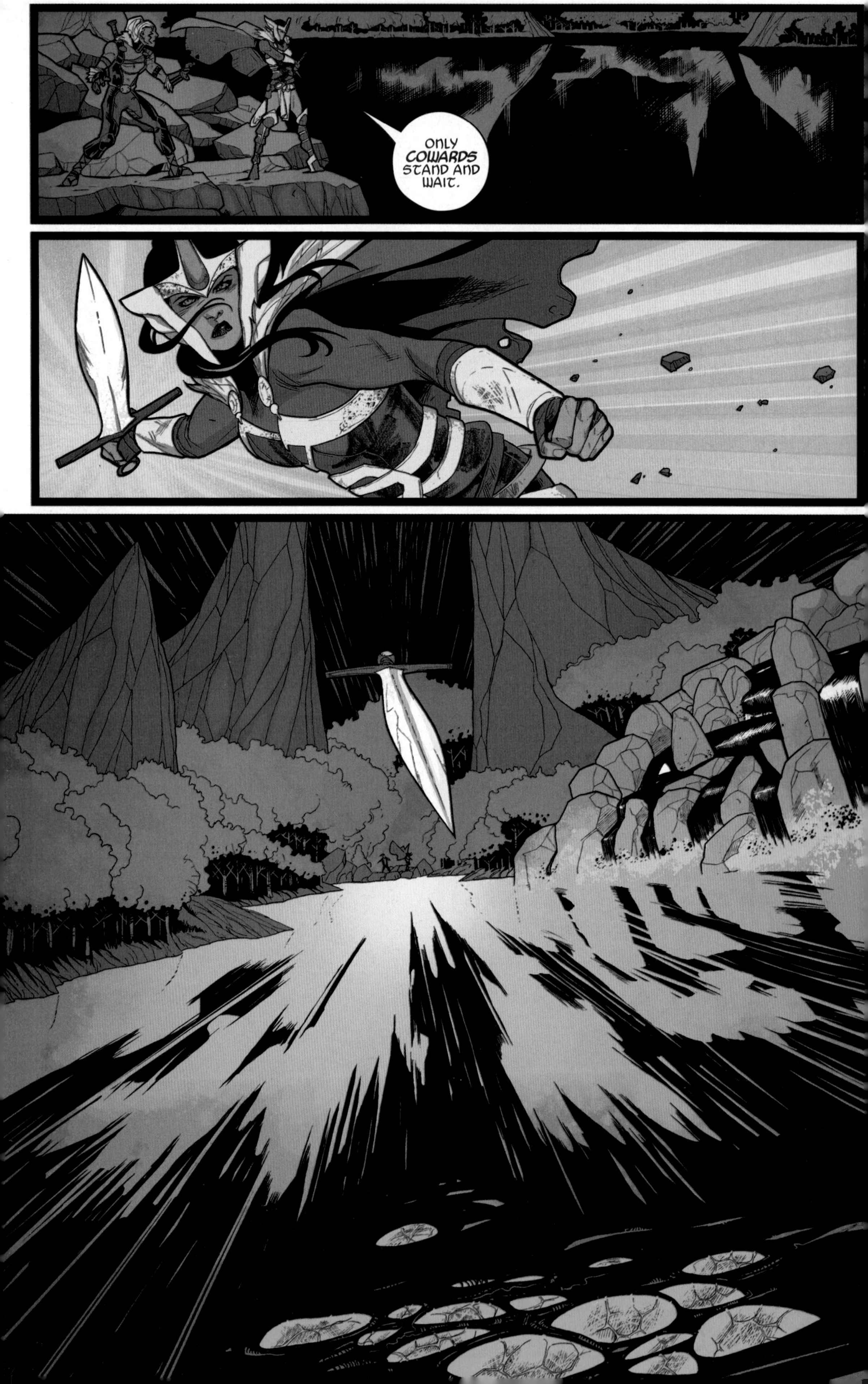
ONLY COWARDS STAND AND WAIT.

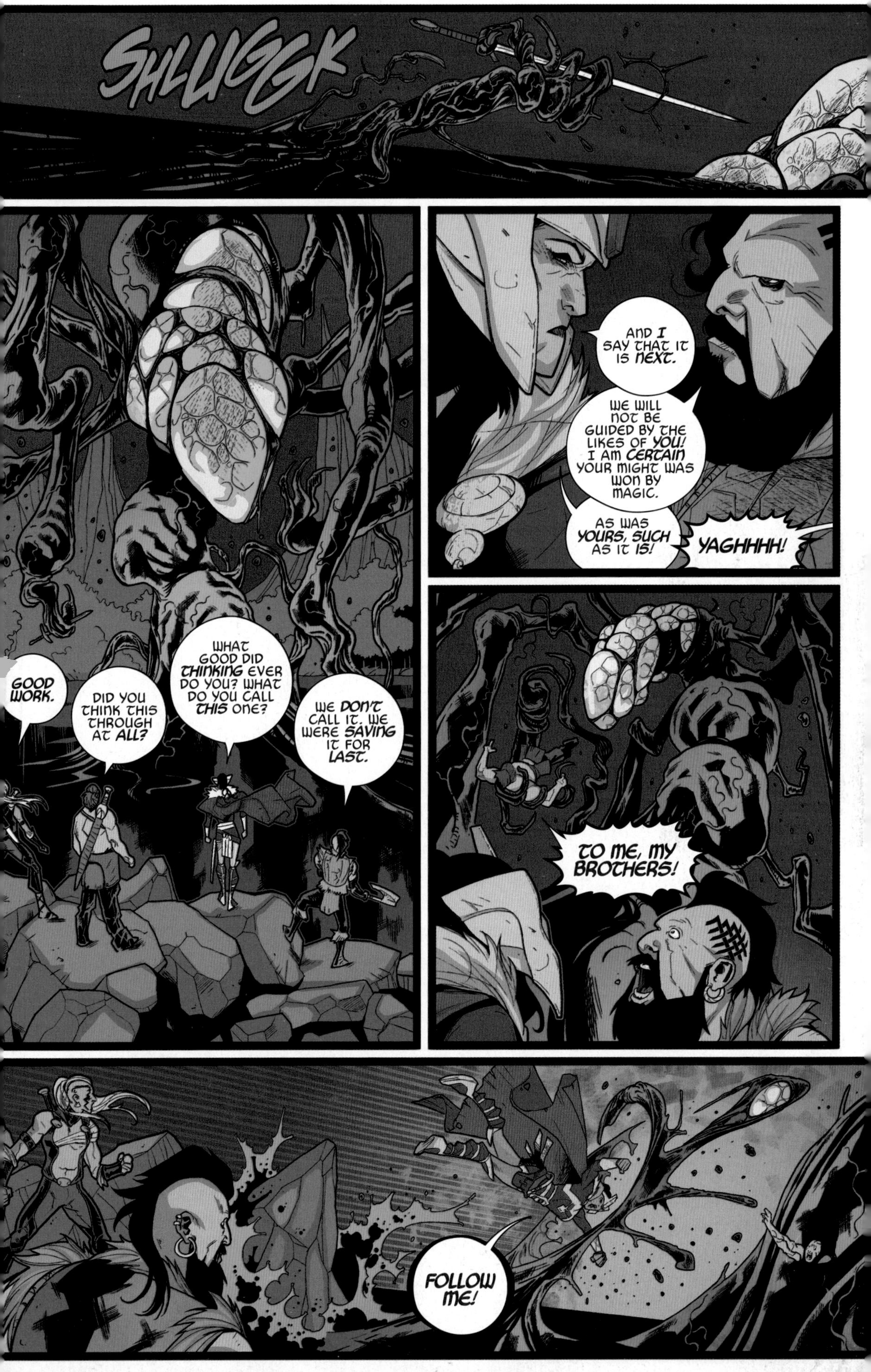
SHLUGGK
AND I SAY THAT IT IS NEXT.
WE WILL NOT BE GUIDED BY THE LIKES OF YOU! I AM CERTAIN YOUR MIGHT WAS WON BY MAGIC.
AS WAS YOURS, SUCH AS IT IS!
YAGHHHH!
GOOD WORK.
DID YOU THINK THIS THROUGH AT ALL?
WHAT GOOD DID THINKING EVER DO YOU? WHAT DO YOU CALL THIS ONE?
WE DON'T CALL IT. WE WERE SAVING IT FOR LAST.
TO ME, MY BROTHERS!
FOLLOW ME!

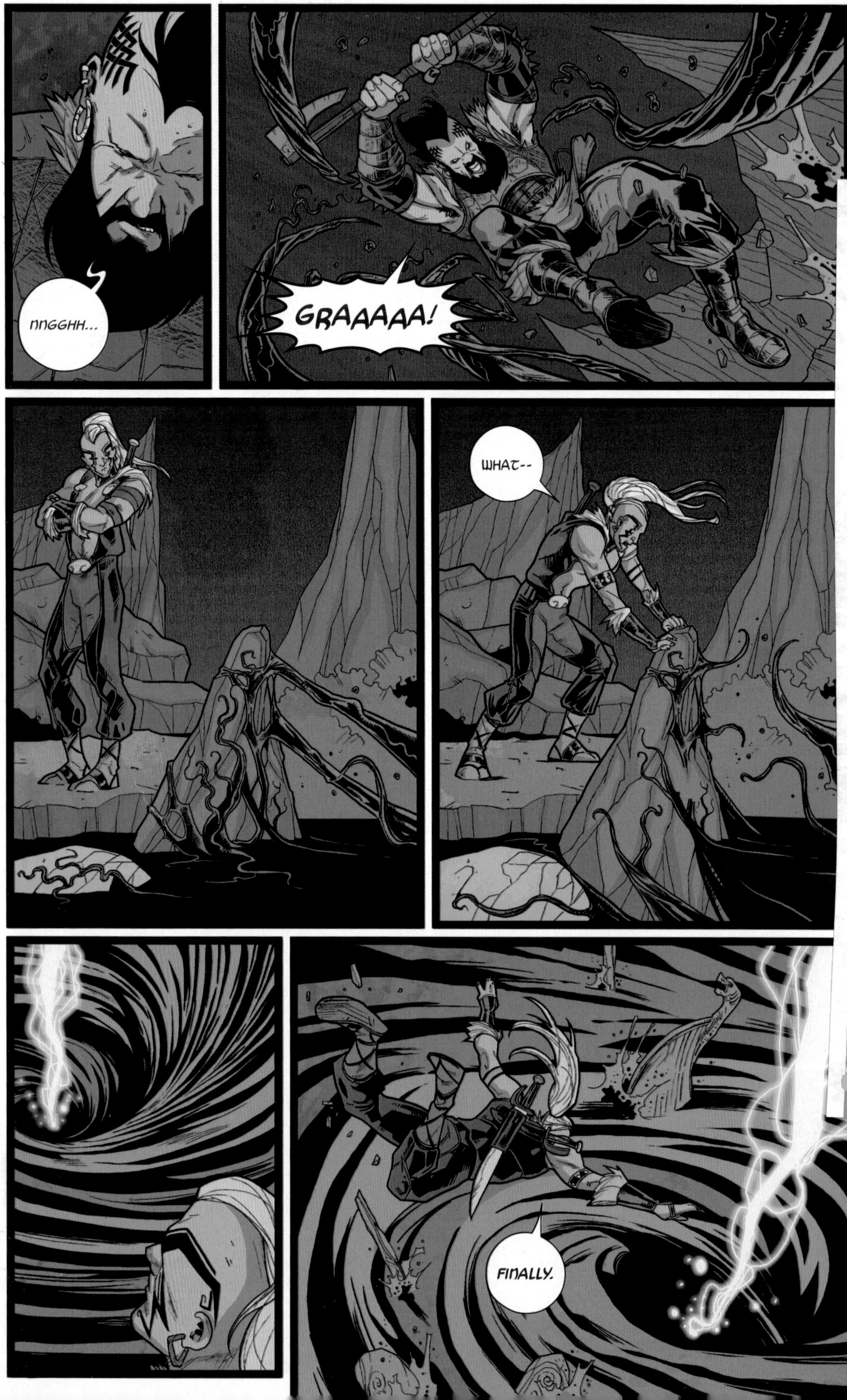
NNGGHH...
GRAAAAA!
WHAT--
FINALLY.

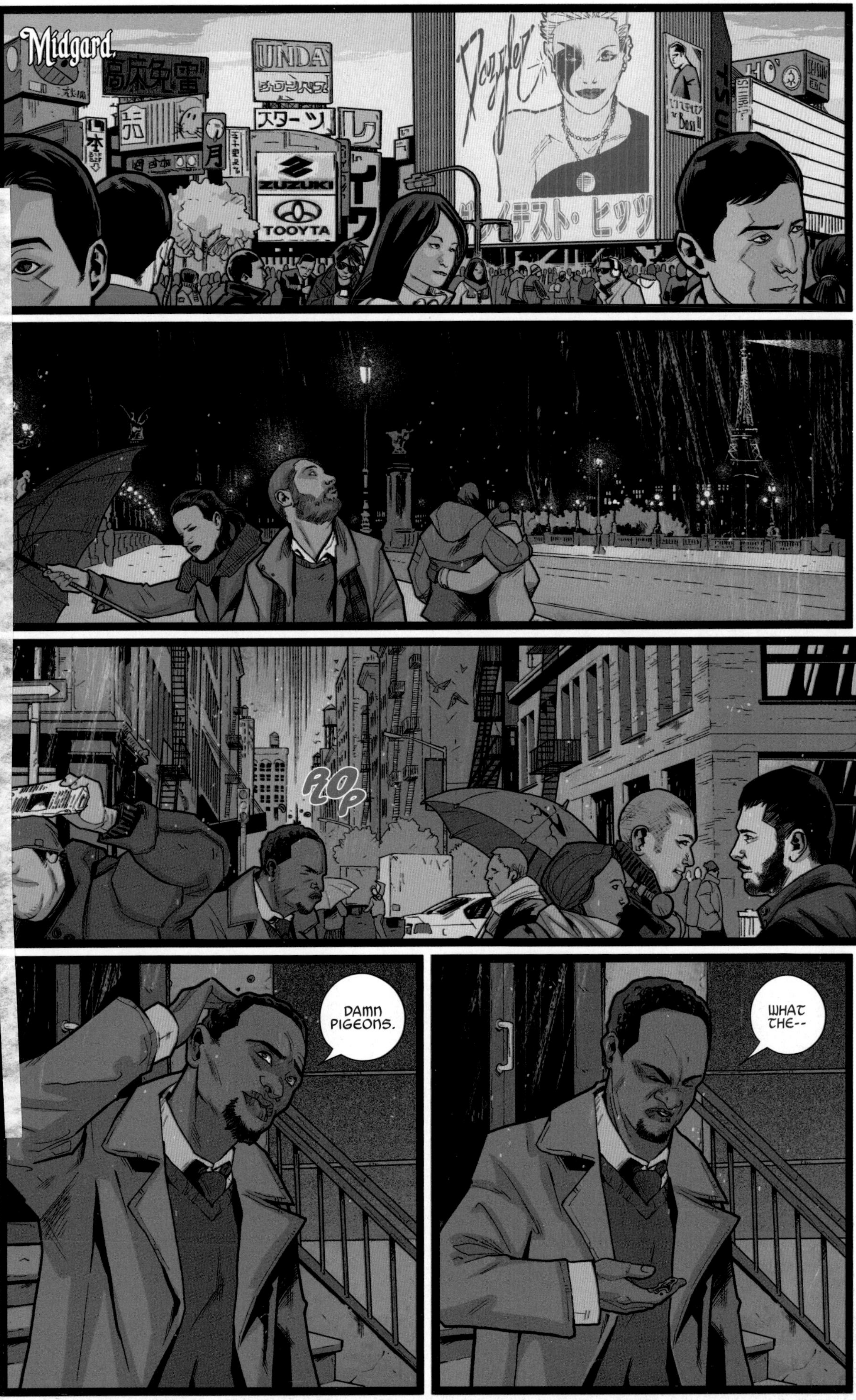
Midgard.
PLOP
DAMN PIGEONS.
WHAT THE--

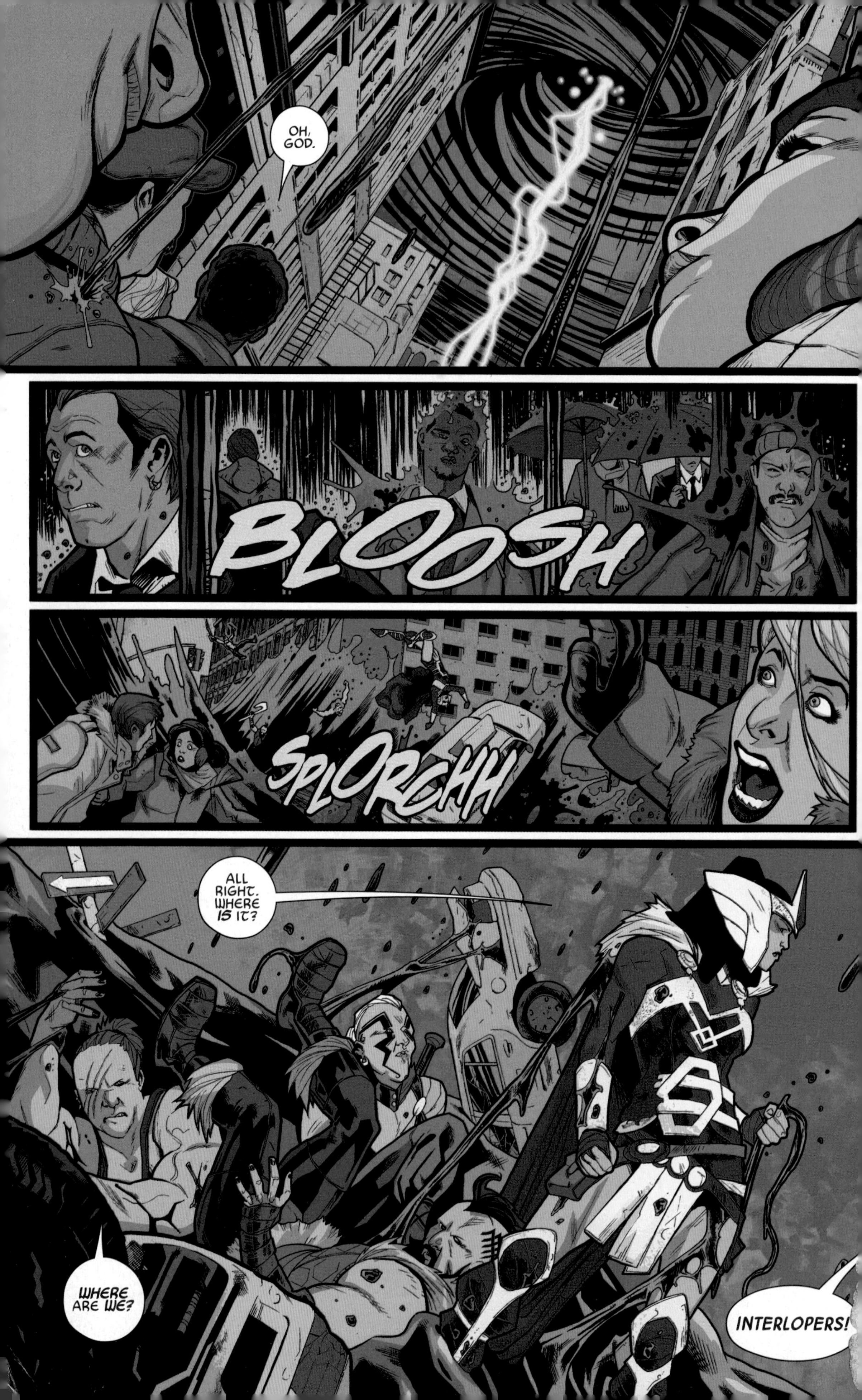
OH, GOD.
BLOOSH
SPLORCHH
ALL RIGHT. WHERE IS IT?
WHERE ARE WE?
INTERLOPERS!

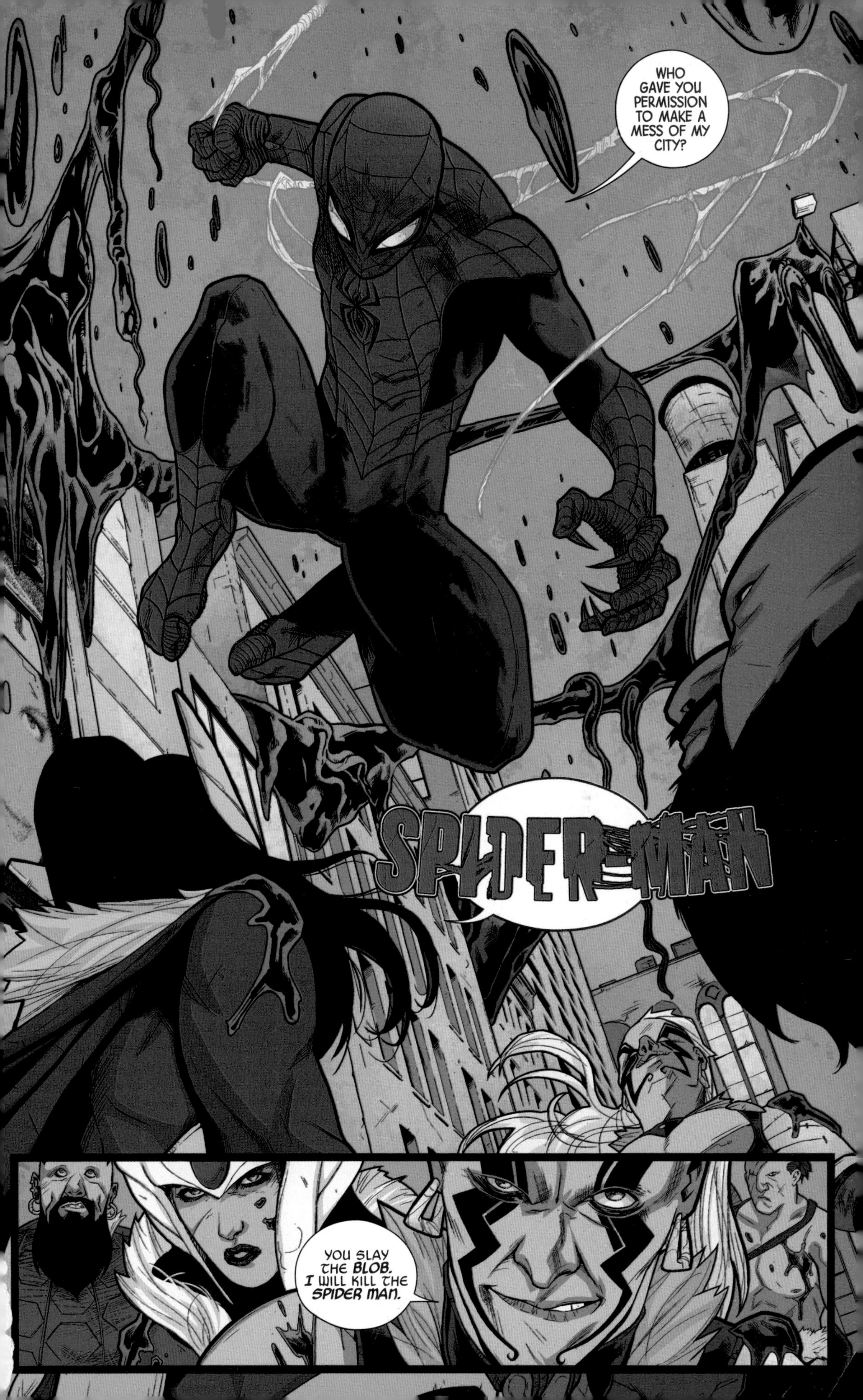
WHO GAVE YOU PERMISSION TO MAKE A MESS OF MY CITY?
SPIDER-MAN
YOU SLAY THE BLOB. I WILL KILL THE SPIDER MAN.

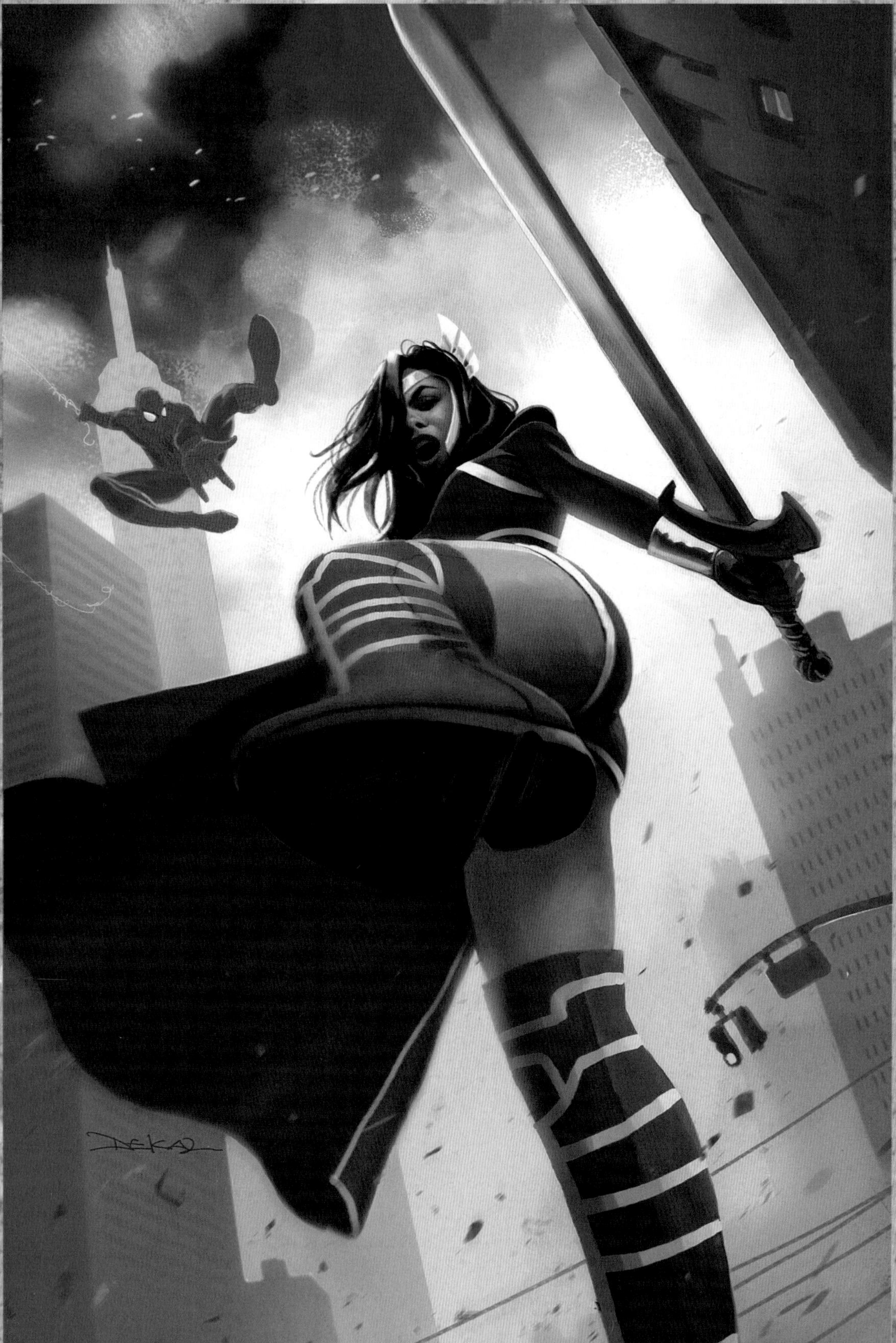

#649

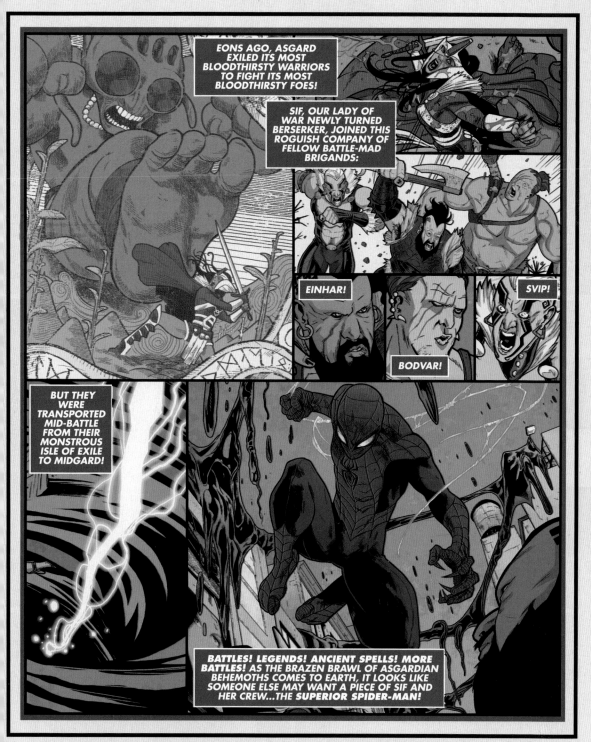

EONS AGO, ASGARD EXILED ITS MOST BLOODTHIRSTY WARRIORS TO FIGHT ITS MOST BLOODTHIRSTY FOES!

SIF, OUR LADY OF WAR NEWLY TURNED BERSERKER, JOINED THIS ROGUISH COMPANY OF FELLOW BATTLE-MAD BRIGANDS:

EINHAR!

BODVAR!

SVIP!

BUT THEY WERE TRANSPORTED MID-BATTLE FROM THEIR MONSTROUS ISLE OF EXILE TO MIDGARD!

BATTLES! LEGENDS! ANCIENT SPELLS! MORE BATTLES! AS THE BRAZEN BRAWL OF ASGARDIAN BEHEMOTHS COMES TO EARTH, IT LOOKS LIKE SOMEONE ELSE MAY WANT A PIECE OF SIF AND HER CREW...THE *SUPERIOR SPIDER-MAN!*

JOURNEY INTO MYSTERY
STRONGER THAN MONSTERS, PART 4 OF 5

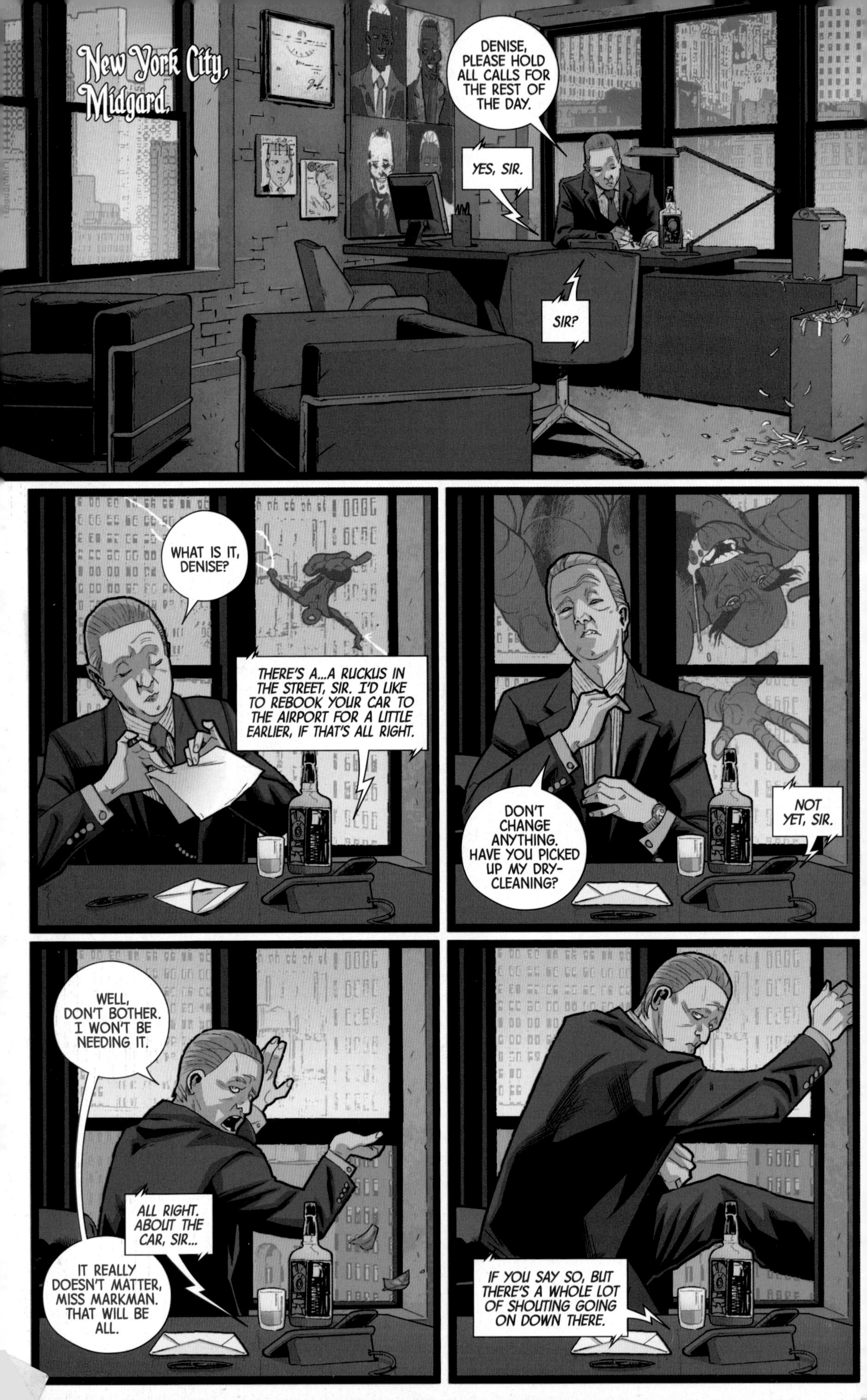
New York City, Midgard.
DENISE, PLEASE HOLD ALL CALLS FOR THE REST OF THE DAY.
YES, SIR.
SIR?
WHAT IS IT, DENISE?
THERE'S A...A RUCKUS IN THE STREET, SIR. I'D LIKE TO REBOOK YOUR CAR TO THE AIRPORT FOR A LITTLE EARLIER, IF THAT'S ALL RIGHT.
DON'T CHANGE ANYTHING. HAVE YOU PICKED UP MY DRY-CLEANING?
NOT YET, SIR.
WELL, DON'T BOTHER. I WON'T BE NEEDING IT.
ALL RIGHT. ABOUT THE CAR, SIR...
IT REALLY DOESN'T MATTER, MISS MARKMAN. THAT WILL BE ALL.
IF YOU SAY SO, BUT THERE'S A WHOLE LOT OF SHOUTING GOING ON DOWN THERE.

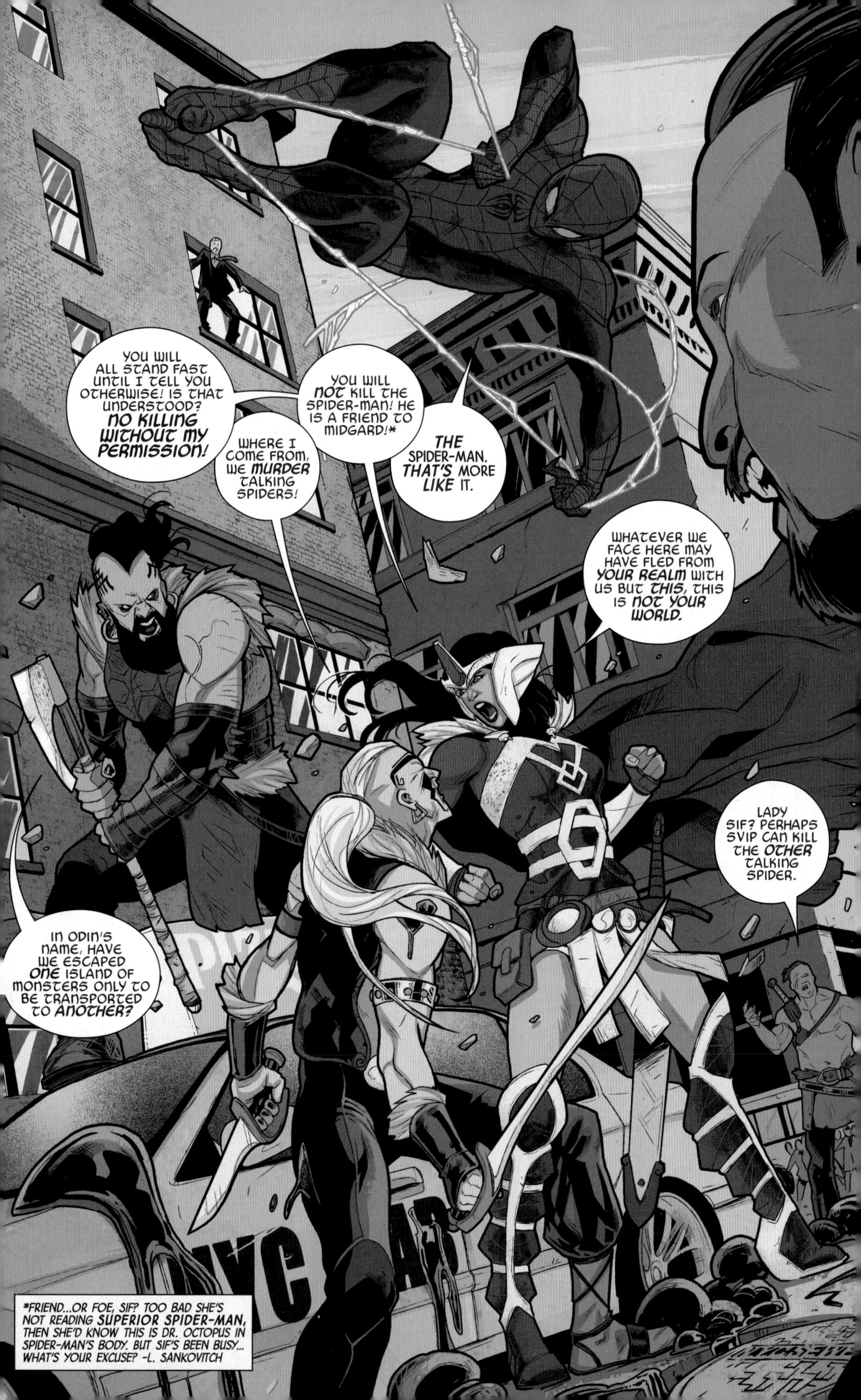
YOU WILL ALL STAND FAST UNTIL I TELL YOU OTHERWISE! IS THAT UNDERSTOOD? NO KILLING WITHOUT MY PERMISSION!
YOU WILL NOT KILL THE SPIDER-MAN! HE IS A FRIEND TO MIDGARD!*
WHERE I COME FROM, WE MURDER TALKING SPIDERS!
THE SPIDER-MAN. THAT'S MORE LIKE IT.
WHATEVER WE FACE HERE MAY HAVE FLED FROM YOUR REALM WITH US BUT THIS, THIS IS NOT YOUR WORLD.
LADY SIF? PERHAPS SVIP CAN KILL THE OTHER TALKING SPIDER.
IN ODIN'S NAME, HAVE WE ESCAPED ONE ISLAND OF MONSTERS ONLY TO BE TRANSPORTED TO ANOTHER?
*FRIEND...OR FOE, SIF? TOO BAD SHE'S NOT READING SUPERIOR SPIDER-MAN, THEN SHE'D KNOW THIS IS DR. OCTOPUS IN SPIDER-MAN'S BODY. BUT SIF'S BEEN BUSY... WHAT'S YOUR EXCUSE? -L. SANKOVITCH

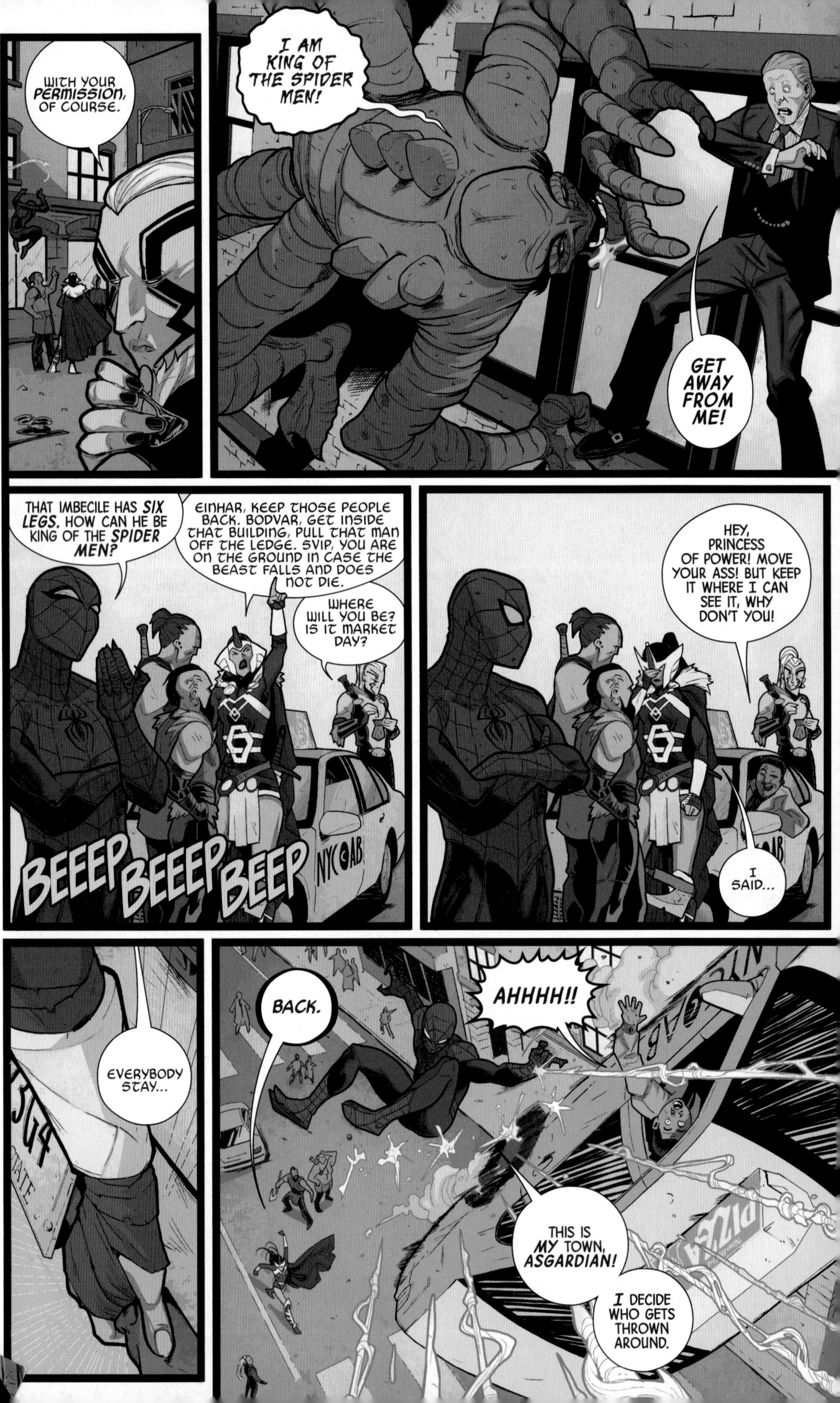
WITH YOUR PERMISSION, OF COURSE.
I AM KING OF THE SPIDER MEN!
GET AWAY FROM ME!
THAT IMBECILE HAS SIX LEGS. HOW CAN HE BE KING OF THE SPIDER MEN?
EINHAR, KEEP THOSE PEOPLE BACK. BODVAR, GET INSIDE THAT BUILDING, PULL THAT MAN OFF THE LEDGE. SVIP, YOU ARE ON THE GROUND IN CASE THE BEAST FALLS AND DOES NOT DIE.
WHERE WILL YOU BE? IS IT MARKET DAY?
BEEEP BEEEP BEEP
NYC CAB
HEY, PRINCESS OF POWER! MOVE YOUR ASS! BUT KEEP IT WHERE I CAN SEE IT, WHY DON'T YOU!
I SAID...
EVERYBODY STAY...
BACK.
AHHHH!!
THIS IS MY TOWN, ASGARDIAN!
I DECIDE WHO GETS THROWN AROUND.

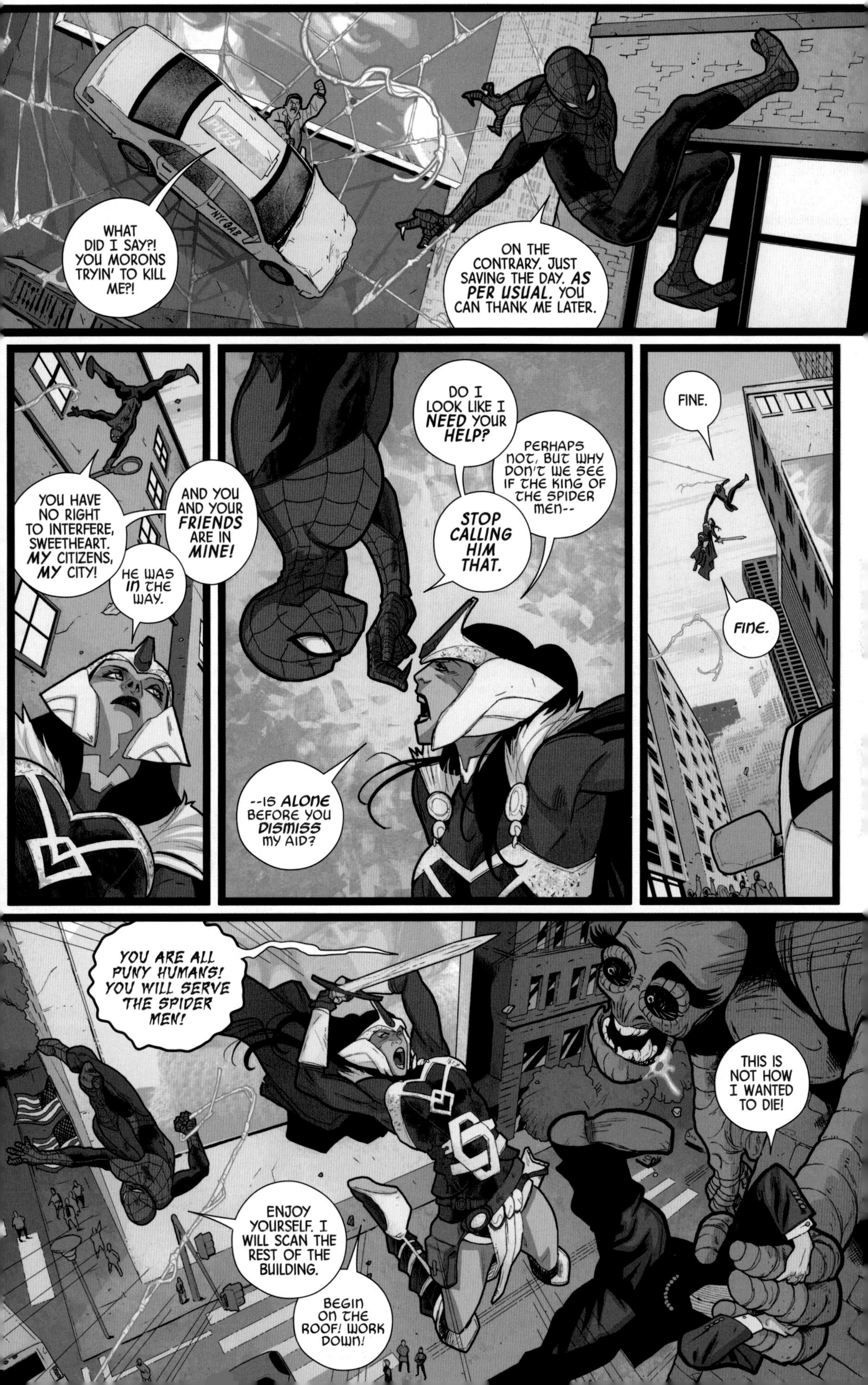
WHAT DID I SAY?! YOU MORONS TRYIN' TO KILL ME?!
ON THE CONTRARY. JUST SAVING THE DAY. AS PER USUAL. YOU CAN THANK ME LATER.
YOU HAVE NO RIGHT TO INTERFERE, SWEETHEART. MY CITIZENS, MY CITY!
AND YOU AND YOUR FRIENDS ARE IN MINE!
HE WAS IN THE WAY.
DO I LOOK LIKE I NEED YOUR HELP?
PERHAPS NOT, BUT WHY DON'T WE SEE IF THE KING OF THE SPIDER MEN--
STOP CALLING HIM THAT.
--IS ALONE BEFORE YOU DISMISS MY AID?
FINE.
FINE.
YOU ARE ALL PUNY HUMANS! YOU WILL SERVE THE SPIDER MEN!
THIS IS NOT HOW I WANTED TO DIE!
ENJOY YOURSELF. I WILL SCAN THE REST OF THE BUILDING.
BEGIN ON THE ROOF! WORK DOWN!

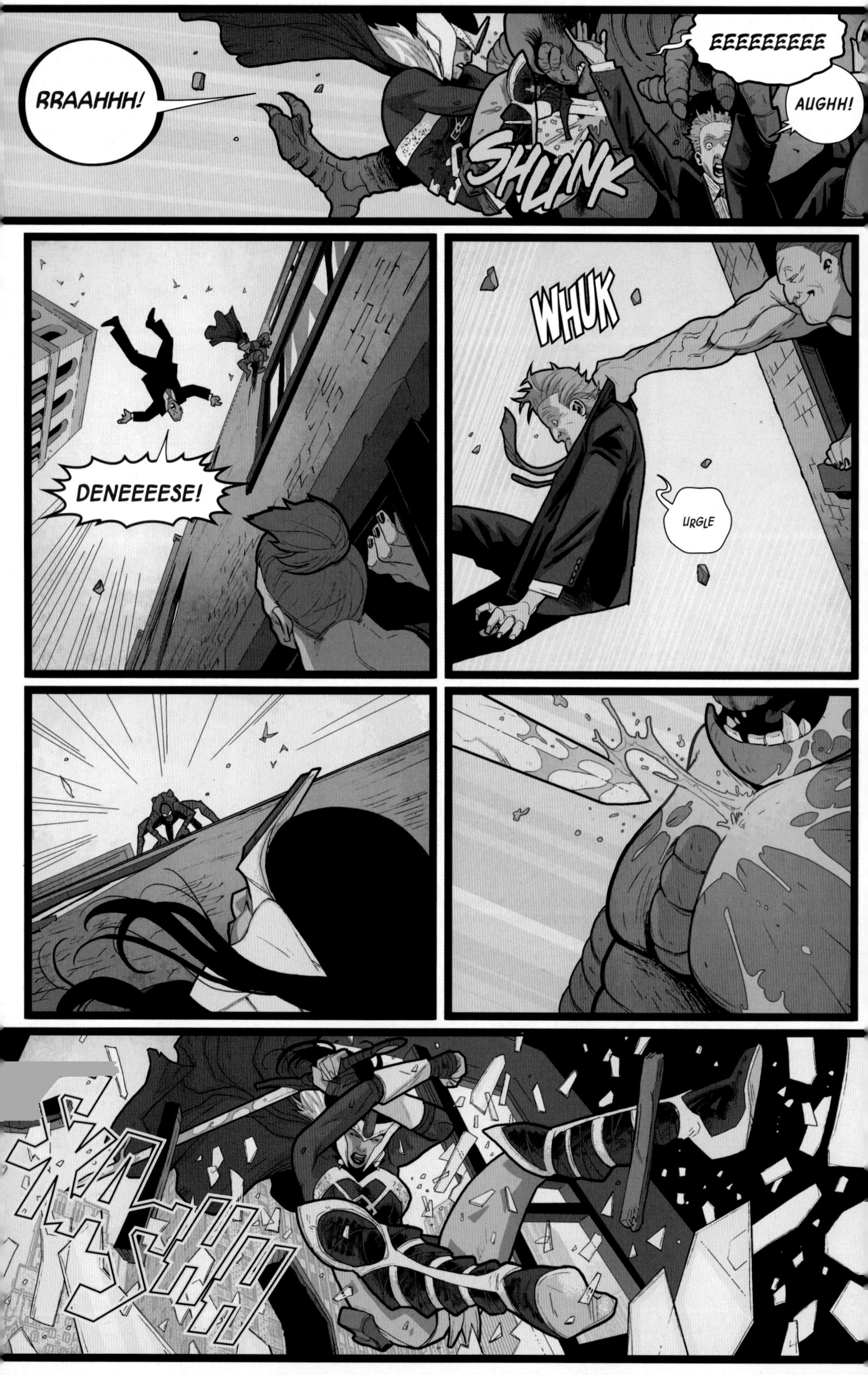
BRAAHHH!
EEEEEEEEE
AUGHH!
SHUNK
DENEEEEESE!
WHUK
URGLE

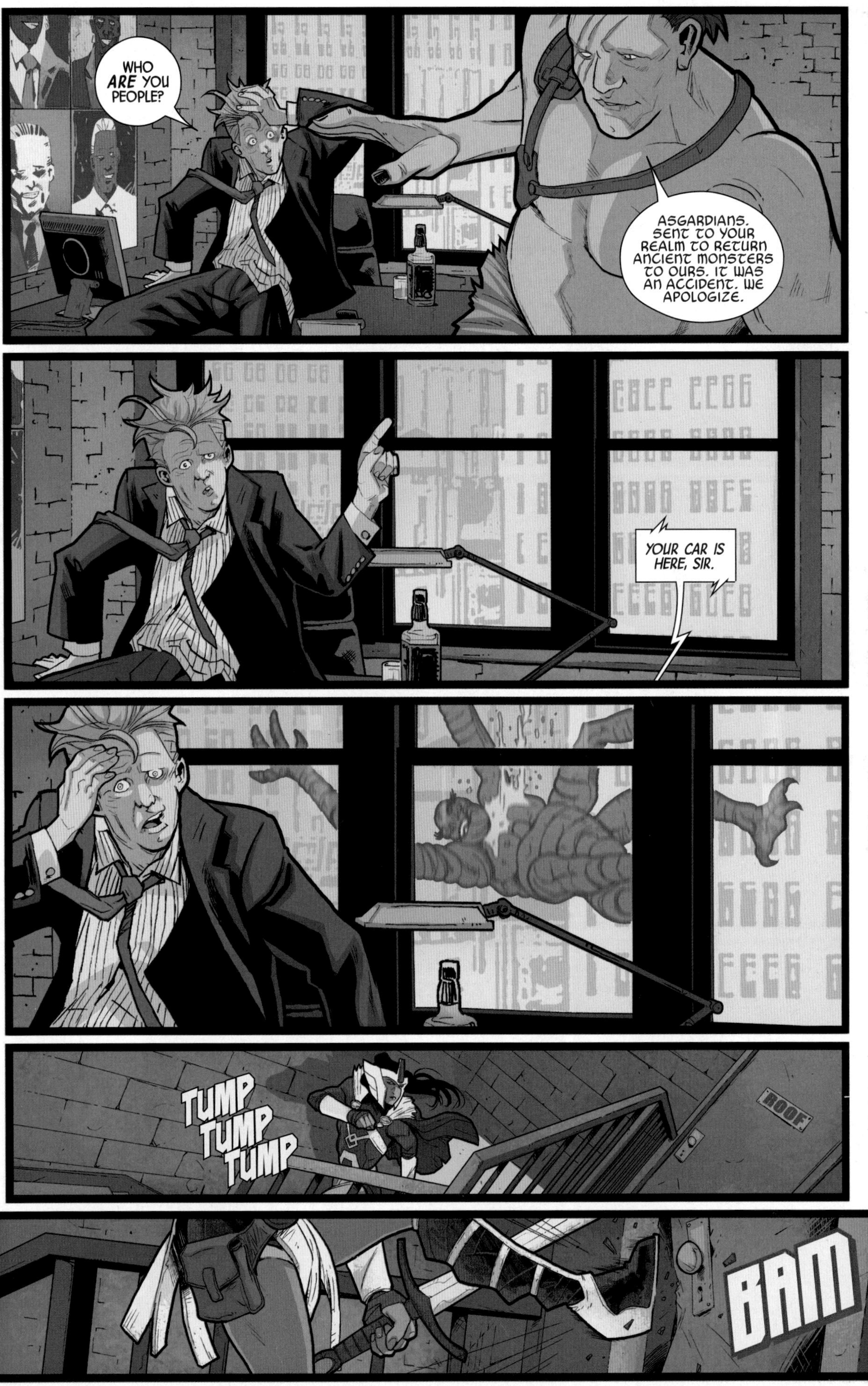
WHO ARE YOU PEOPLE?
ASGARDIANS. SENT TO YOUR REALM TO RETURN ANCIENT MONSTERS TO OURS. IT WAS AN ACCIDENT. WE APOLOGIZE.
YOUR CAR IS HERE, SIR.
TUMP TUMP TUMP
ROOF
BAM

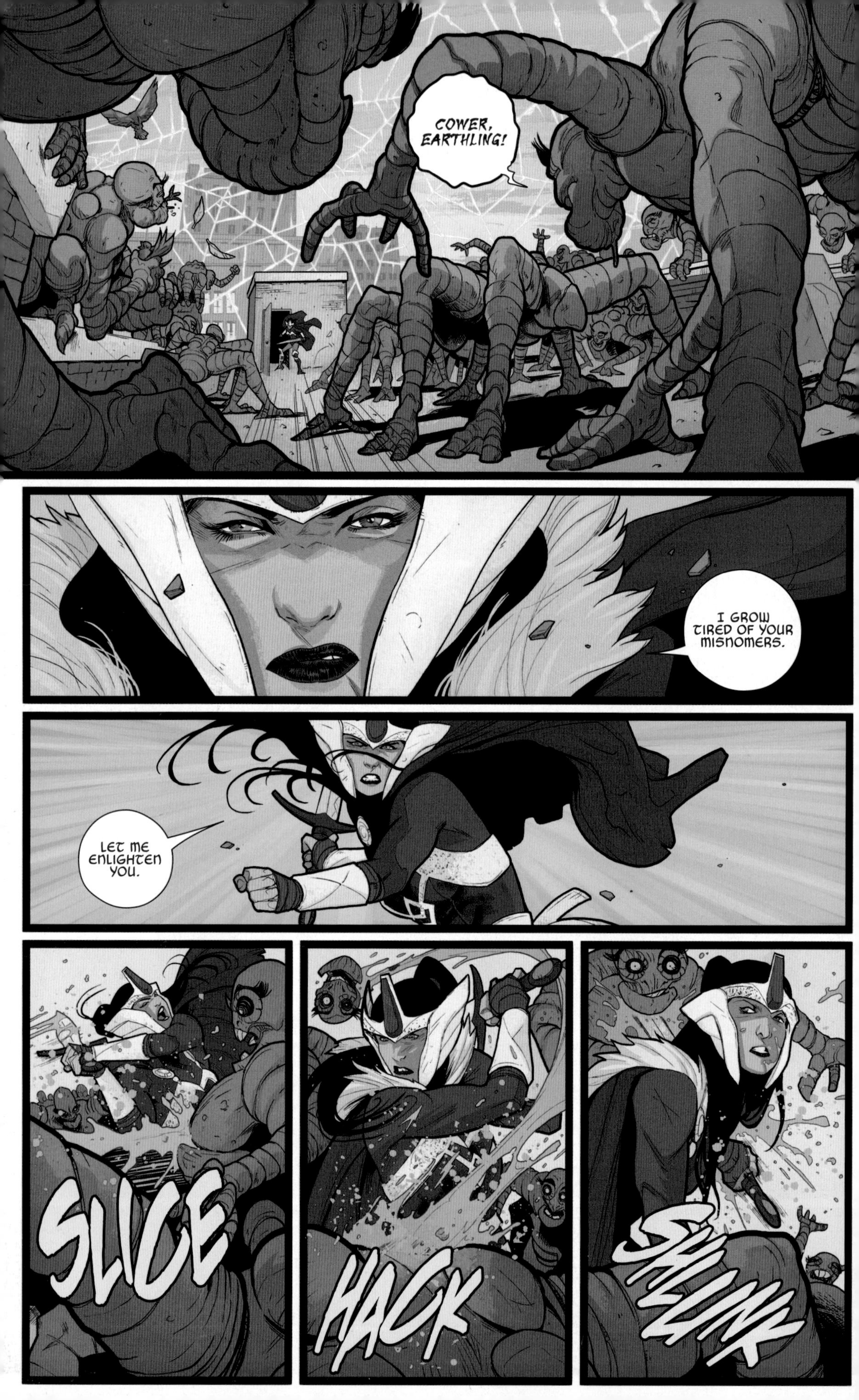
COWER, EARTHLING!
I GROW TIRED OF YOUR MISNOMERS.
LET ME ENLIGHTEN YOU.
SLICE
HACK
SHUNK

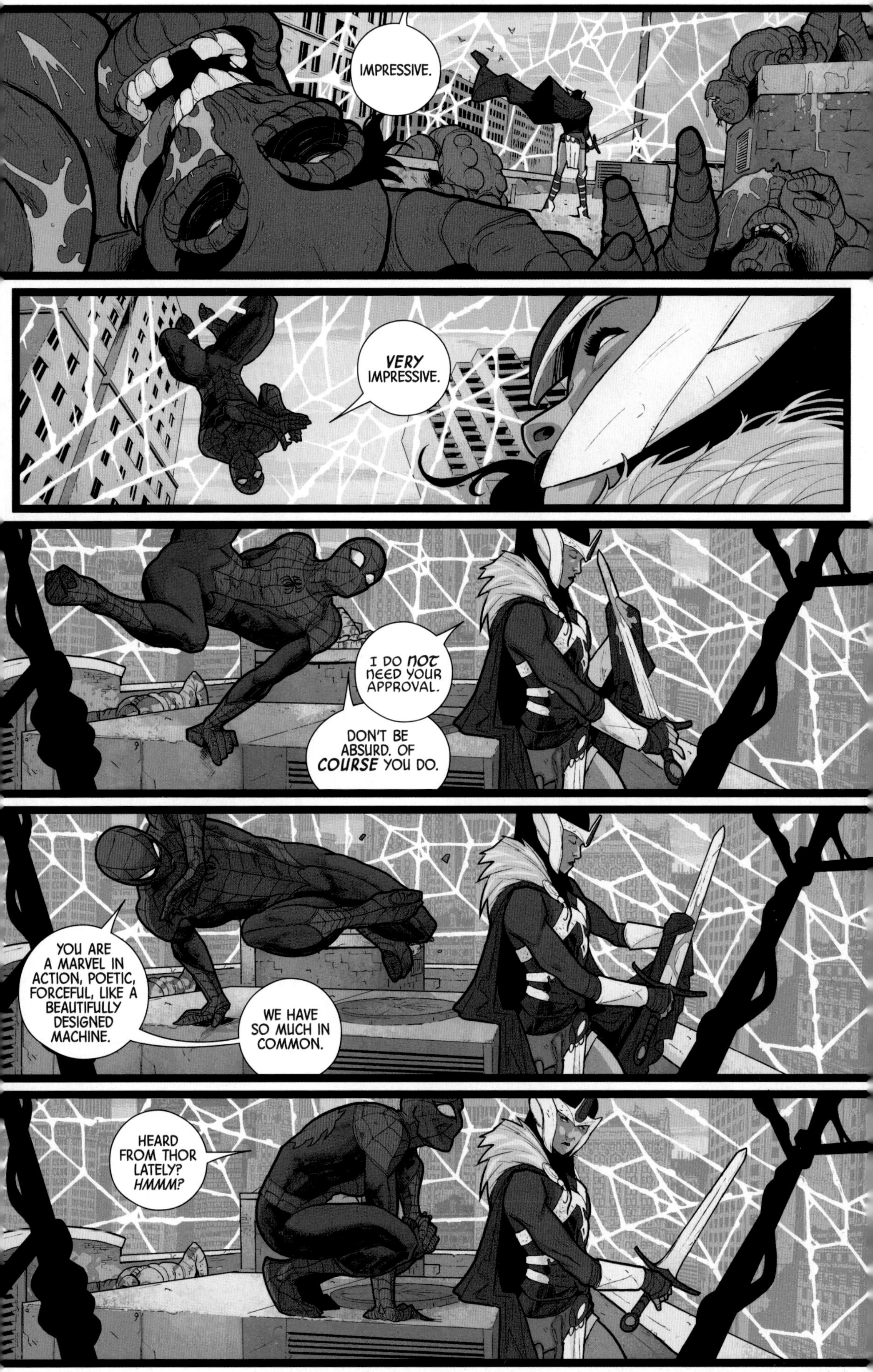
IMPRESSIVE.
VERY IMPRESSIVE.
I DO NOT NEED YOUR APPROVAL.
DON'T BE ABSURD. OF COURSE YOU DO.
YOU ARE A MARVEL IN ACTION, POETIC, FORCEFUL, LIKE A BEAUTIFULLY DESIGNED MACHINE.
WE HAVE SO MUCH IN COMMON.
HEARD FROM THOR LATELY? HMMM?

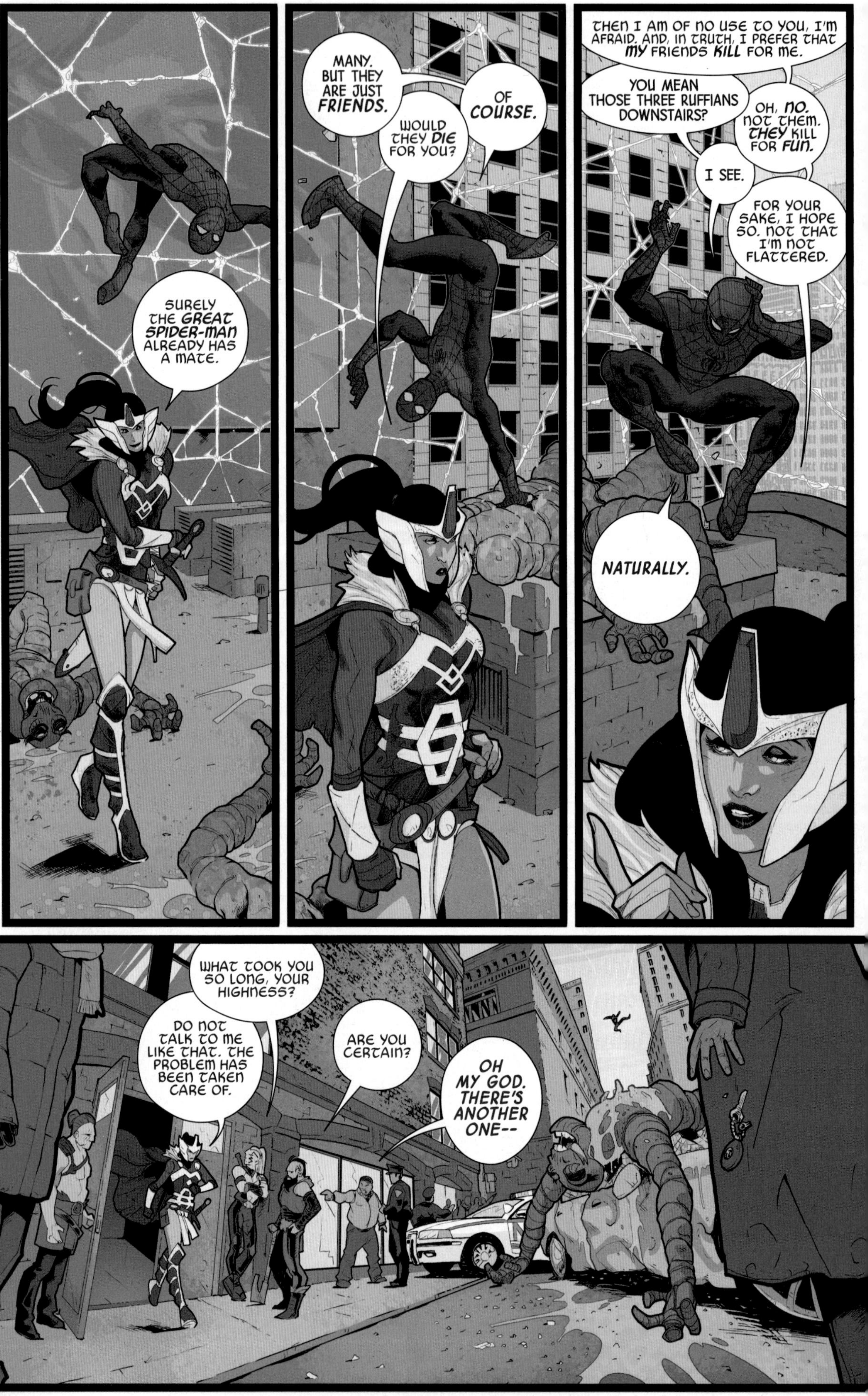
SURELY THE GREAT SPIDER-MAN ALREADY HAS A MATE.
MANY. BUT THEY ARE JUST FRIENDS.
WOULD THEY DIE FOR YOU?
OF COURSE.
THEN I AM OF NO USE TO YOU, I'M AFRAID. AND, IN TRUTH, I PREFER THAT MY FRIENDS KILL FOR ME.
YOU MEAN THOSE THREE RUFFIANS DOWNSTAIRS?
OH, NO. NOT THEM. THEY KILL FOR FUN.
I SEE.
FOR YOUR SAKE, I HOPE SO. NOT THAT I'M NOT FLATTERED.
NATURALLY.
WHAT TOOK YOU SO LONG, YOUR HIGHNESS?
DO NOT TALK TO ME LIKE THAT. THE PROBLEM HAS BEEN TAKEN CARE OF.
ARE YOU CERTAIN?
OH MY GOD. THERE'S ANOTHER ONE--

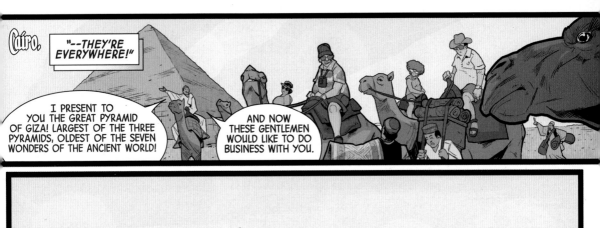

Cairo,

"--THEY'RE EVERYWHERE!"

I PRESENT TO YOU THE GREAT PYRAMID OF GIZA! LARGEST OF THE THREE PYRAMIDS, OLDEST OF THE SEVEN WONDERS OF THE ANCIENT WORLD!

AND NOW THESE GENTLEMEN WOULD LIKE TO DO BUSINESS WITH YOU.

FRANKINCENSE! MYRRH! SAFFRON! CUMIN!

GOMDULLA!

PERHAPS! LET ME CHECK IN THE BACK!

I AM GOMDULLA, THE LIVING PHARAOH! TREMBLE BEFORE ME, MORTALS!

AHHHHHHH!

AUGGHH!

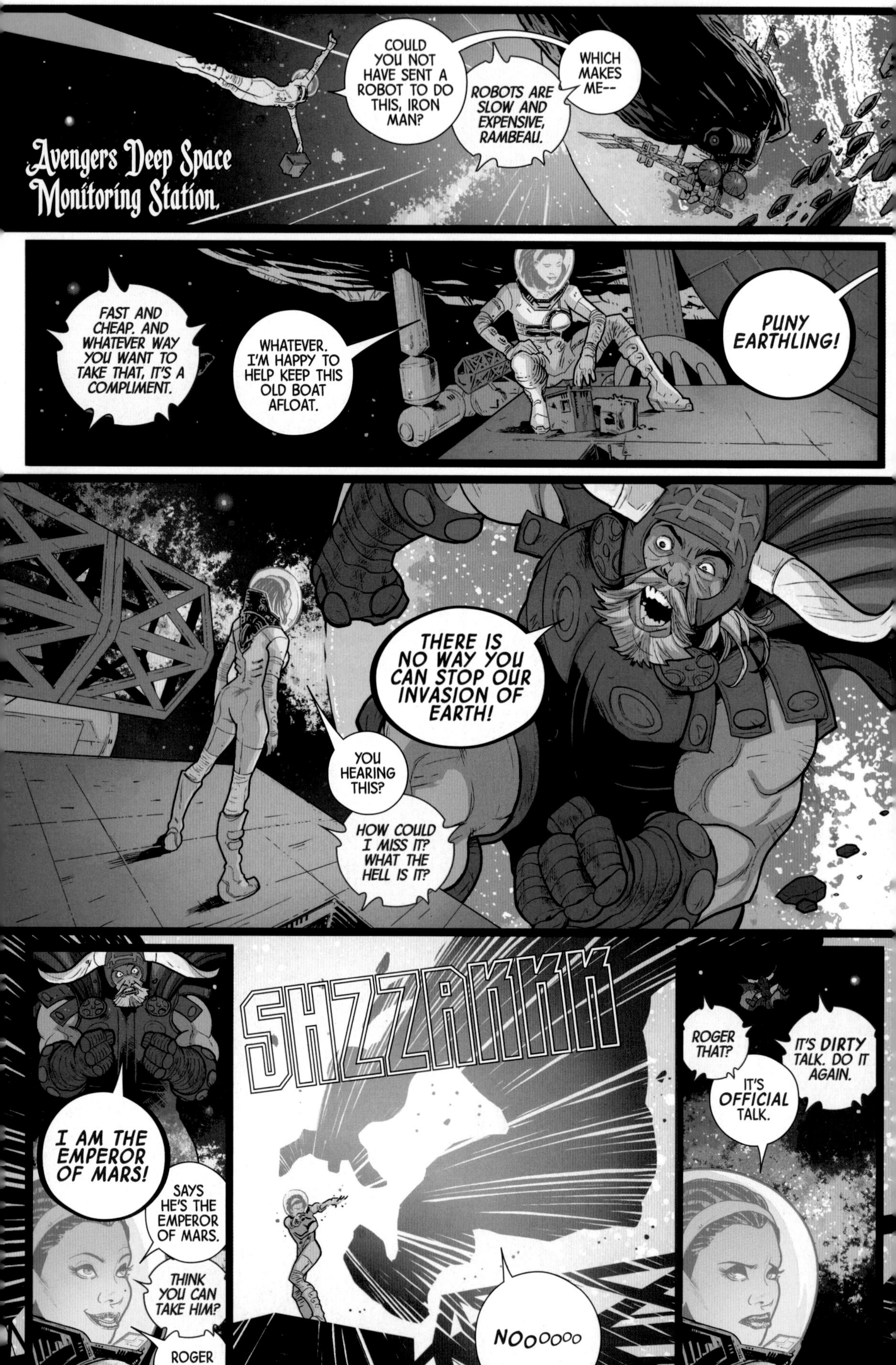
Avengers Deep Space Monitoring Station.
COULD YOU NOT HAVE SENT A ROBOT TO DO THIS, IRON MAN?
ROBOTS ARE SLOW AND EXPENSIVE, RAMBEAU.
WHICH MAKES ME--
FAST AND CHEAP. AND WHATEVER WAY YOU WANT TO TAKE THAT, IT'S A COMPLIMENT.
WHATEVER. I'M HAPPY TO HELP KEEP THIS OLD BOAT AFLOAT.
PUNY EARTHLING!
THERE IS NO WAY YOU CAN STOP OUR INVASION OF EARTH!
YOU HEARING THIS?
HOW COULD I MISS IT? WHAT THE HELL IS IT?
I AM THE EMPEROR OF MARS!
SAYS HE'S THE EMPEROR OF MARS.
THINK YOU CAN TAKE HIM?
ROGER THAT.
SHZZAKKK
NOooooo
ROGER THAT?
IT'S OFFICIAL TALK.
IT'S DIRTY TALK. DO IT AGAIN.

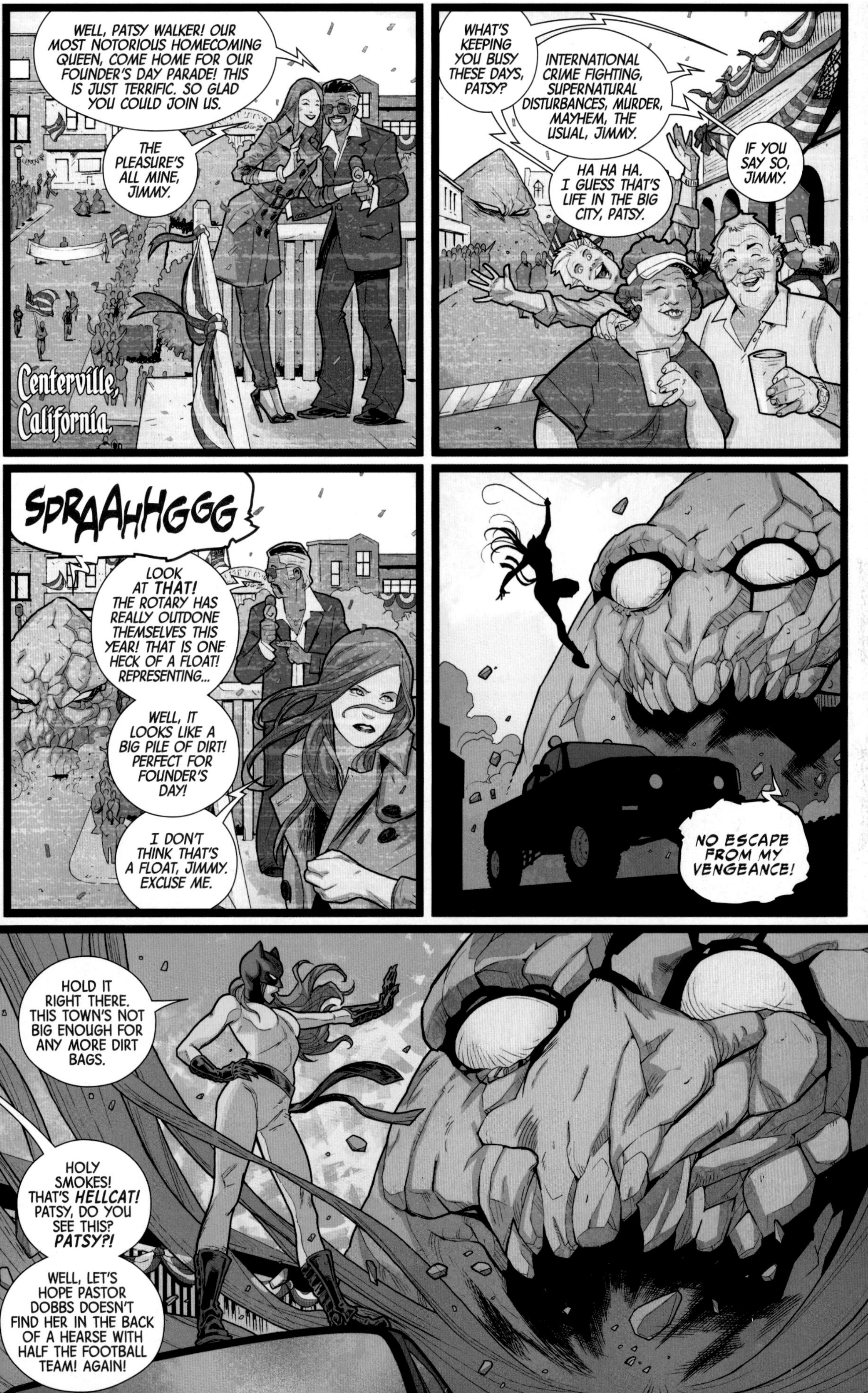
WELL, PATSY WALKER! OUR MOST NOTORIOUS HOMECOMING QUEEN, COME HOME FOR OUR FOUNDER'S DAY PARADE! THIS IS JUST TERRIFIC. SO GLAD YOU COULD JOIN US.
THE PLEASURE'S ALL MINE, JIMMY.
Centerville, California.
WHAT'S KEEPING YOU BUSY THESE DAYS, PATSY?
INTERNATIONAL CRIME FIGHTING, SUPERNATURAL DISTURBANCES, MURDER, MAYHEM, THE USUAL, JIMMY.
HA HA HA. I GUESS THAT'S LIFE IN THE BIG CITY, PATSY.
IF YOU SAY SO, JIMMY.
SPRAAHHGGG
LOOK AT THAT! THE ROTARY HAS REALLY OUTDONE THEMSELVES THIS YEAR! THAT IS ONE HECK OF A FLOAT! REPRESENTING...
WELL, IT LOOKS LIKE A BIG PILE OF DIRT! PERFECT FOR FOUNDER'S DAY!
I DON'T THINK THAT'S A FLOAT, JIMMY. EXCUSE ME.
NO ESCAPE FROM MY VENGEANCE!
HOLD IT RIGHT THERE. THIS TOWN'S NOT BIG ENOUGH FOR ANY MORE DIRT BAGS.
HOLY SMOKES! THAT'S HELLCAT! PATSY, DO YOU SEE THIS? PATSY?!
WELL, LET'S HOPE PASTOR DOBBS DOESN'T FIND HER IN THE BACK OF A HEARSE WITH HALF THE FOOTBALL TEAM! AGAIN!

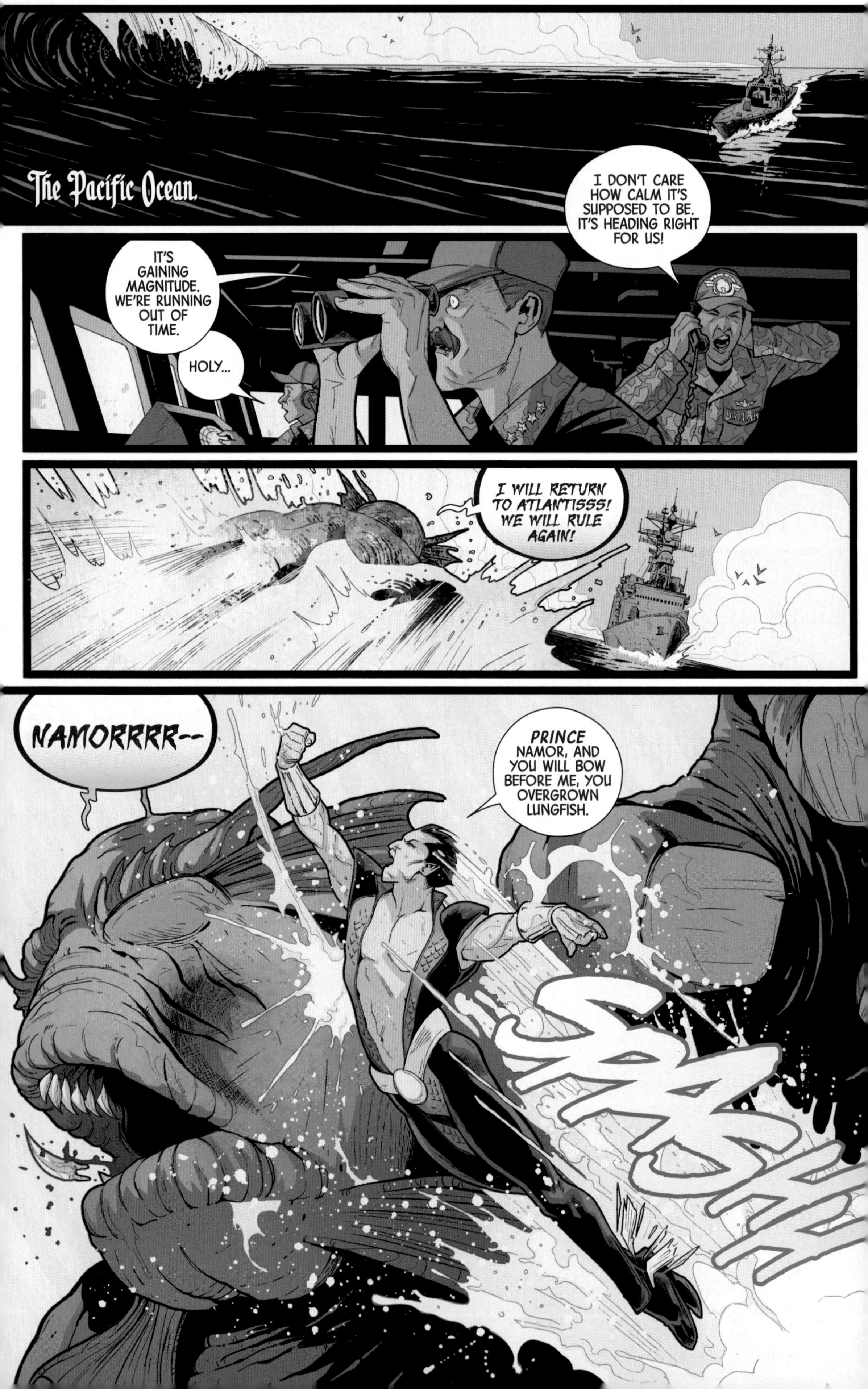
The Pacific Ocean.
I DON'T CARE HOW CALM IT'S SUPPOSED TO BE. IT'S HEADING RIGHT FOR US!
IT'S GAINING MAGNITUDE. WE'RE RUNNING OUT OF TIME.
HOLY...
I WILL RETURN TO ATLANTISSS! WE WILL RULE AGAIN!
NAMORRRR--
PRINCE NAMOR, AND YOU WILL BOW BEFORE ME, YOU OVERGROWN LUNGFISH.

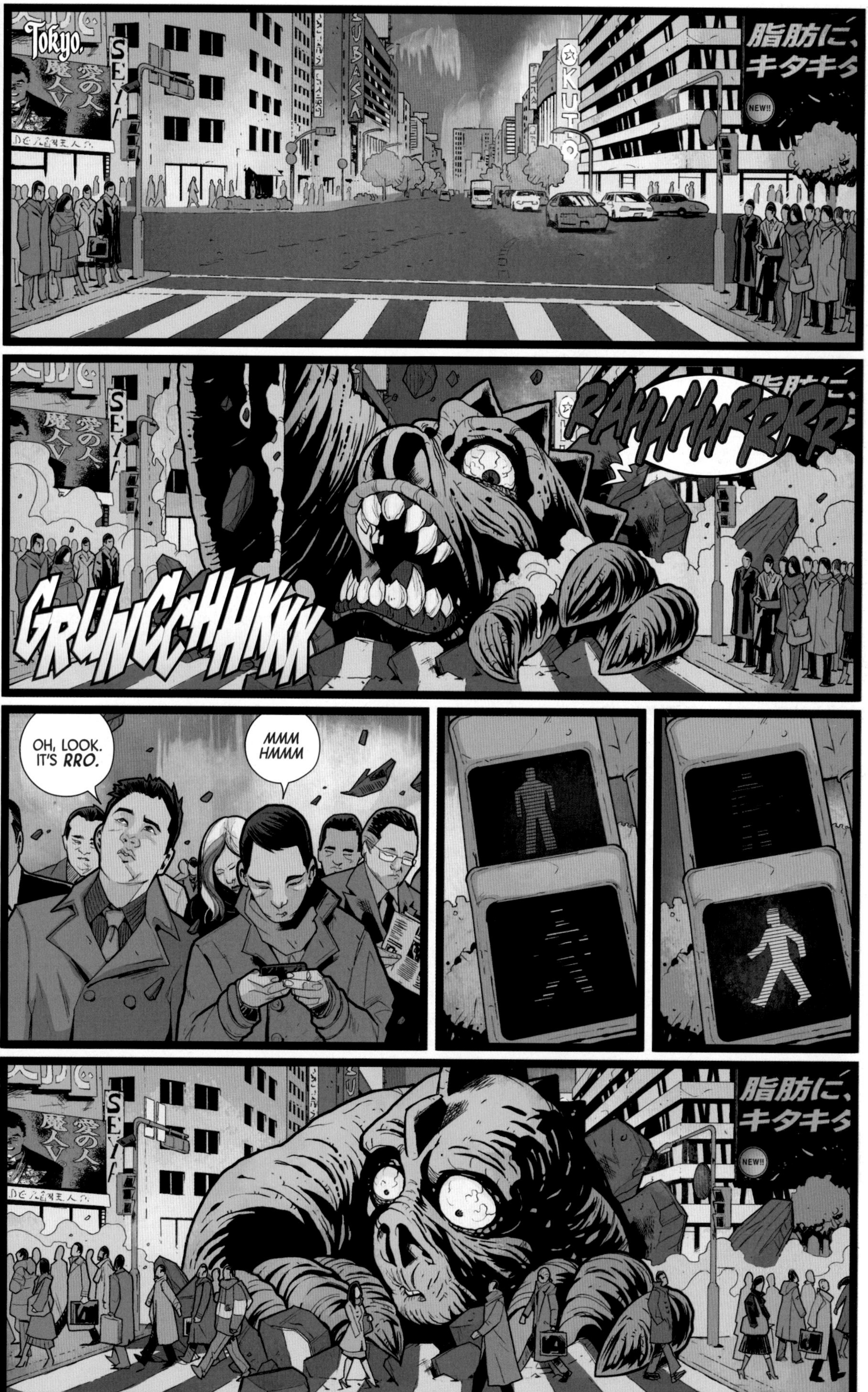

Tokyo.
脂肪に、
キタキタ
NEW!!
RAHHHURRRR
GRUNCCHHKKK
OH, LOOK. IT'S RRO.
MMM HMMM

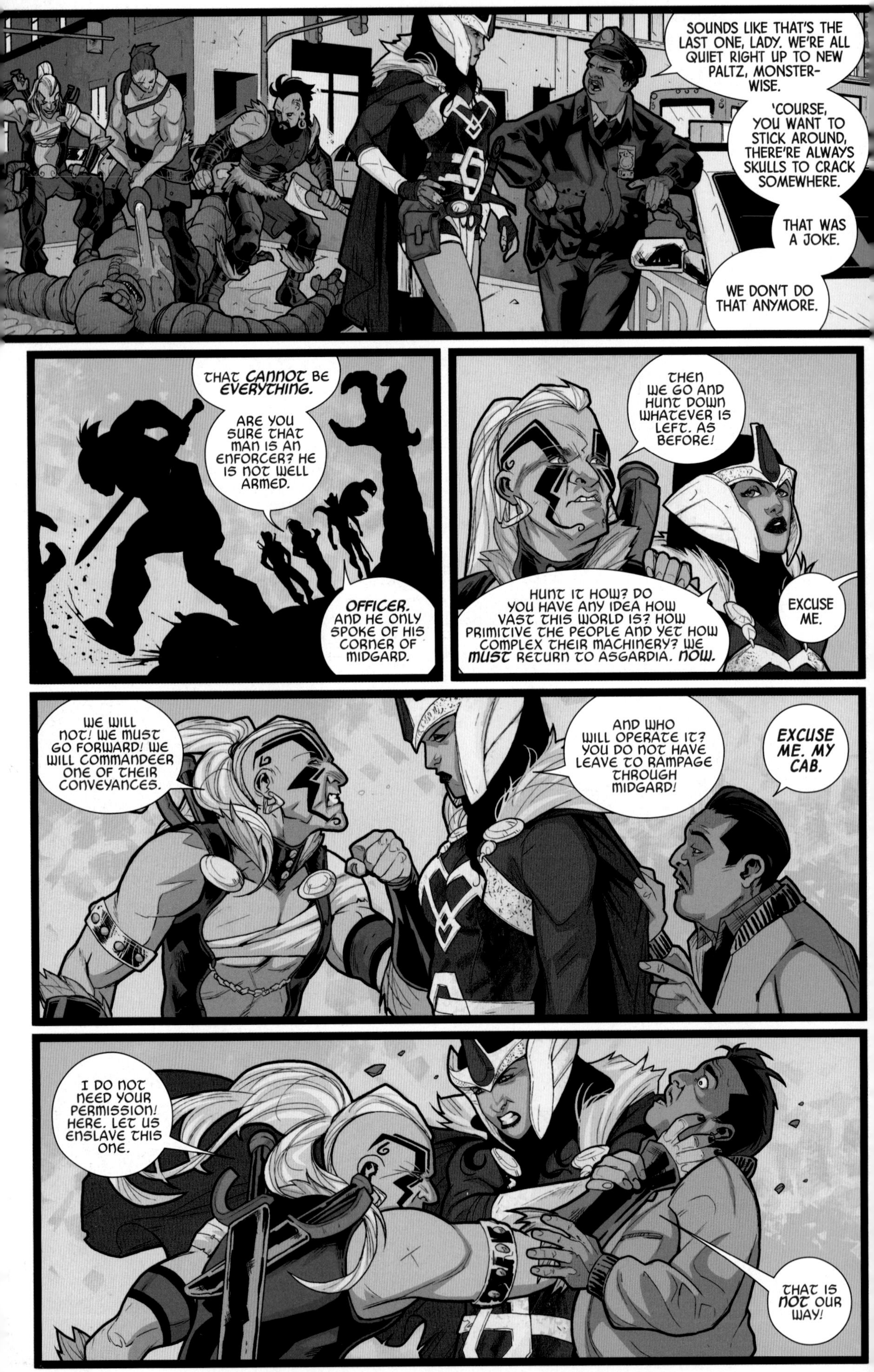
SOUNDS LIKE THAT'S THE LAST ONE, LADY. WE'RE ALL QUIET RIGHT UP TO NEW PALTZ, MONSTER-WISE.
'COURSE, YOU WANT TO STICK AROUND, THERE'RE ALWAYS SKULLS TO CRACK SOMEWHERE.
THAT WAS A JOKE.
WE DON'T DO THAT ANYMORE.
THAT CANNOT BE EVERYTHING.
ARE YOU SURE THAT MAN IS AN ENFORCER? HE IS NOT WELL ARMED.
OFFICER. AND HE ONLY SPOKE OF HIS CORNER OF MIDGARD.
THEN WE GO AND HUNT DOWN WHATEVER IS LEFT. AS BEFORE!
HUNT IT HOW? DO YOU HAVE ANY IDEA HOW VAST THIS WORLD IS? HOW PRIMITIVE THE PEOPLE AND YET HOW COMPLEX THEIR MACHINERY? WE MUST RETURN TO ASGARDIA. NOW.
EXCUSE ME.
WE WILL NOT! WE MUST GO FORWARD! WE WILL COMMANDEER ONE OF THEIR CONVEYANCES.
AND WHO WILL OPERATE IT? YOU DO NOT HAVE LEAVE TO RAMPAGE THROUGH MIDGARD!
EXCUSE ME. MY CAB.
I DO NOT NEED YOUR PERMISSION! HERE. LET US ENSLAVE THIS ONE.
THAT IS NOT OUR WAY!

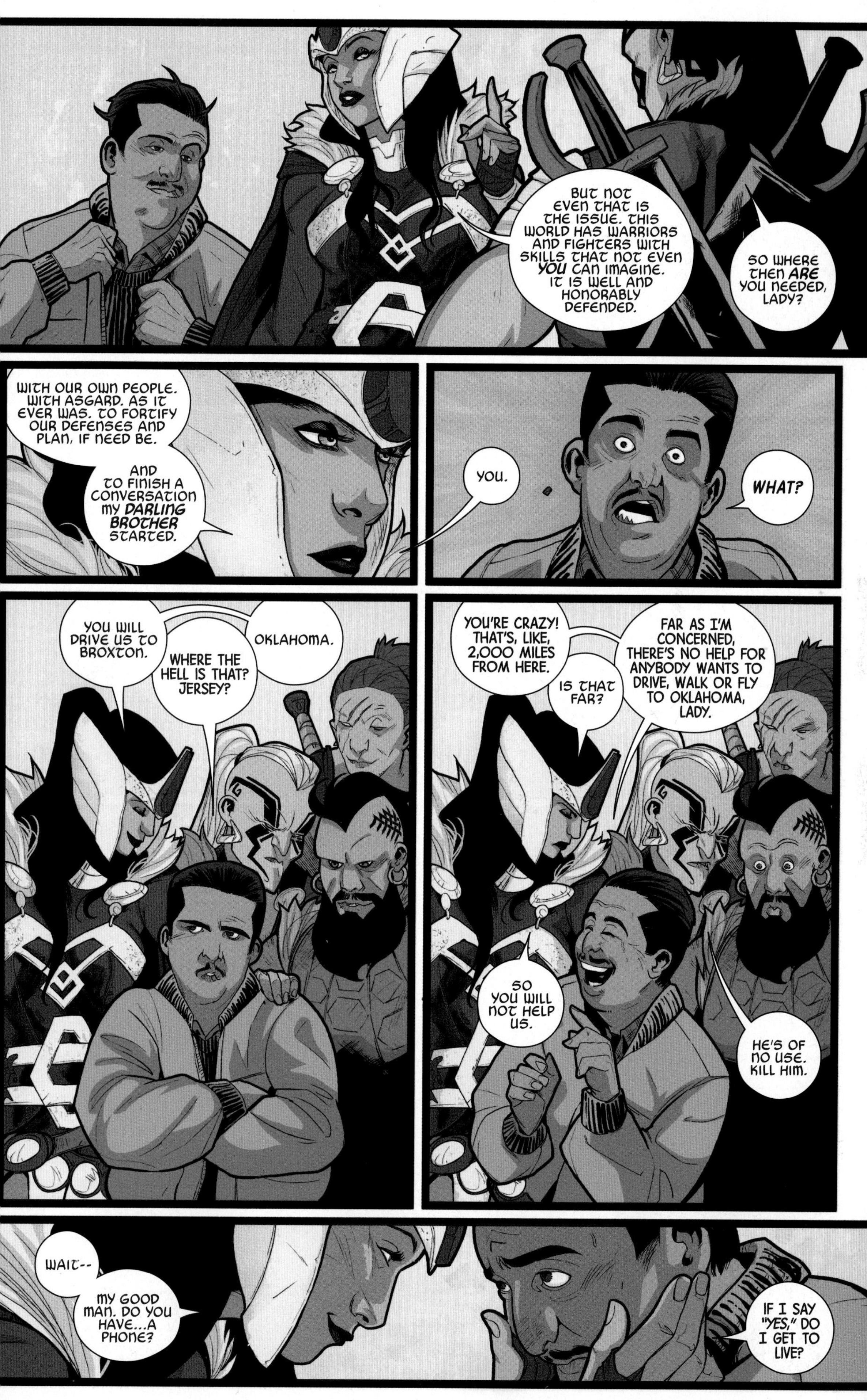
BUT NOT EVEN THAT IS THE ISSUE. THIS WORLD HAS WARRIORS AND FIGHTERS WITH SKILLS THAT NOT EVEN YOU CAN IMAGINE. IT IS WELL AND HONORABLY DEFENDED.
SO WHERE THEN ARE YOU NEEDED, LADY?
WITH OUR OWN PEOPLE. WITH ASGARD. AS IT EVER WAS. TO FORTIFY OUR DEFENSES AND PLAN, IF NEED BE.
AND TO FINISH A CONVERSATION MY DARLING BROTHER STARTED.
YOU.
WHAT?
YOU WILL DRIVE US TO BROXTON.
WHERE THE HELL IS THAT? JERSEY?
OKLAHOMA.
YOU'RE CRAZY! THAT'S, LIKE, 2,000 MILES FROM HERE.
IS THAT FAR?
FAR AS I'M CONCERNED, THERE'S NO HELP FOR ANYBODY WANTS TO DRIVE, WALK OR FLY TO OKLAHOMA, LADY.
SO YOU WILL NOT HELP US.
HE'S OF NO USE. KILL HIM.
WAIT--
MY GOOD MAN. DO YOU HAVE...A PHONE?
IF I SAY "YES," DO I GET TO LIVE?

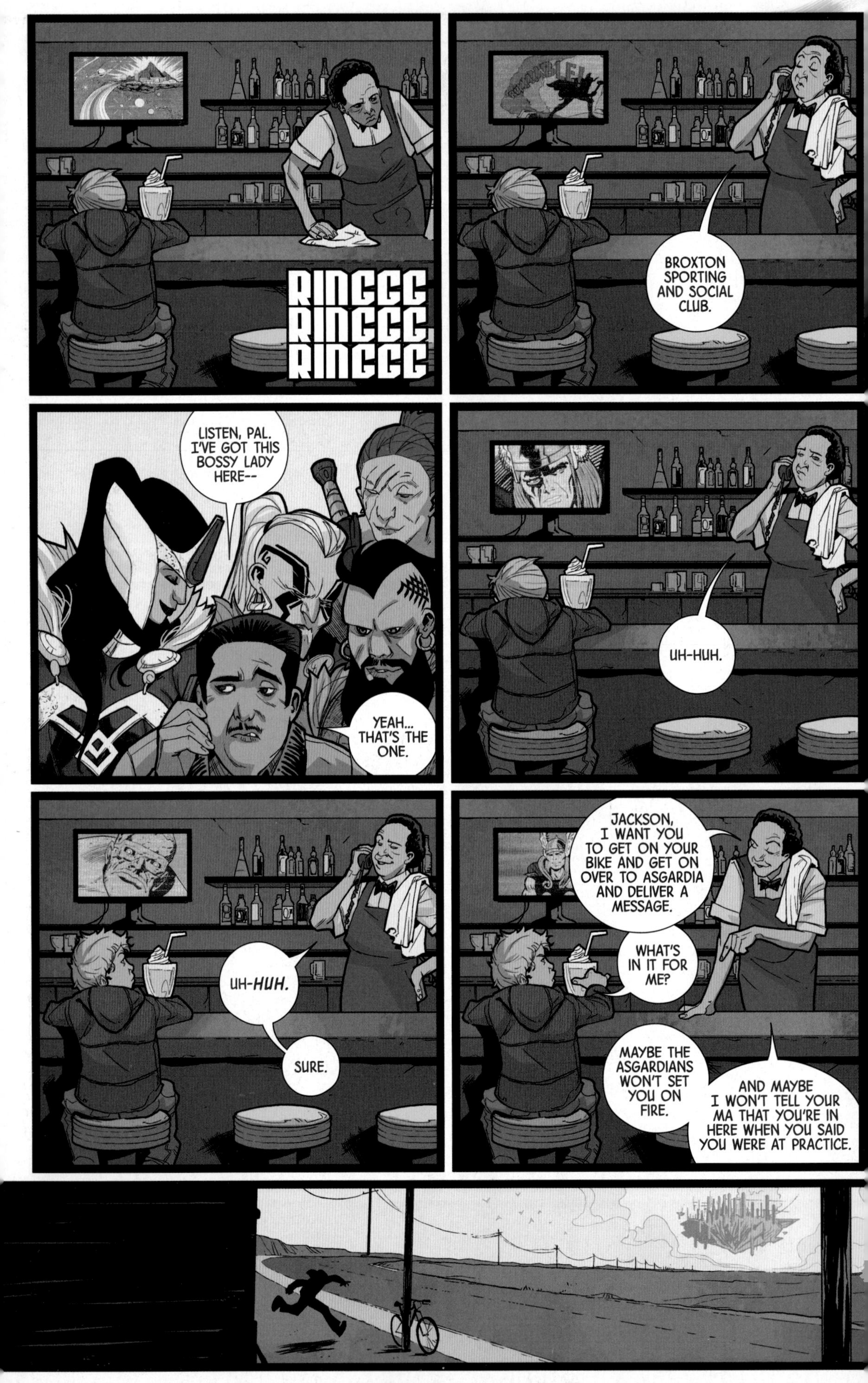
RINGGG
RINGGG
RINGGG
BROXTON SPORTING AND SOCIAL CLUB.
LISTEN, PAL. I'VE GOT THIS BOSSY LADY HERE--
YEAH... THAT'S THE ONE.
UH-HUH.
UH-HUH.
SURE.
JACKSON, I WANT YOU TO GET ON YOUR BIKE AND GET ON OVER TO ASGARDIA AND DELIVER A MESSAGE.
WHAT'S IN IT FOR ME?
MAYBE THE ASGARDIANS WON'T SET YOU ON FIRE.
AND MAYBE I WON'T TELL YOUR MA THAT YOU'RE IN HERE WHEN YOU SAID YOU WERE AT PRACTICE.

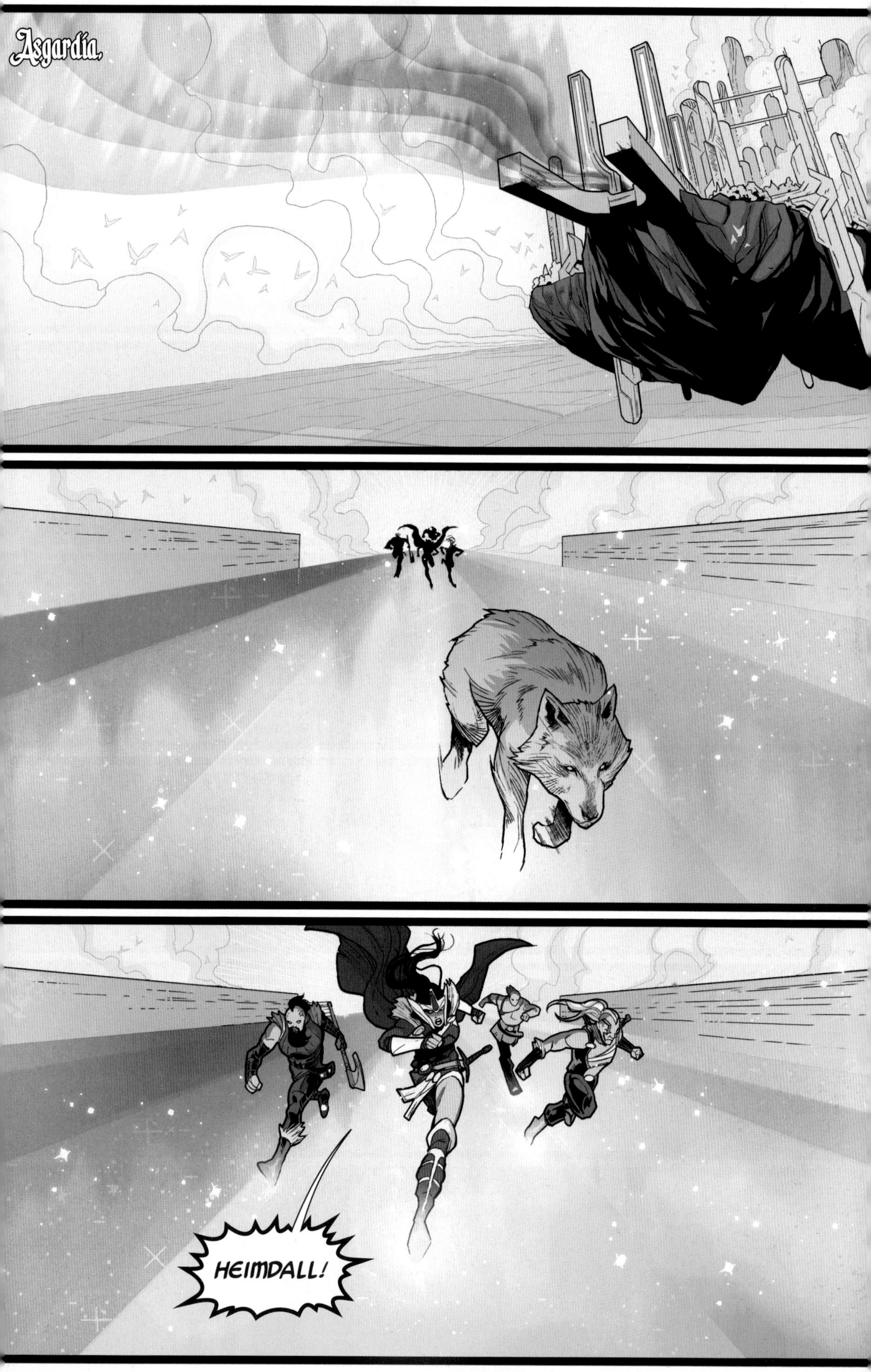
Asgardia,
HEIMDALL!

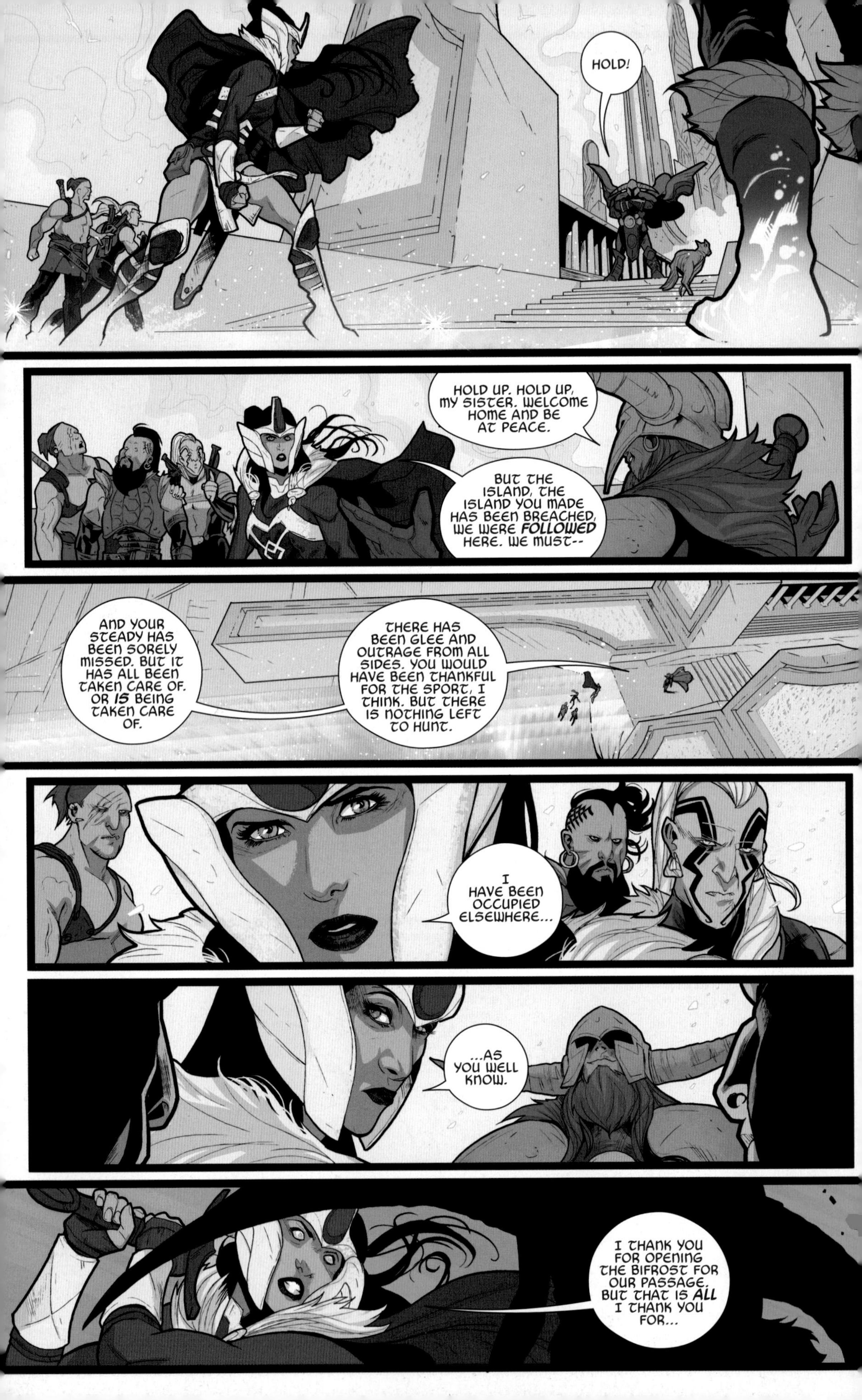
HOLD!
HOLD UP. HOLD UP, MY SISTER. WELCOME HOME AND BE AT PEACE.
BUT THE ISLAND, THE ISLAND YOU MADE HAS BEEN BREACHED, WE WERE FOLLOWED HERE. WE MUST--
THERE HAS BEEN GLEE AND OUTRAGE FROM ALL SIDES. YOU WOULD HAVE BEEN THANKFUL FOR THE SPORT, I THINK. BUT THERE IS NOTHING LEFT TO HUNT.
AND YOUR STEADY HAS BEEN SORELY MISSED. BUT IT HAS ALL BEEN TAKEN CARE OF. OR IS BEING TAKEN CARE OF.
I HAVE BEEN OCCUPIED ELSEWHERE...
...AS YOU WELL KNOW.
I THANK YOU FOR OPENING THE BIFROST FOR OUR PASSAGE. BUT THAT IS ALL I THANK YOU FOR...

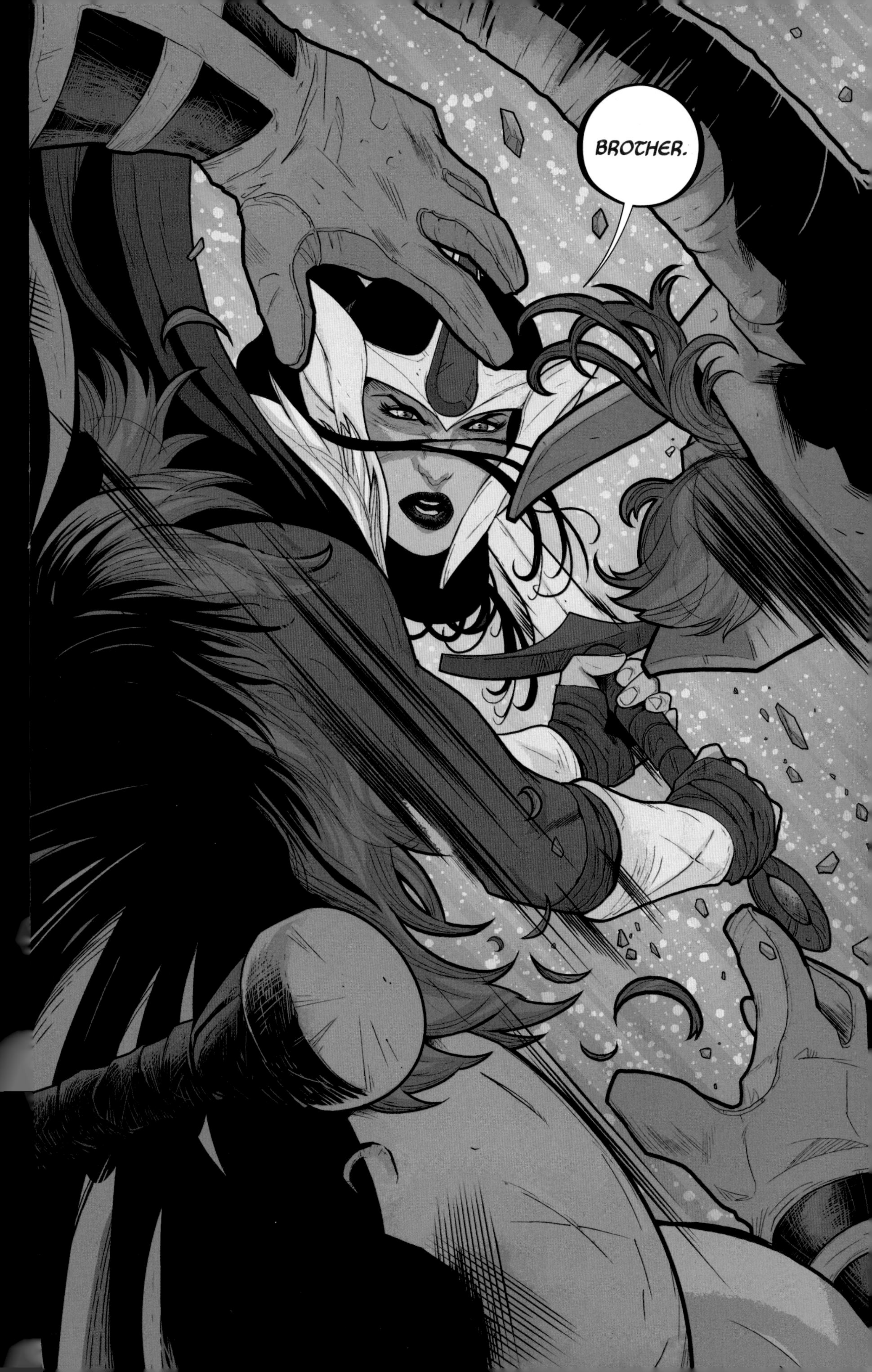
BROTHER.

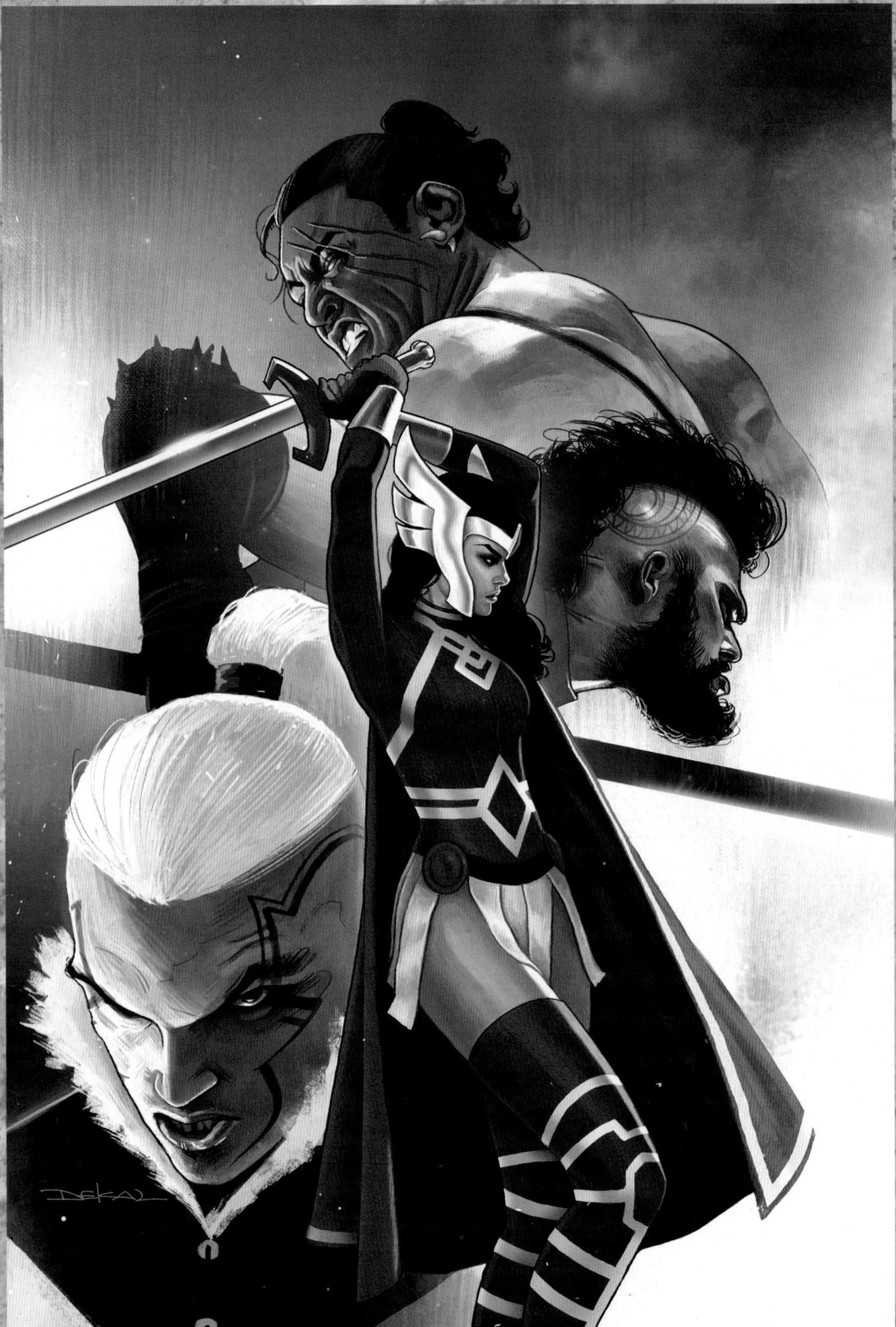

#650

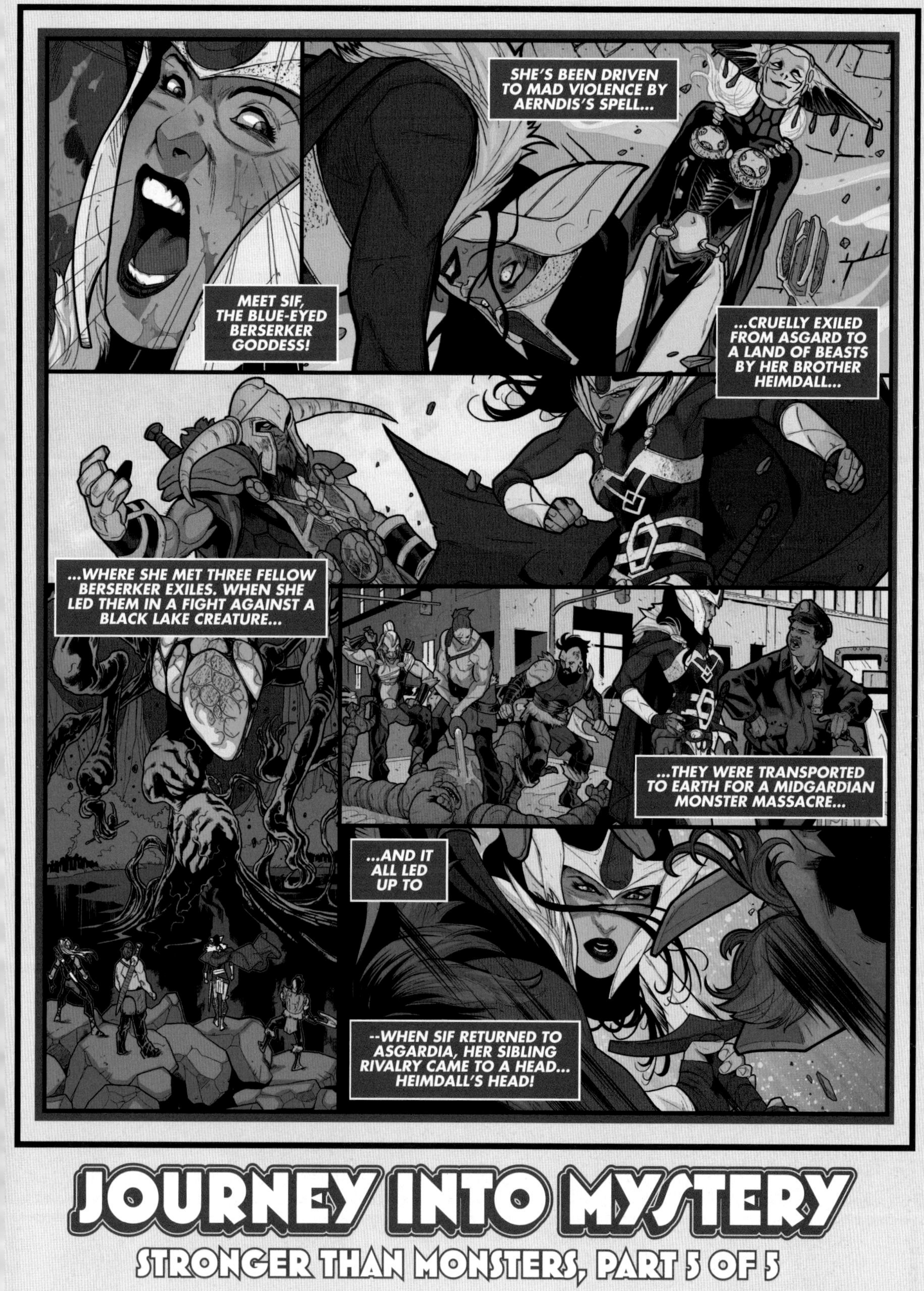
SHE'S BEEN DRIVEN TO MAD VIOLENCE BY AERNDIS'S SPELL...
MEET SIF, THE BLUE-EYED BERSERKER GODDESS!
...CRUELLY EXILED FROM ASGARD TO A LAND OF BEASTS BY HER BROTHER HEIMDALL...
...WHERE SHE MET THREE FELLOW BERSERKER EXILES. WHEN SHE LED THEM IN A FIGHT AGAINST A BLACK LAKE CREATURE...
...THEY WERE TRANSPORTED TO EARTH FOR A MIDGARDIAN MONSTER MASSACRE...
...AND IT ALL LED UP TO
--WHEN SIF RETURNED TO ASGARDIA, HER SIBLING RIVALRY CAME TO A HEAD... HEIMDALL'S HEAD!

JOURNEY INTO MYSTERY

STRONGER THAN MONSTERS, PART 5 OF 5

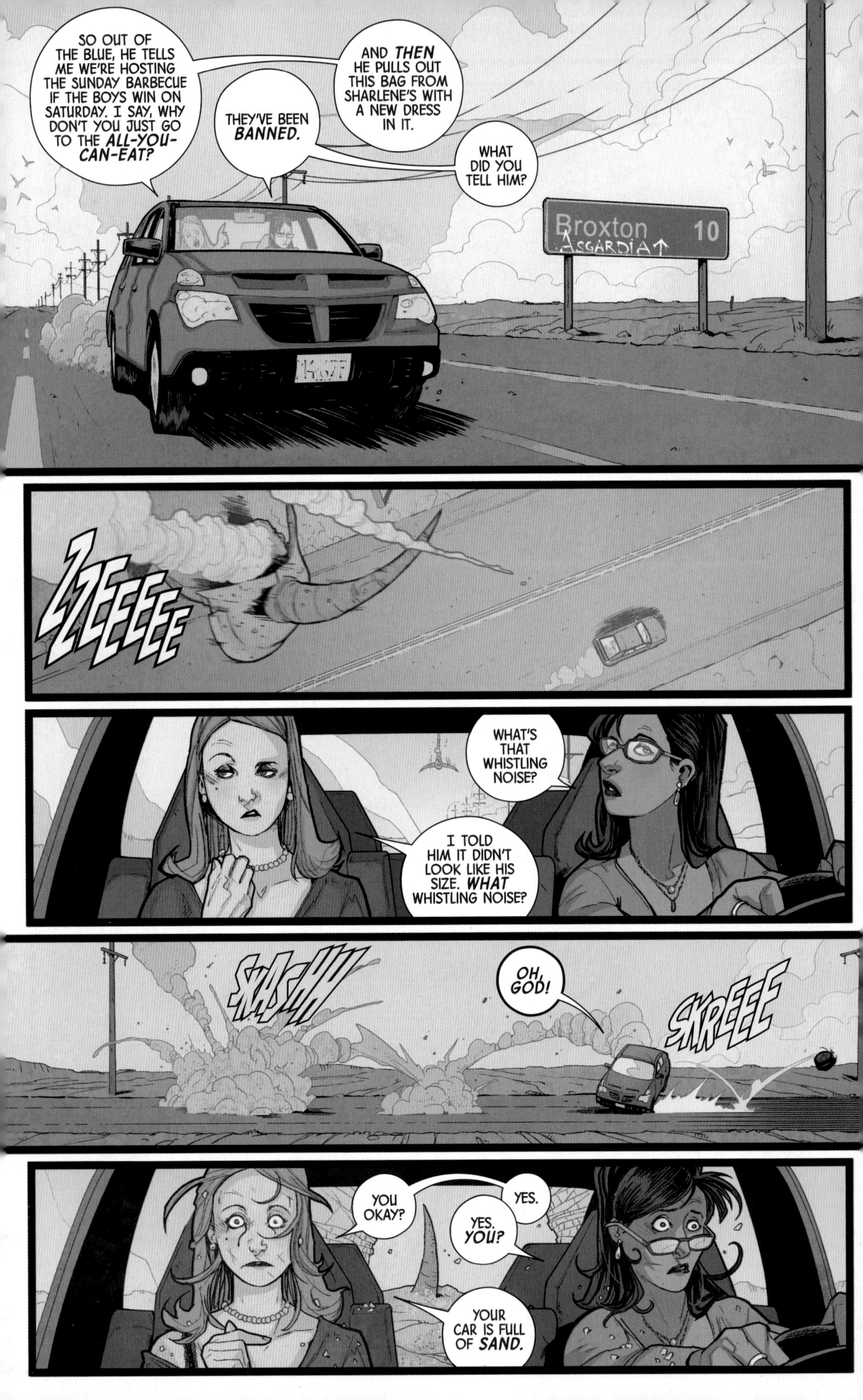
SO OUT OF THE BLUE, HE TELLS ME WE'RE HOSTING THE SUNDAY BARBECUE IF THE BOYS WIN ON SATURDAY. I SAY, WHY DON'T YOU JUST GO TO THE ALL-YOU-CAN-EAT?
THEY'VE BEEN BANNED.
AND THEN HE PULLS OUT THIS BAG FROM SHARLENE'S WITH A NEW DRESS IN IT.
WHAT DID YOU TELL HIM?
Broxton 10
ASGARDIA ↑
ZZEEEEEE
WHAT'S THAT WHISTLING NOISE?
I TOLD HIM IT DIDN'T LOOK LIKE HIS SIZE. WHAT WHISTLING NOISE?
SKASHH
OH, GOD!
SKREEEE
YOU OKAY?
YES.
YES. YOU?
YOUR CAR IS FULL OF SAND.

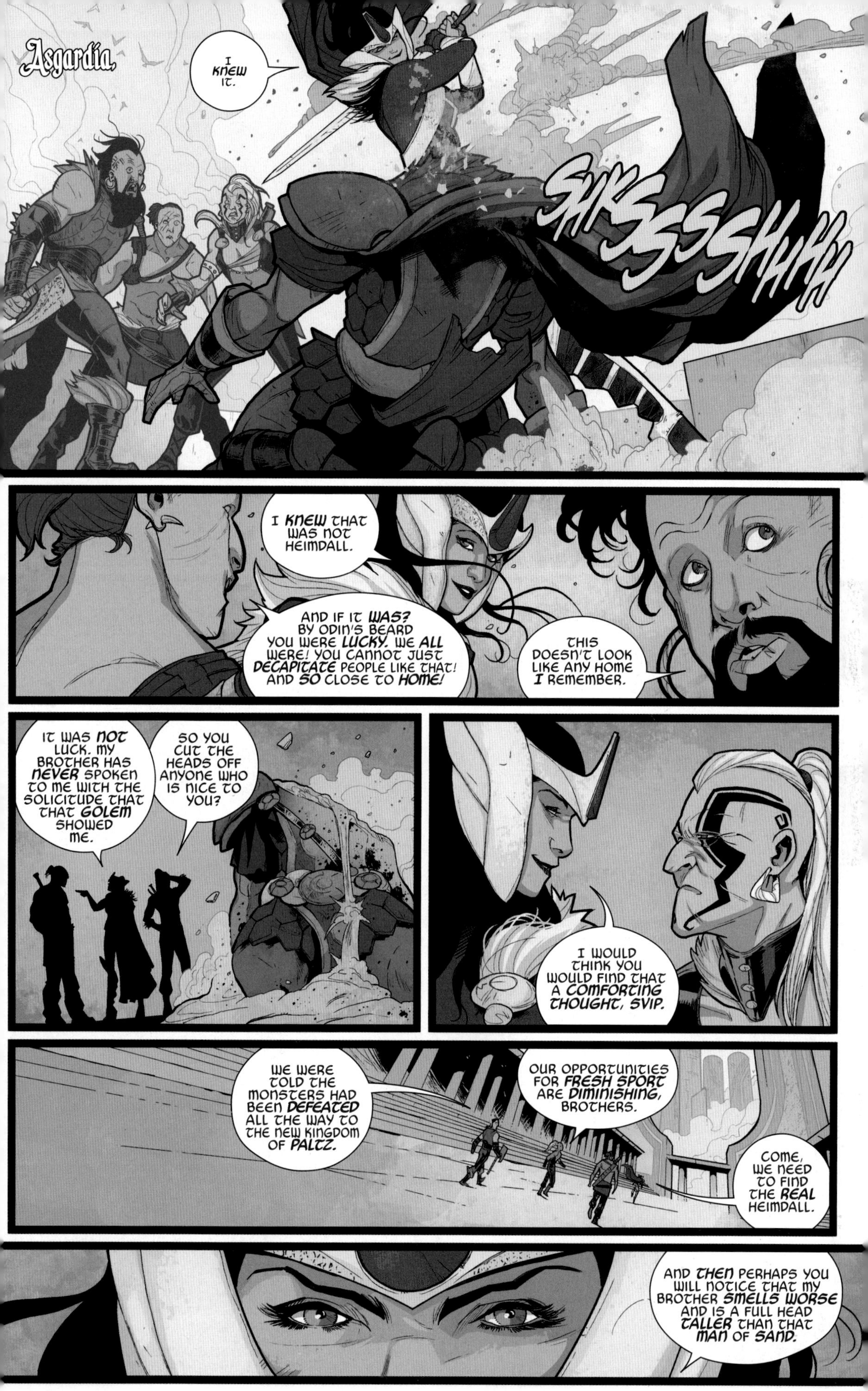
Asgardia,
I KNEW IT.
SHKSSSSHHHH
I KNEW THAT WAS NOT HEIMDALL.
AND IF IT WAS? BY ODIN'S BEARD YOU WERE LUCKY. WE ALL WERE! YOU CANNOT JUST DECAPITATE PEOPLE LIKE THAT! AND SO CLOSE TO HOME!
THIS DOESN'T LOOK LIKE ANY HOME I REMEMBER.
IT WAS NOT LUCK. MY BROTHER HAS NEVER SPOKEN TO ME WITH THE SOLICITUDE THAT THAT GOLEM SHOWED ME.
SO YOU CUT THE HEADS OFF ANYONE WHO IS NICE TO YOU?
I WOULD THINK YOU WOULD FIND THAT A COMFORTING THOUGHT, SVIP.
WE WERE TOLD THE MONSTERS HAD BEEN DEFEATED ALL THE WAY TO THE NEW KINGDOM OF PALTZ.
OUR OPPORTUNITIES FOR FRESH SPORT ARE DIMINISHING, BROTHERS.
COME, WE NEED TO FIND THE REAL HEIMDALL.
AND THEN PERHAPS YOU WILL NOTICE THAT MY BROTHER SMELLS WORSE AND IS A FULL HEAD TALLER THAN THAT MAN OF SAND.

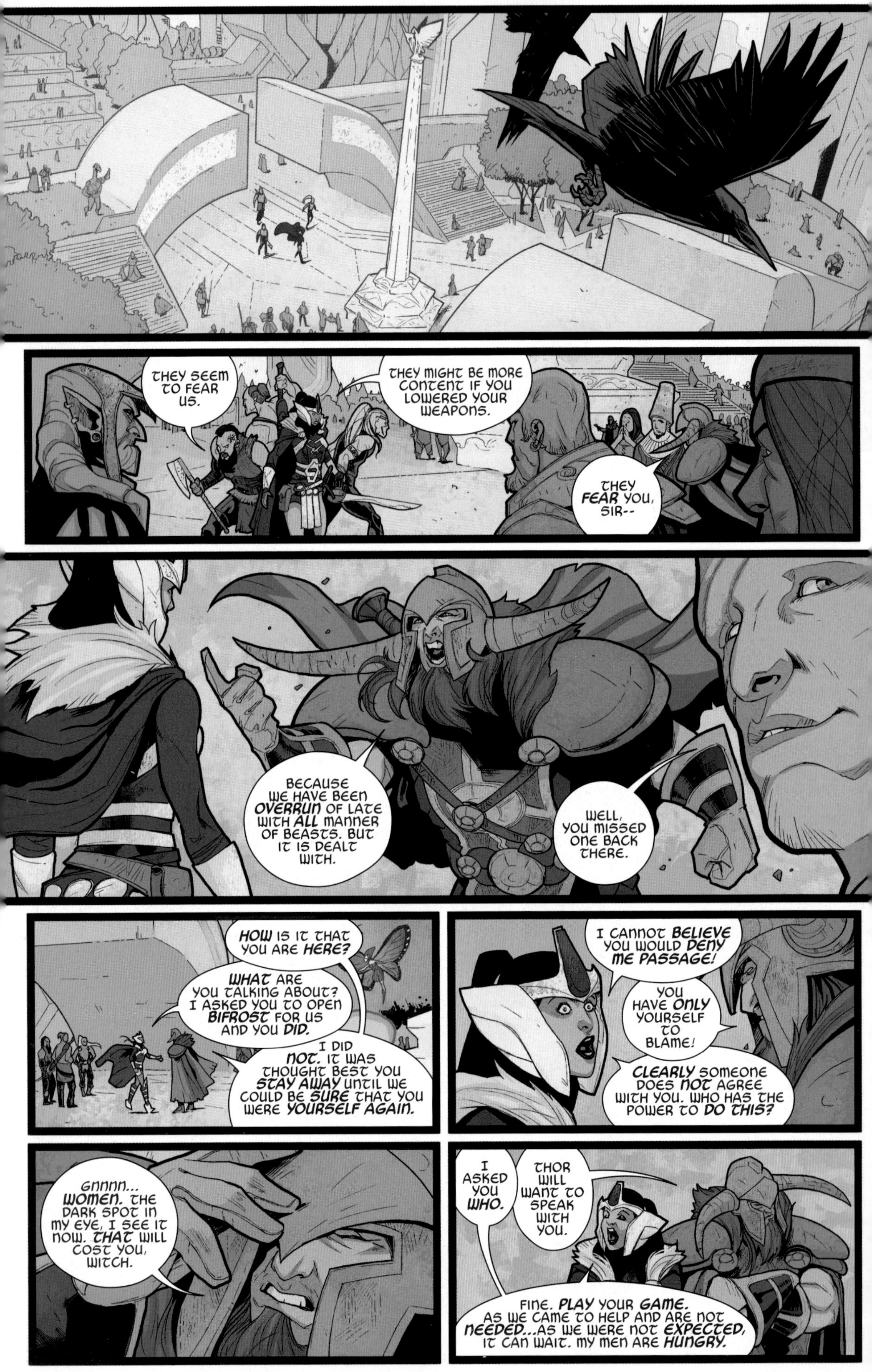
THEY SEEM TO FEAR US.
THEY MIGHT BE MORE CONTENT IF YOU LOWERED YOUR WEAPONS.
THEY FEAR YOU, SIR--
BECAUSE WE HAVE BEEN OVERRUN OF LATE WITH ALL MANNER OF BEASTS. BUT IT IS DEALT WITH.
WELL, YOU MISSED ONE BACK THERE.
HOW IS IT THAT YOU ARE HERE?
WHAT ARE YOU TALKING ABOUT? I ASKED YOU TO OPEN BIFROST FOR US AND YOU DID.
I DID NOT. IT WAS THOUGHT BEST YOU STAY AWAY UNTIL WE COULD BE SURE THAT YOU WERE YOURSELF AGAIN.
I CANNOT BELIEVE YOU WOULD DENY ME PASSAGE!
YOU HAVE ONLY YOURSELF TO BLAME!
CLEARLY SOMEONE DOES NOT AGREE WITH YOU. WHO HAS THE POWER TO DO THIS?
GNNNN... WOMEN. THE DARK SPOT IN MY EYE, I SEE IT NOW. THAT WILL COST YOU, WITCH.
I ASKED YOU WHO.
THOR WILL WANT TO SPEAK WITH YOU.
FINE. PLAY YOUR GAME. AS WE CAME TO HELP AND ARE NOT NEEDED...AS WE WERE NOT EXPECTED, IT CAN WAIT. MY MEN ARE HUNGRY.

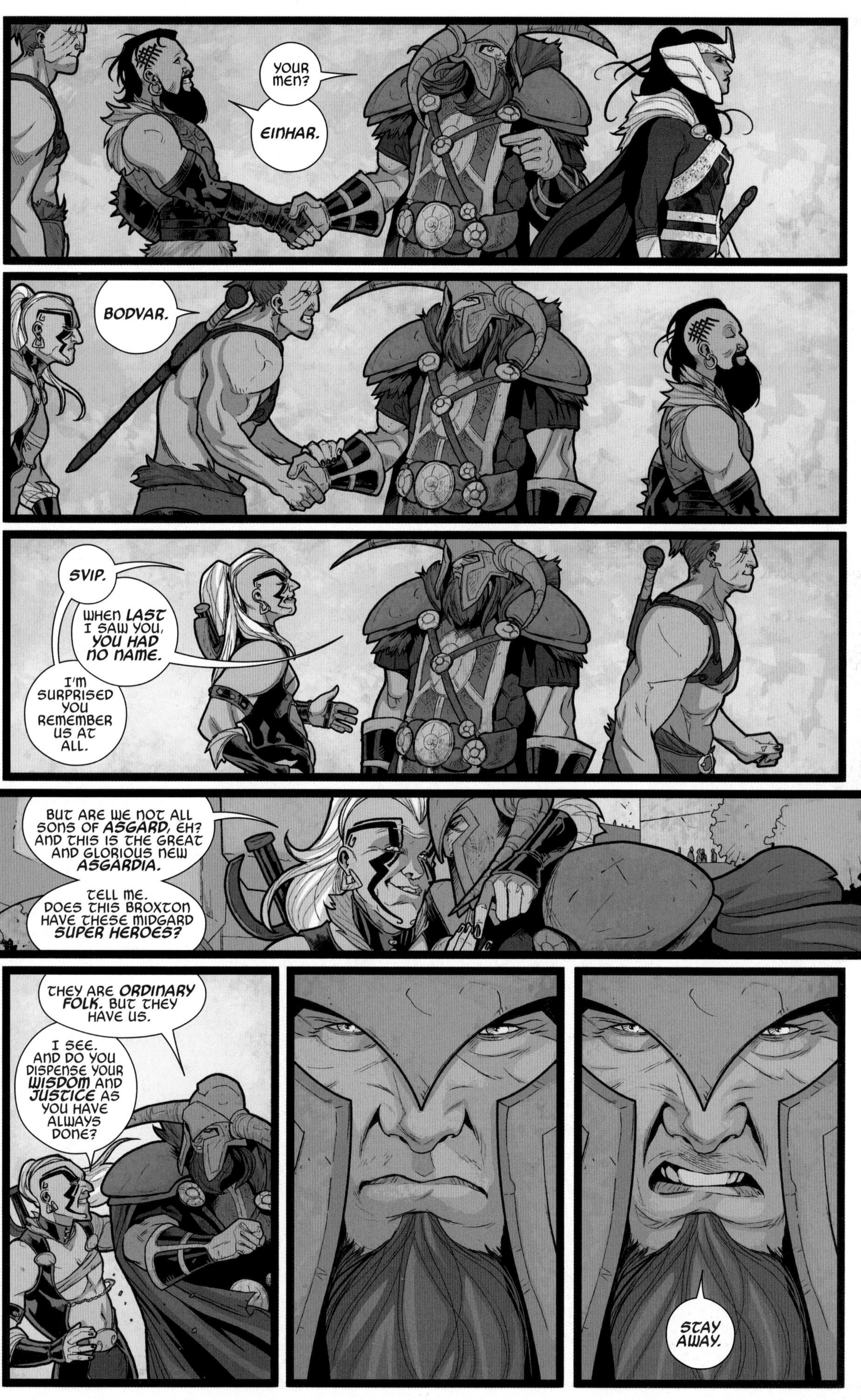

YOUR MEN?
EINHAR.
BODVAR.
SVIP.
WHEN LAST I SAW YOU, YOU HAD NO NAME.
I'M SURPRISED YOU REMEMBER US AT ALL.
BUT ARE WE NOT ALL SONS OF ASGARD, EH? AND THIS IS THE GREAT AND GLORIOUS NEW ASGARDIA.
TELL ME. DOES THIS BROXTON HAVE THESE MIDGARD SUPER HEROES?
THEY ARE ORDINARY FOLK. BUT THEY HAVE US.
I SEE. AND DO YOU DISPENSE YOUR WISDOM AND JUSTICE AS YOU HAVE ALWAYS DONE?
STAY AWAY.

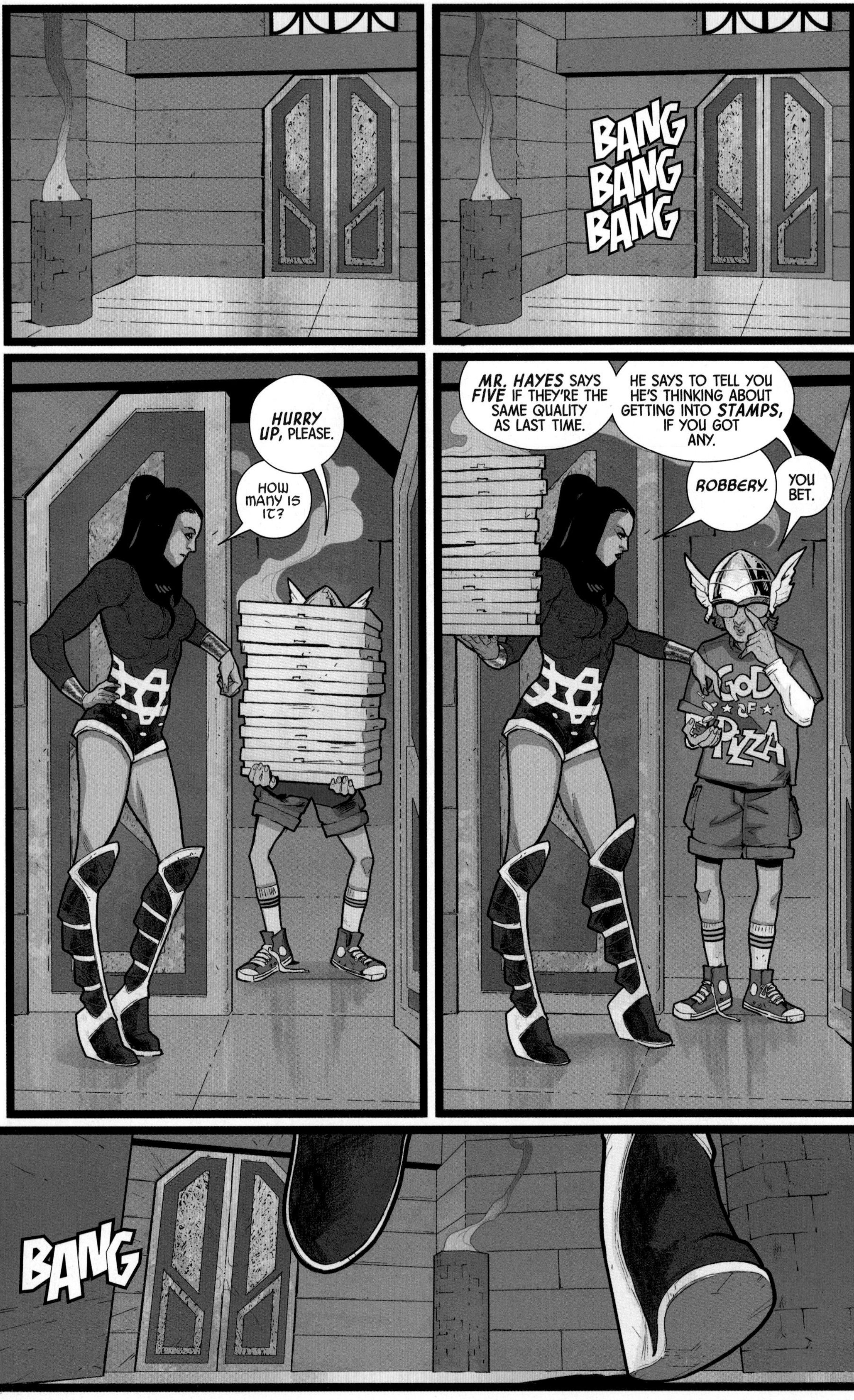
BANG BANG BANG
HURRY UP, PLEASE.
HOW MANY IS IT?
MR. HAYES SAYS FIVE IF THEY'RE THE SAME QUALITY AS LAST TIME.
HE SAYS TO TELL YOU HE'S THINKING ABOUT GETTING INTO STAMPS, IF YOU GOT ANY.
ROBBERY.
YOU BET.
GOD OF PIZZA
BANG

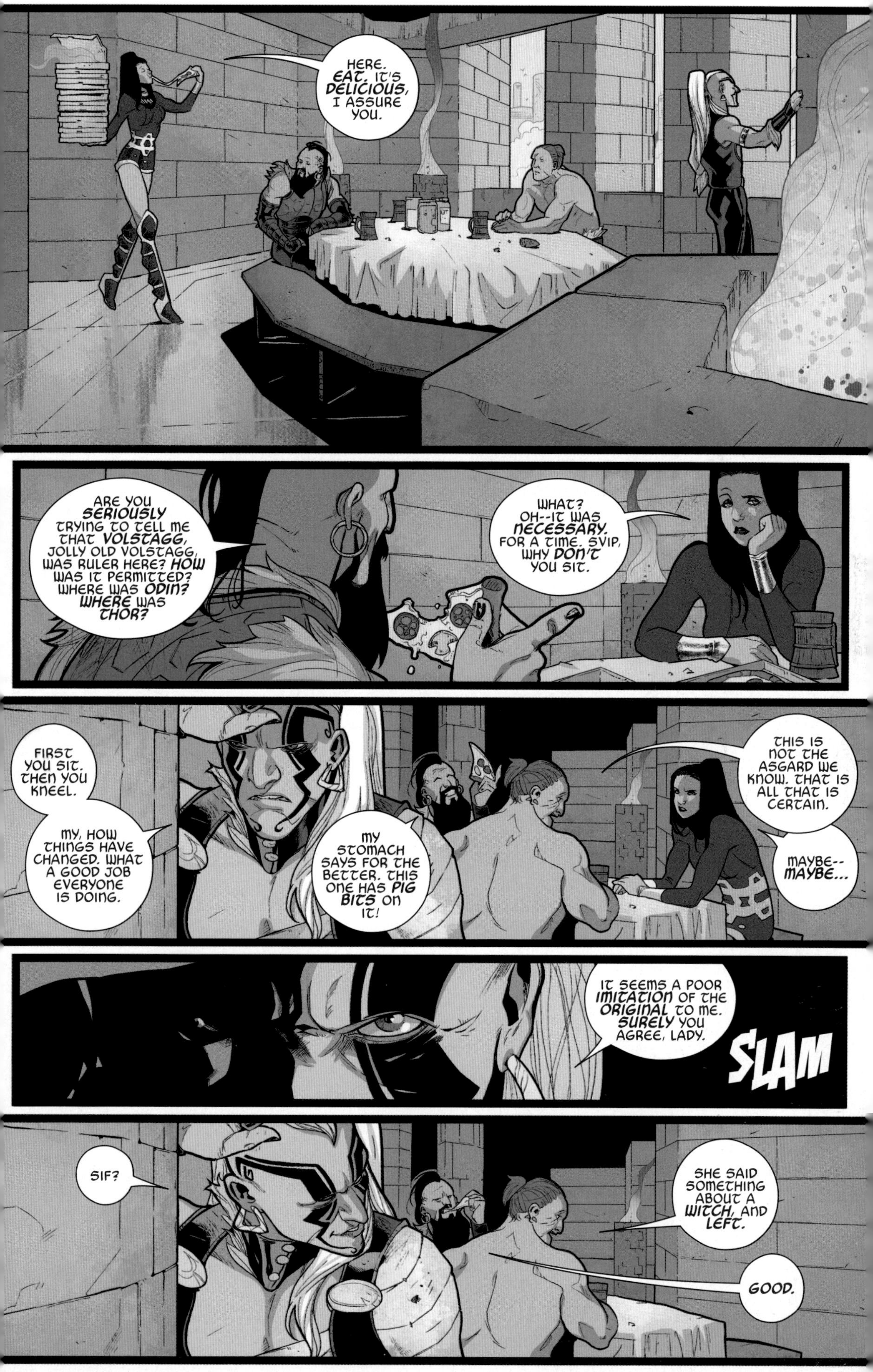
HERE. EAT. IT'S DELICIOUS, I ASSURE YOU.
ARE YOU SERIOUSLY TRYING TO TELL ME THAT VOLSTAGG, JOLLY OLD VOLSTAGG, WAS RULER HERE? HOW WAS IT PERMITTED? WHERE WAS ODIN? WHERE WAS THOR?
WHAT? OH--IT WAS NECESSARY. FOR A TIME. SVIP, WHY DON'T YOU SIT.
FIRST YOU SIT. THEN YOU KNEEL.
MY, HOW THINGS HAVE CHANGED. WHAT A GOOD JOB EVERYONE IS DOING.
MY STOMACH SAYS FOR THE BETTER. THIS ONE HAS PIG BITS ON IT!
THIS IS NOT THE ASGARD WE KNOW. THAT IS ALL THAT IS CERTAIN.
MAYBE--MAYBE...
IT SEEMS A POOR IMITATION OF THE ORIGINAL TO ME. SURELY YOU AGREE, LADY.
SLAM
SIF?
SHE SAID SOMETHING ABOUT A WITCH, AND LEFT.
GOOD.

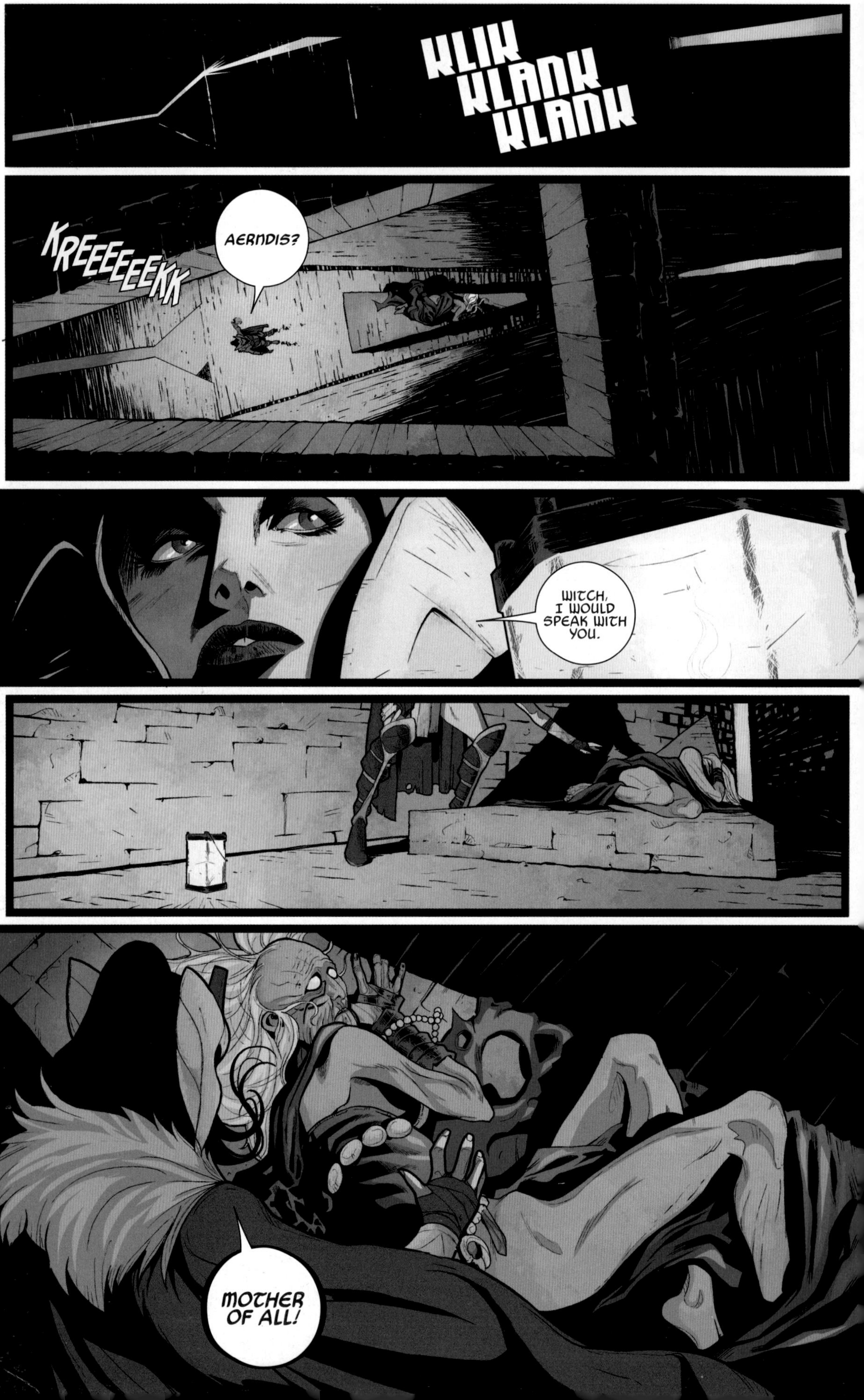
KLIK KLANK KLANK
KREEEEEEKK
AERNDIS?
WITCH, I WOULD SPEAK WITH YOU.
MOTHER OF ALL!

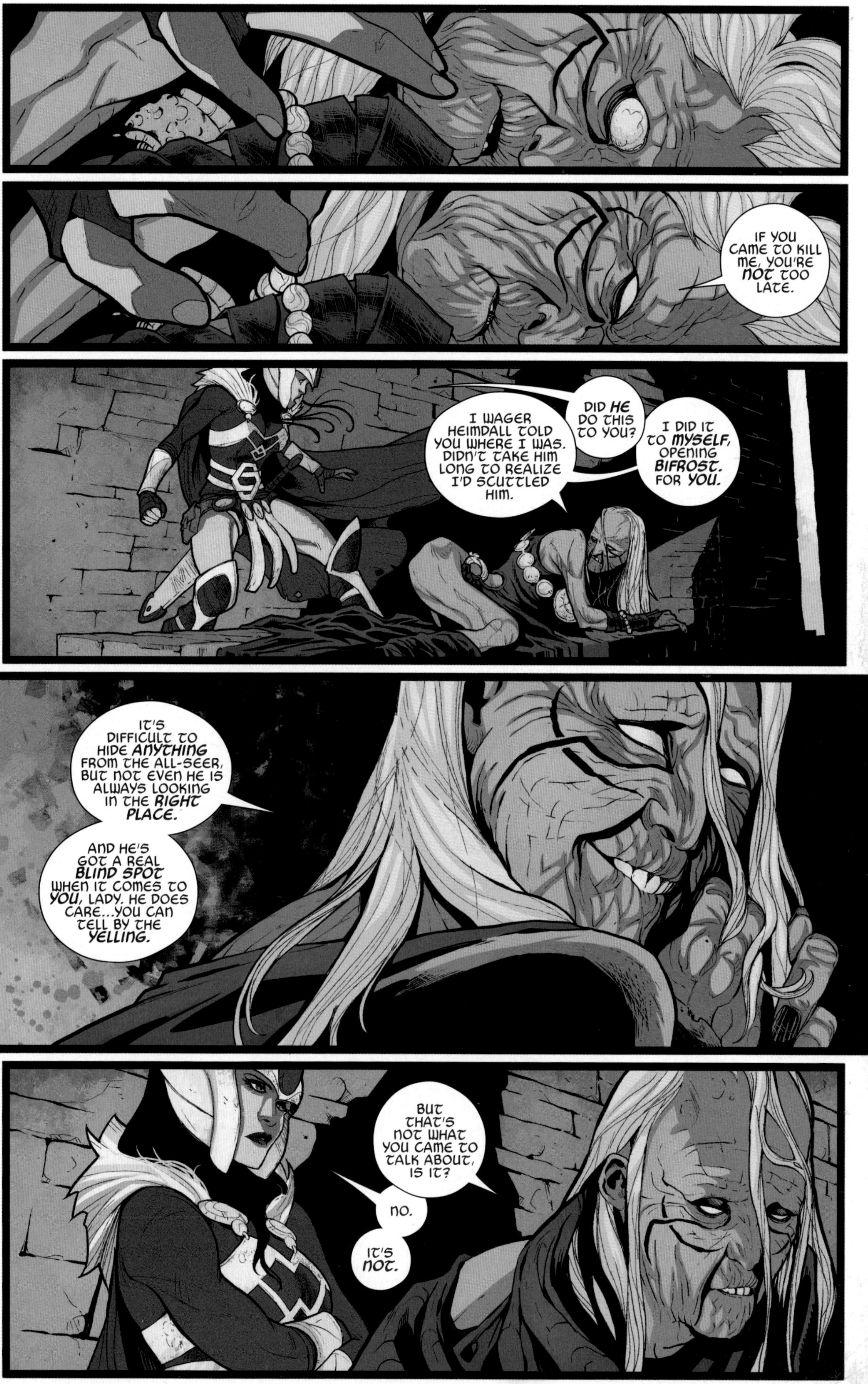

IF YOU CAME TO KILL ME, YOU'RE NOT TOO LATE.
I WAGER HEIMDALL TOLD YOU WHERE I WAS. DIDN'T TAKE HIM LONG TO REALIZE I'D SCUTTLED HIM.
DID HE DO THIS TO YOU?
I DID IT TO MYSELF, OPENING BIFROST. FOR YOU.
IT'S DIFFICULT TO HIDE ANYTHING FROM THE ALL-SEER, BUT NOT EVEN HE IS ALWAYS LOOKING IN THE RIGHT PLACE.
AND HE'S GOT A REAL BLIND SPOT WHEN IT COMES TO YOU, LADY. HE DOES CARE...YOU CAN TELL BY THE YELLING.
BUT THAT'S NOT WHAT YOU CAME TO TALK ABOUT, IS IT?
NO.
IT'S NOT.

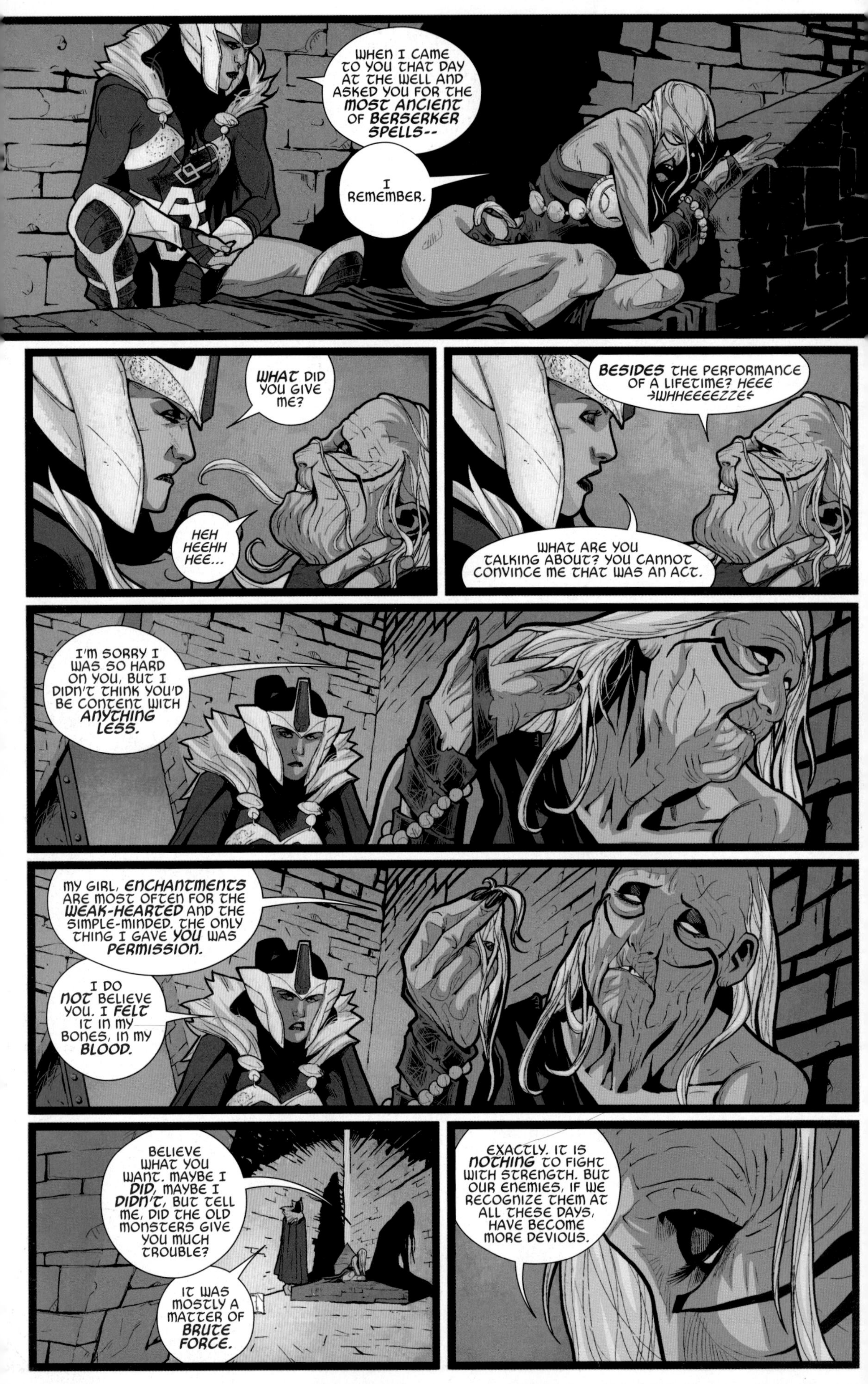
WHEN I CAME TO YOU THAT DAY AT THE WELL AND ASKED YOU FOR THE MOST ANCIENT OF BERSERKER SPELLS--
I REMEMBER.
WHAT DID YOU GIVE ME?
HEH HEEHH HEE...
BESIDES THE PERFORMANCE OF A LIFETIME? HEEE →WHHEEEEZZE←
WHAT ARE YOU TALKING ABOUT? YOU CANNOT CONVINCE ME THAT WAS AN ACT.
I'M SORRY I WAS SO HARD ON YOU, BUT I DIDN'T THINK YOU'D BE CONTENT WITH ANYTHING LESS.
MY GIRL, ENCHANTMENTS ARE MOST OFTEN FOR THE WEAK-HEARTED AND THE SIMPLE-MINDED. THE ONLY THING I GAVE YOU WAS PERMISSION.
I DO NOT BELIEVE YOU. I FELT IT IN MY BONES, IN MY BLOOD.
BELIEVE WHAT YOU WANT. MAYBE I DID, MAYBE I DIDN'T, BUT TELL ME, DID THE OLD MONSTERS GIVE YOU MUCH TROUBLE?
IT WAS MOSTLY A MATTER OF BRUTE FORCE.
EXACTLY. IT IS NOTHING TO FIGHT WITH STRENGTH. BUT OUR ENEMIES, IF WE RECOGNIZE THEM AT ALL THESE DAYS, HAVE BECOME MORE DEVIOUS.

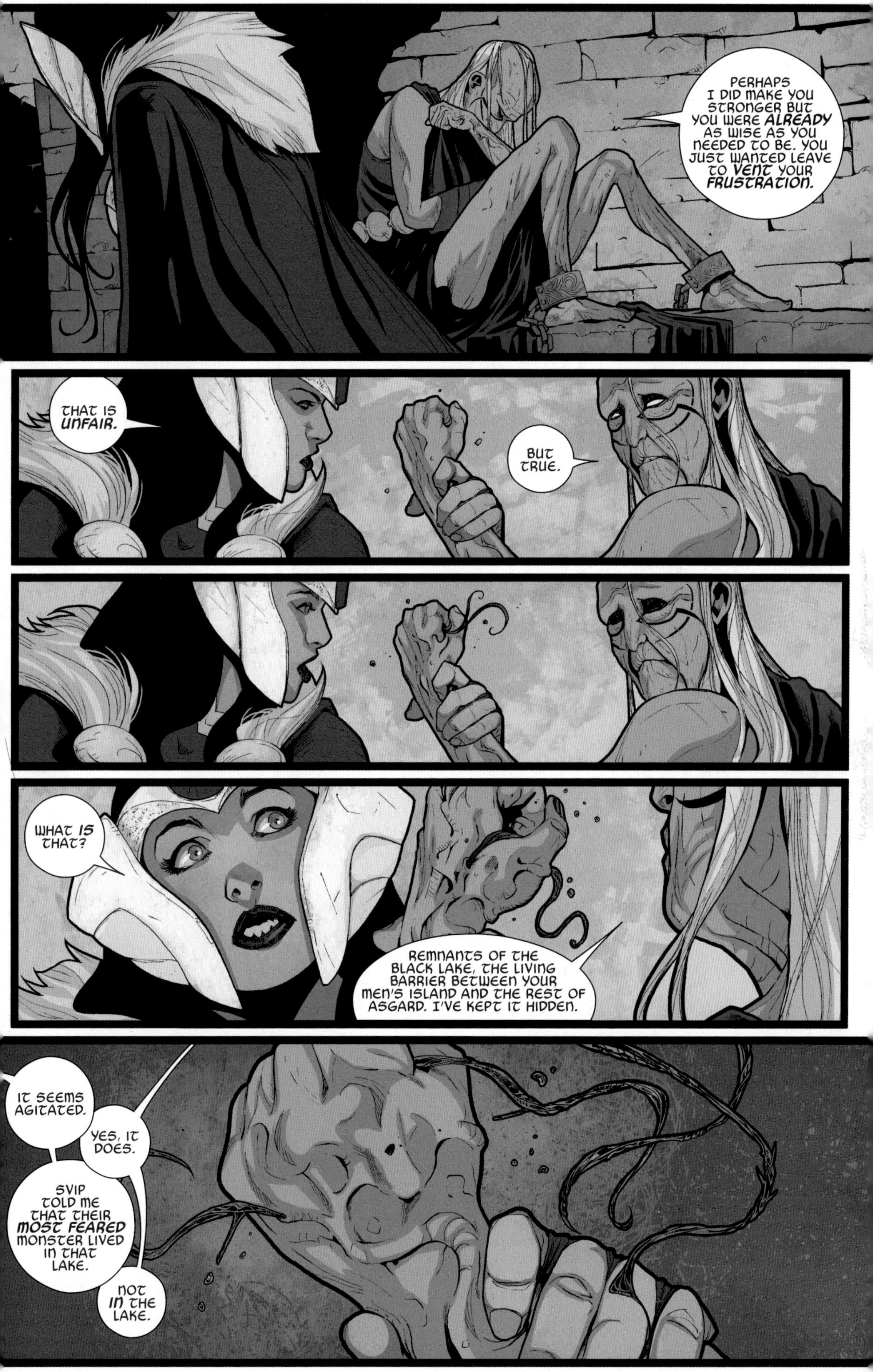
PERHAPS I DID MAKE YOU STRONGER BUT YOU WERE ALREADY AS WISE AS YOU NEEDED TO BE. YOU JUST WANTED LEAVE TO VENT YOUR FRUSTRATION.
THAT IS UNFAIR.
BUT TRUE.
WHAT IS THAT?
REMNANTS OF THE BLACK LAKE, THE LIVING BARRIER BETWEEN YOUR MEN'S ISLAND AND THE REST OF ASGARD. I'VE KEPT IT HIDDEN.
IT SEEMS AGITATED.
YES, IT DOES.
SVIP TOLD ME THAT THEIR MOST FEARED MONSTER LIVED IN THAT LAKE.
NOT IN THE LAKE.

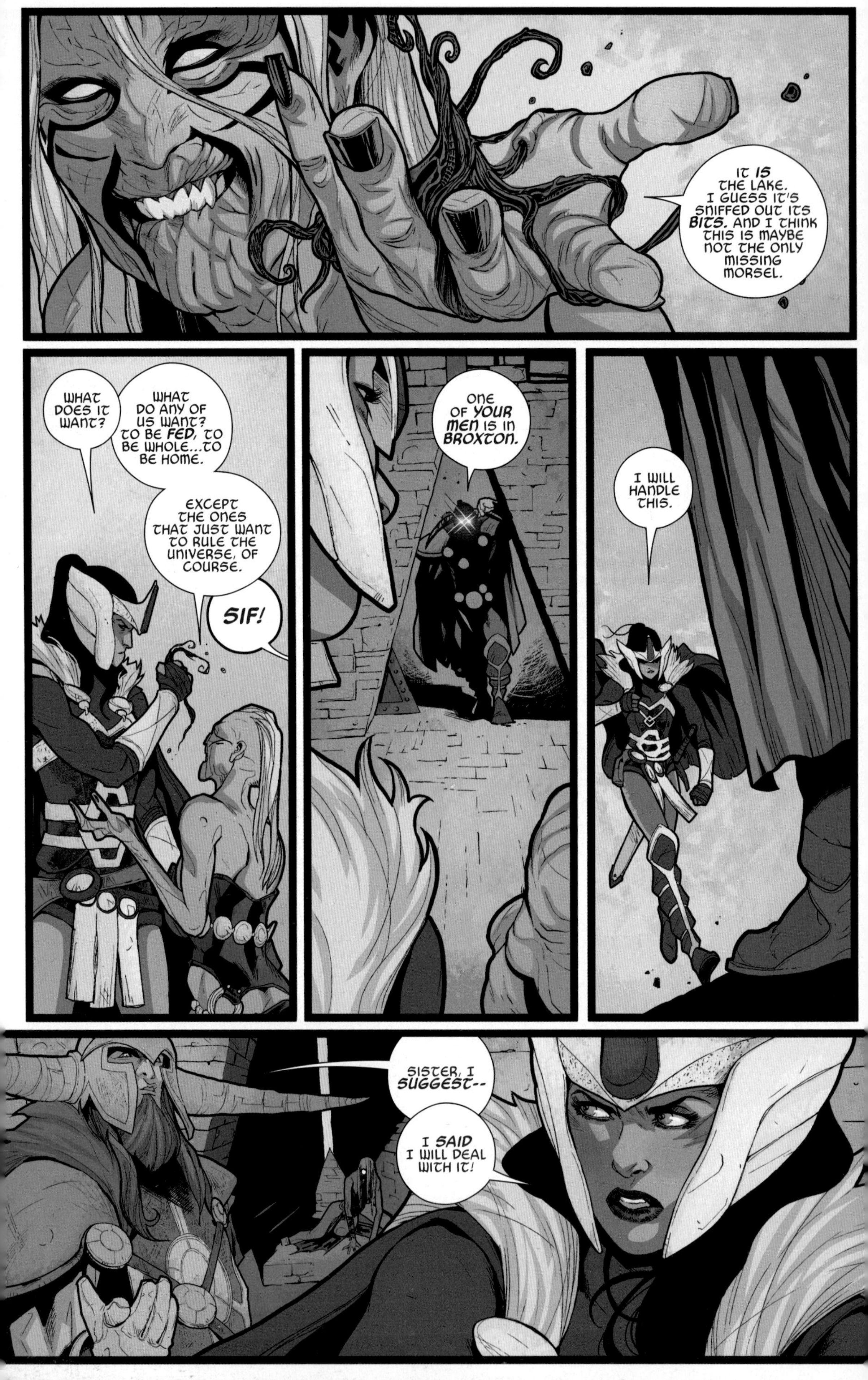
IT IS THE LAKE. I GUESS IT'S SNIFFED OUT ITS BITS. AND I THINK THIS IS MAYBE NOT THE ONLY MISSING MORSEL.
WHAT DOES IT WANT?
WHAT DO ANY OF US WANT? TO BE FED, TO BE WHOLE...TO BE HOME.
EXCEPT THE ONES THAT JUST WANT TO RULE THE UNIVERSE, OF COURSE.
SIF!
ONE OF YOUR MEN IS IN BROXTON.
I WILL HANDLE THIS.
SISTER, I SUGGEST--
I SAID I WILL DEAL WITH IT!

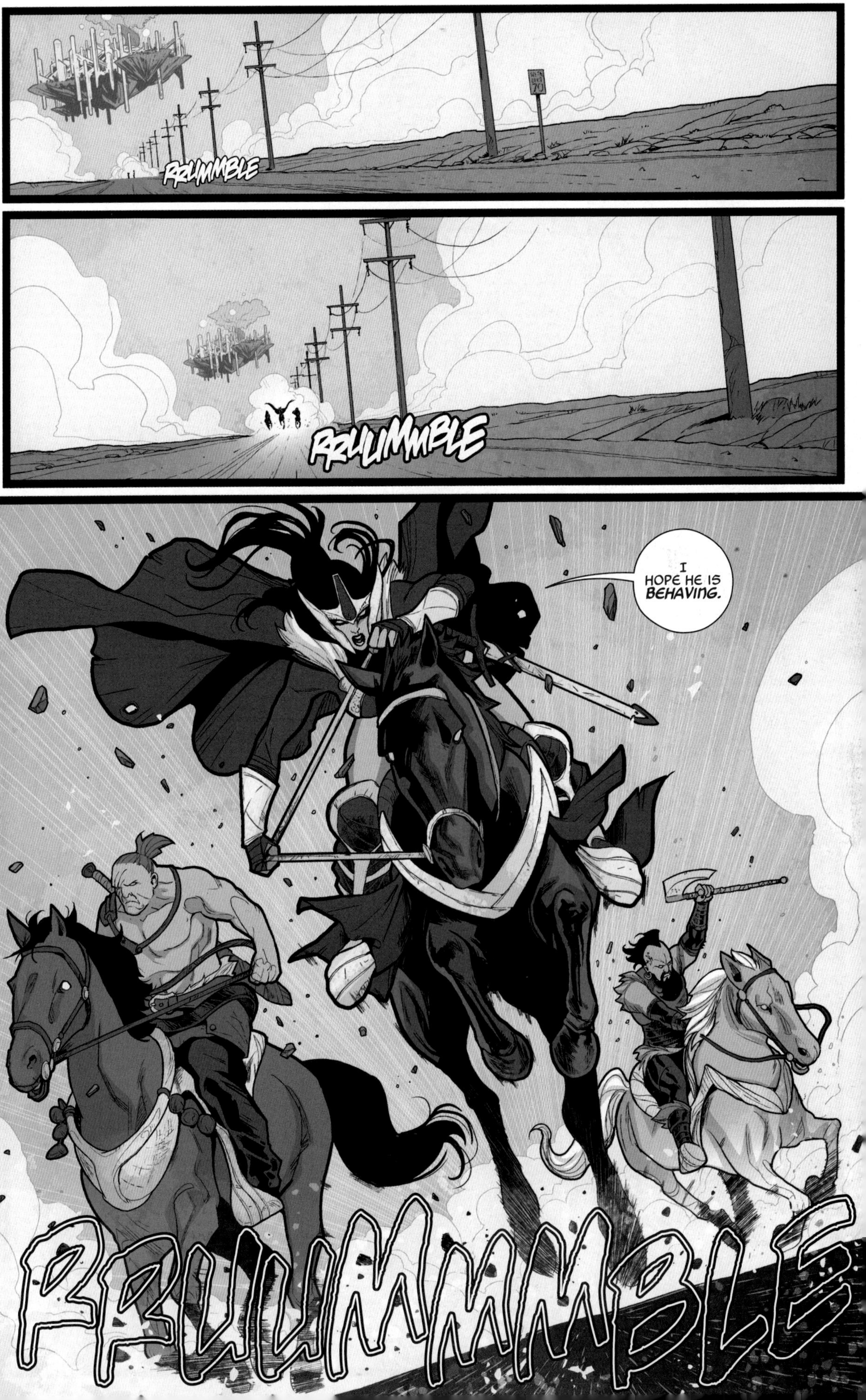
RRUMMBLE
RRRUMMBLE
I HOPE HE IS BEHAVING.
RRUUMMMBLE

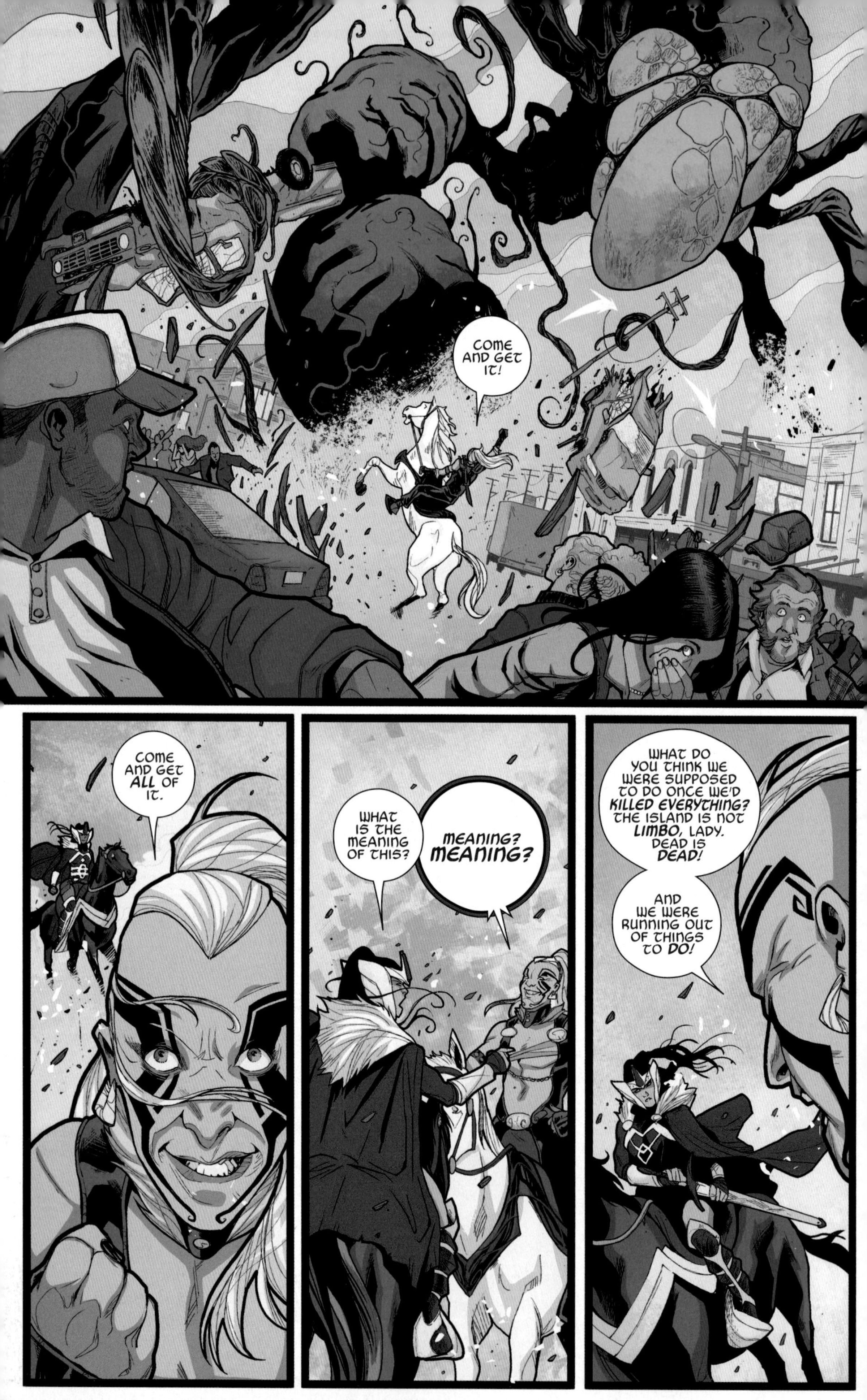

COME AND GET IT!
COME AND GET ALL OF IT.
WHAT IS THE MEANING OF THIS?
MEANING? MEANING?
WHAT DO YOU THINK WE WERE SUPPOSED TO DO ONCE WE'D KILLED EVERYTHING? THE ISLAND IS NOT LIMBO, LADY. DEAD IS DEAD!
AND WE WERE RUNNING OUT OF THINGS TO DO!

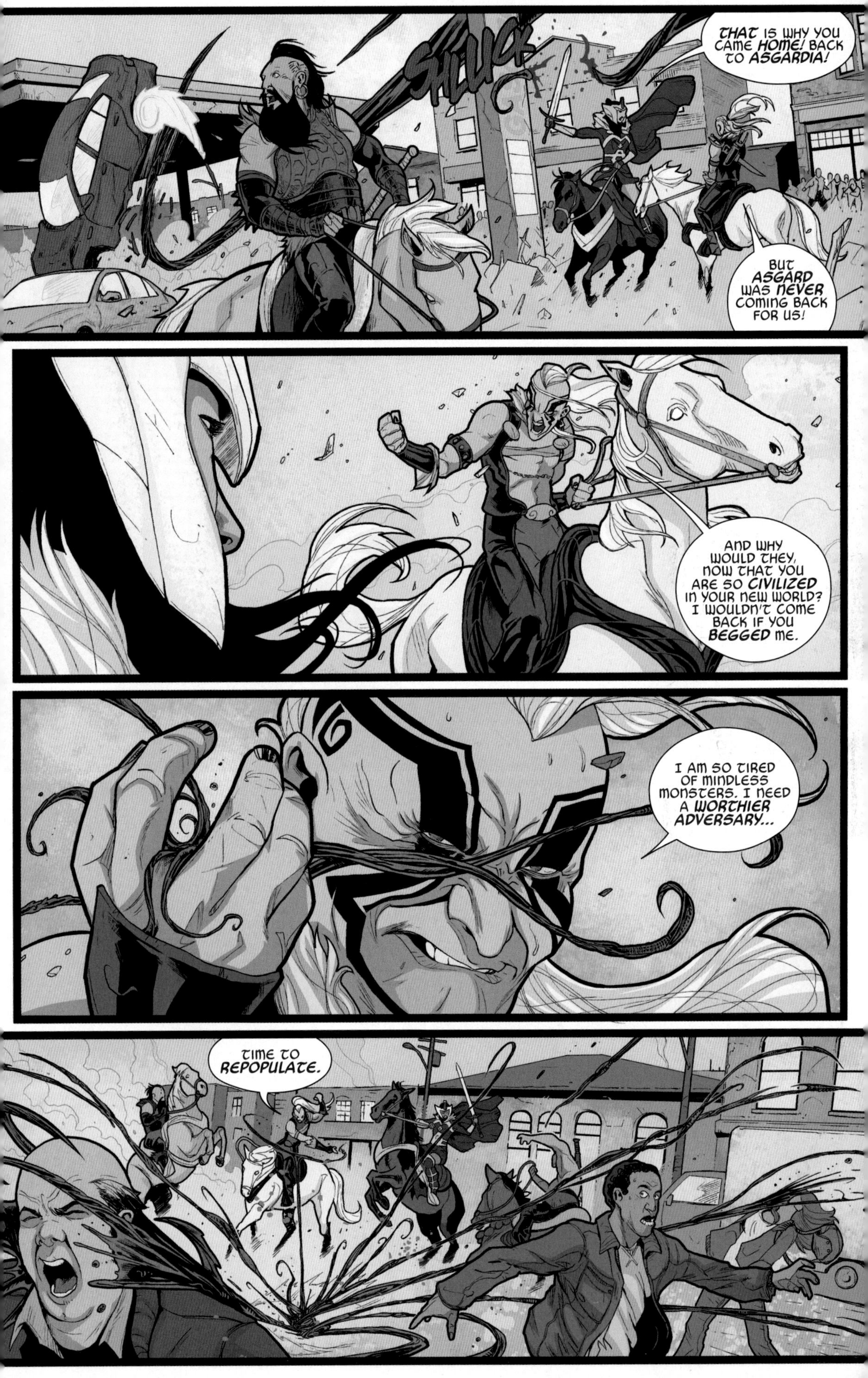
SHLICK
THAT is why you came HOME! Back to ASGARDIA!
But ASGARD was NEVER coming back for us!
And why would they, now that you are so CIVILIZED in your new world? I wouldn't come back if you BEGGED me.
I am so tired of mindless monsters. I need a WORTHIER ADVERSARY...
Time to REPOPULATE.

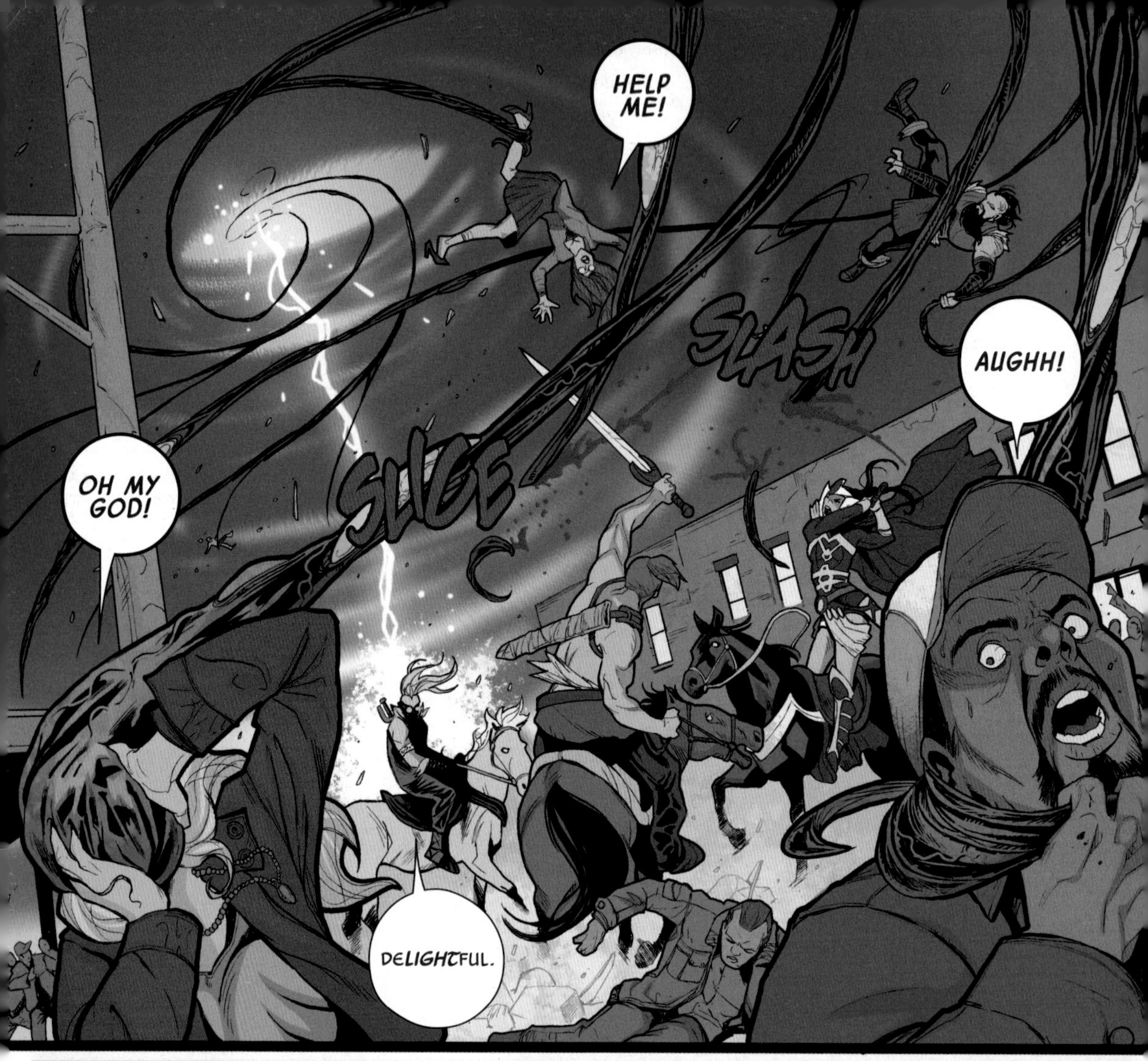
HELP ME!
OH MY GOD!
SLICE
SLASH
AUGHH!
DELIGHTFUL.

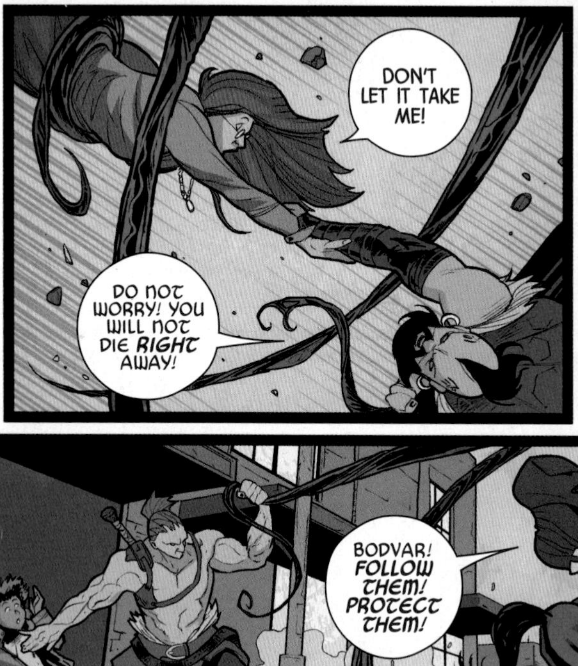
DON'T LET IT TAKE ME!
DO NOT WORRY! YOU WILL NOT DIE RIGHT AWAY!

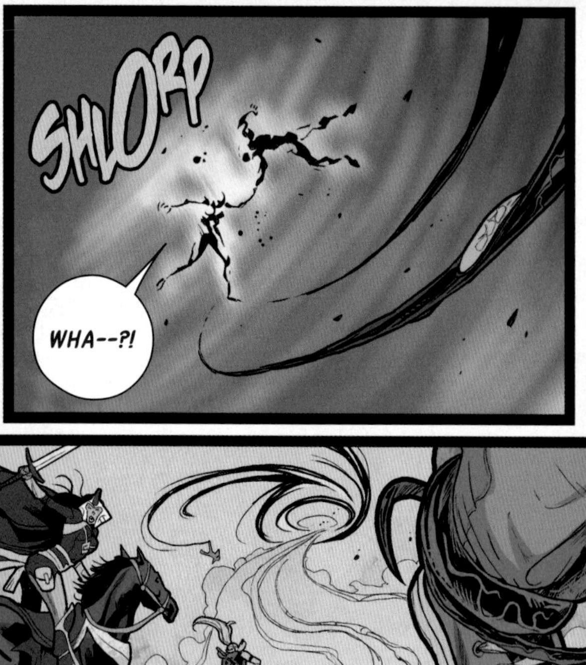
SHLORP
WHA--?!

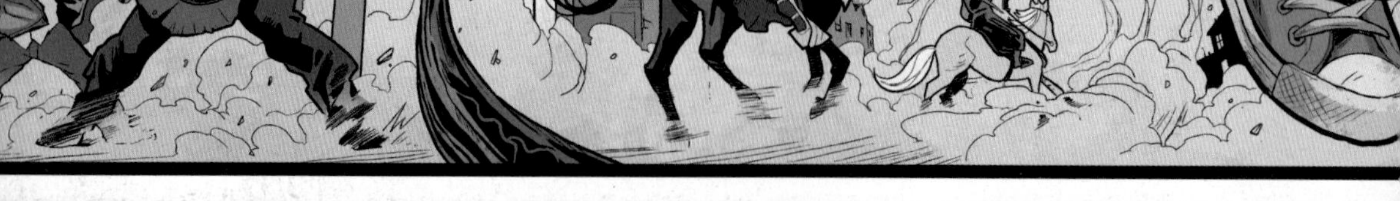
BODVAR! FOLLOW THEM! PROTECT THEM!

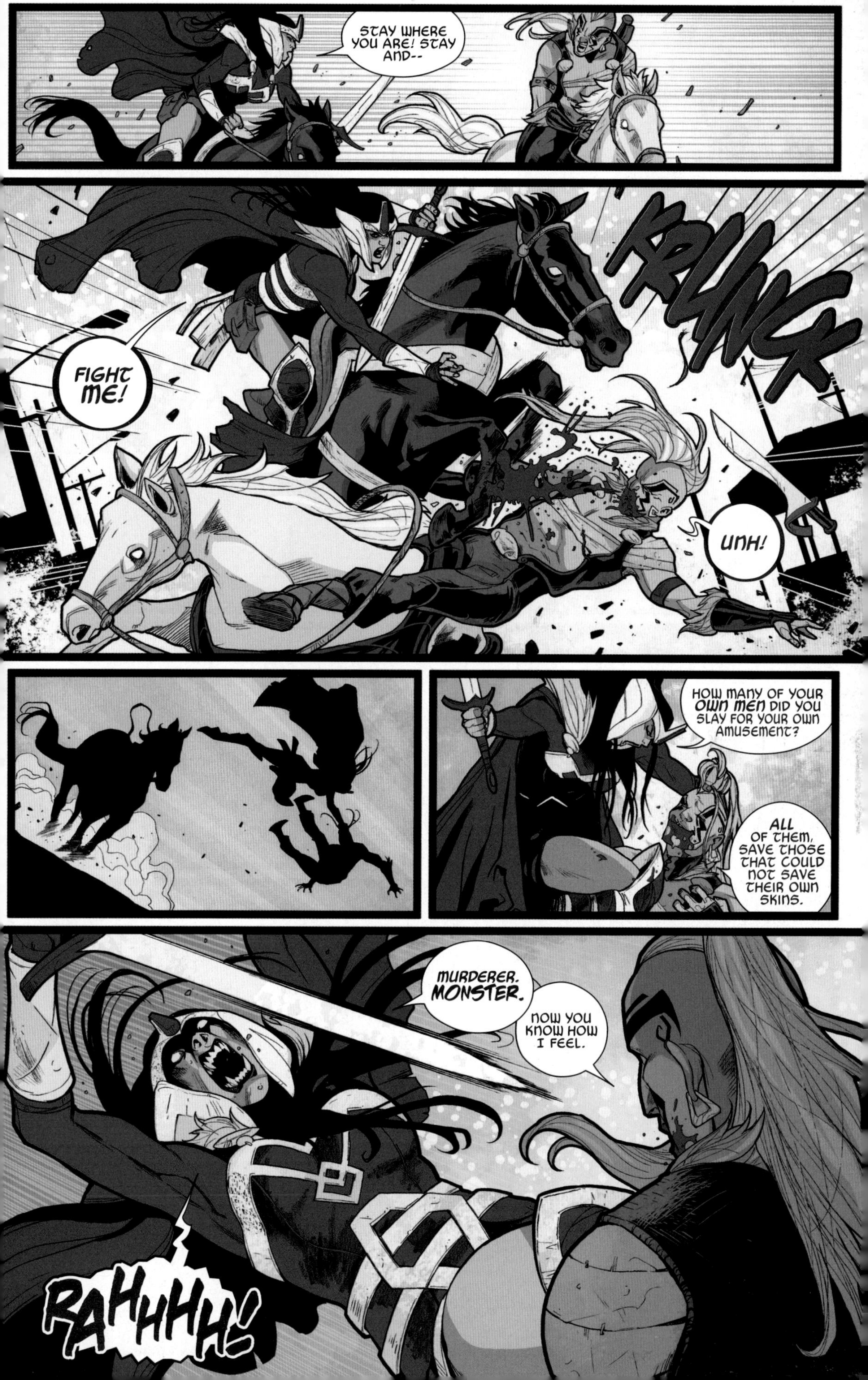
STAY WHERE YOU ARE! STAY AND--
KRUNCK
FIGHT ME!
UNH!
HOW MANY OF YOUR OWN MEN DID YOU SLAY FOR YOUR OWN AMUSEMENT?
ALL OF THEM, SAVE THOSE THAT COULD NOT SAVE THEIR OWN SKINS.
MURDERER. MONSTER.
NOW YOU KNOW HOW I FEEL.
RAHHHH!

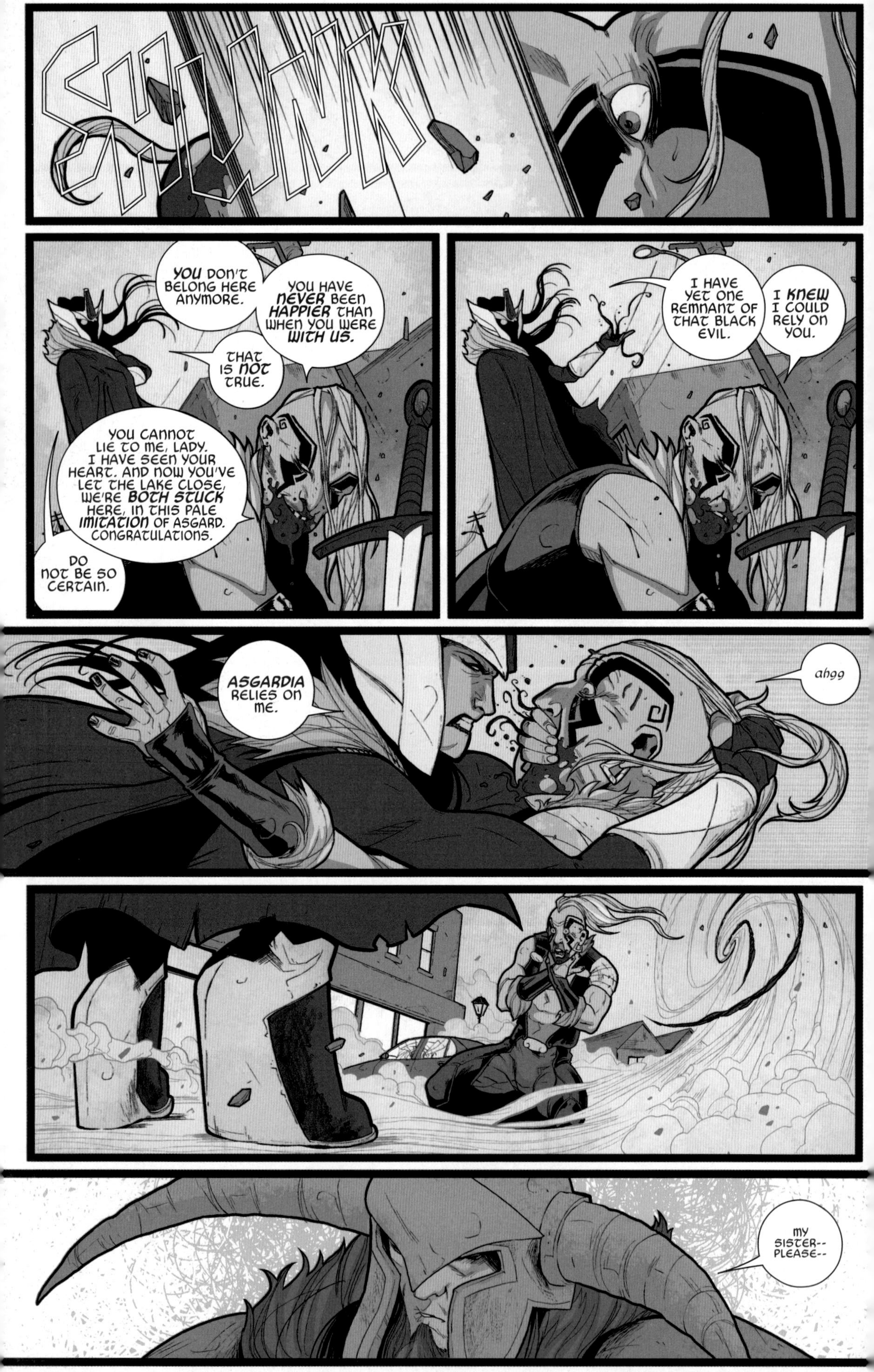
SHUNK
YOU DON'T BELONG HERE ANYMORE.
YOU HAVE NEVER BEEN HAPPIER THAN WHEN YOU WERE WITH US.
THAT IS NOT TRUE.
YOU CANNOT LIE TO ME, LADY. I HAVE SEEN YOUR HEART. AND NOW YOU'VE LET THE LAKE CLOSE, WE'RE BOTH STUCK HERE, IN THIS PALE IMITATION OF ASGARD. CONGRATULATIONS.
DO NOT BE SO CERTAIN.
I HAVE YET ONE REMNANT OF THAT BLACK EVIL.
I KNEW I COULD RELY ON YOU.
ASGARDIA RELIES ON ME.
ahgg
MY SISTER-- PLEASE--

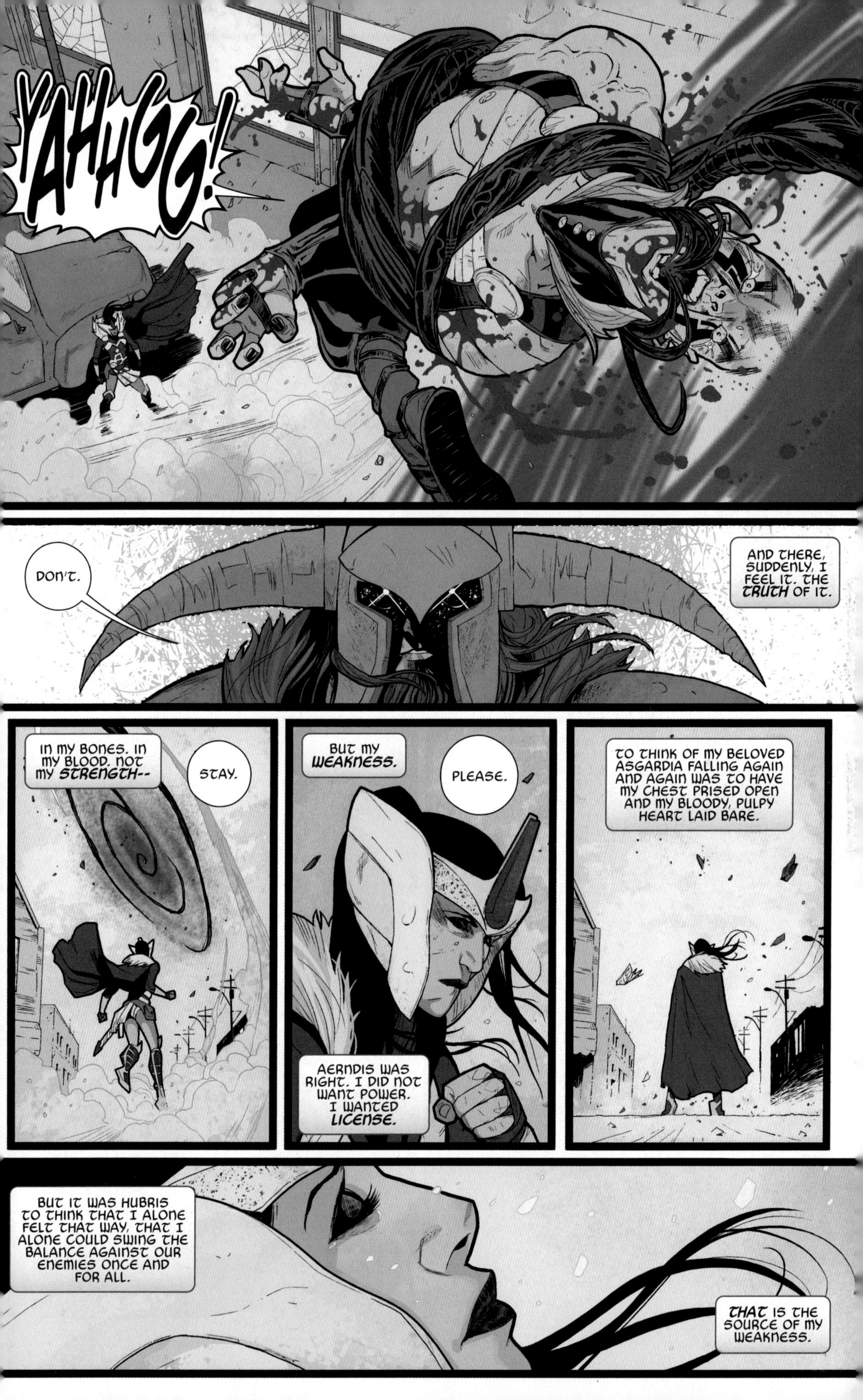
YAHHGG!
DON'T.
AND THERE, SUDDENLY, I FEEL IT. THE TRUTH OF IT.
IN MY BONES. IN MY BLOOD. NOT MY STRENGTH--
STAY.
BUT MY WEAKNESS.
PLEASE.
AERNDIS WAS RIGHT. I DID NOT WANT POWER. I WANTED LICENSE.
TO THINK OF MY BELOVED ASGARDIA FALLING AGAIN AND AGAIN WAS TO HAVE MY CHEST PRISED OPEN AND MY BLOODY, PULPY HEART LAID BARE.
BUT IT WAS HUBRIS TO THINK THAT I ALONE FELT THAT WAY, THAT I ALONE COULD SWING THE BALANCE AGAINST OUR ENEMIES ONCE AND FOR ALL.
THAT IS THE SOURCE OF MY WEAKNESS.

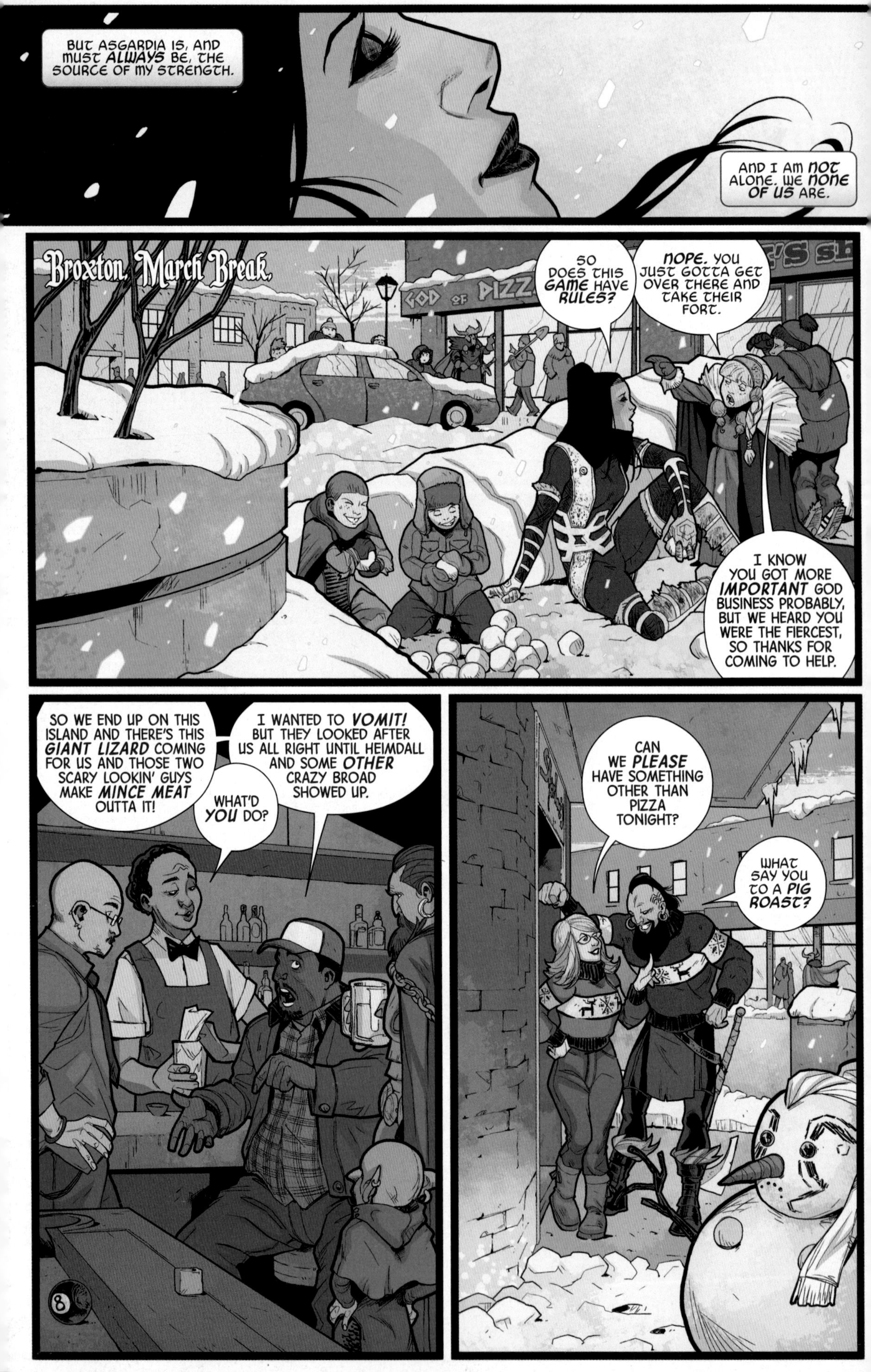

BUT ASGARDIA IS, AND MUST ALWAYS BE, THE SOURCE OF MY STRENGTH.
AND I AM NOT ALONE. WE NONE OF US ARE.
Broxton, March Break.
GOD OF PIZZ
SO DOES THIS GAME HAVE RULES?
NOPE. YOU JUST GOTTA GET OVER THERE AND TAKE THEIR FORT.
I KNOW YOU GOT MORE IMPORTANT GOD BUSINESS PROBABLY, BUT WE HEARD YOU WERE THE FIERCEST, SO THANKS FOR COMING TO HELP.
SO WE END UP ON THIS ISLAND AND THERE'S THIS GIANT LIZARD COMING FOR US AND THOSE TWO SCARY LOOKIN' GUYS MAKE MINCE MEAT OUTTA IT!
WHAT'D YOU DO?
I WANTED TO VOMIT! BUT THEY LOOKED AFTER US ALL RIGHT UNTIL HEIMDALL AND SOME OTHER CRAZY BROAD SHOWED UP.
CAN WE PLEASE HAVE SOMETHING OTHER THAN PIZZA TONIGHT?
WHAT SAY YOU TO A PIG ROAST?

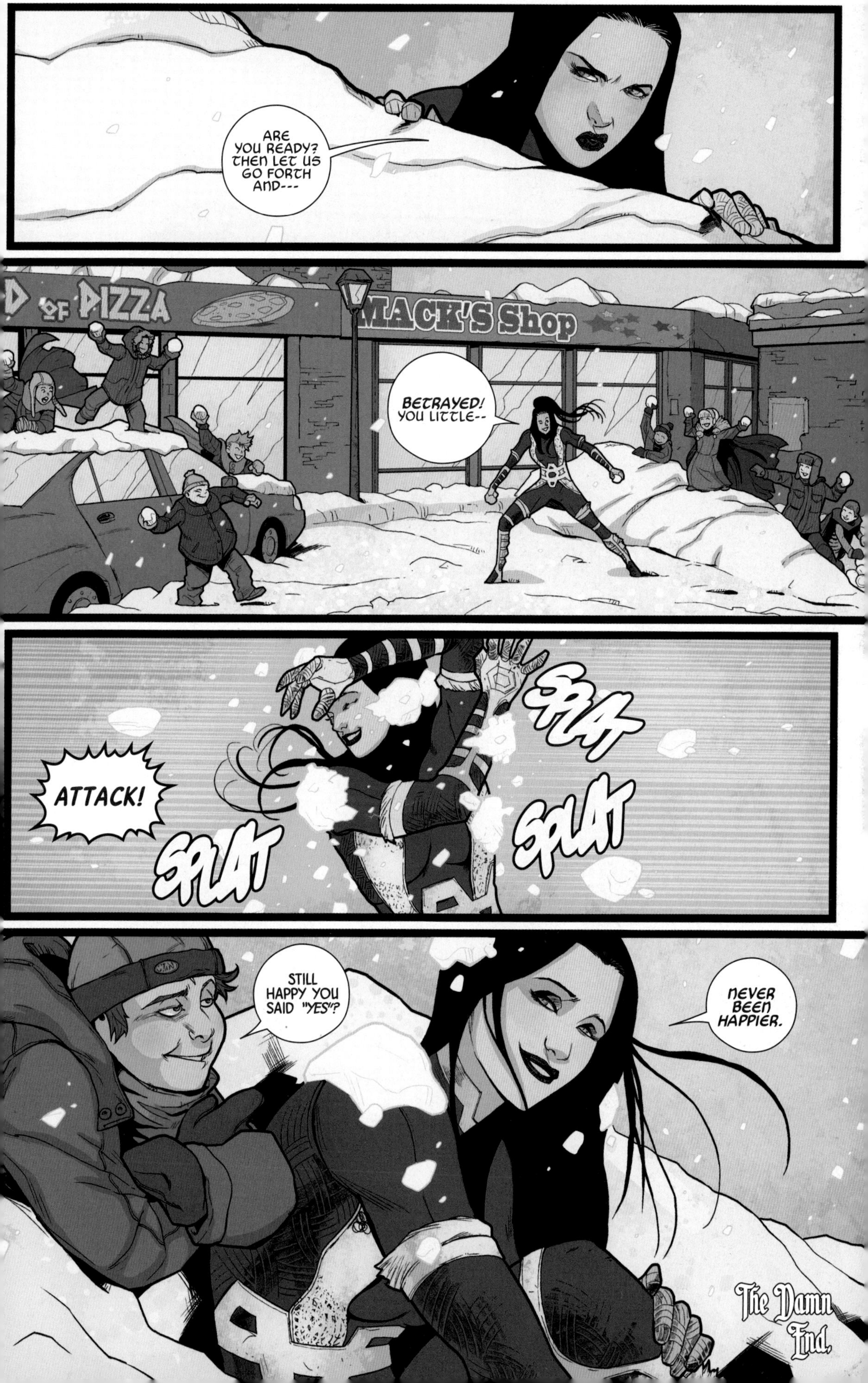
ARE YOU READY? THEN LET US GO FORTH AND---
D OF PIZZA
MACK'S Shop
BETRAYED! YOU LITTLE--
ATTACK!
SPLAT
SPLAT
SPLAT
STILL HAPPY YOU SAID "YES"?
NEVER BEEN HAPPIER.
The Damn End.

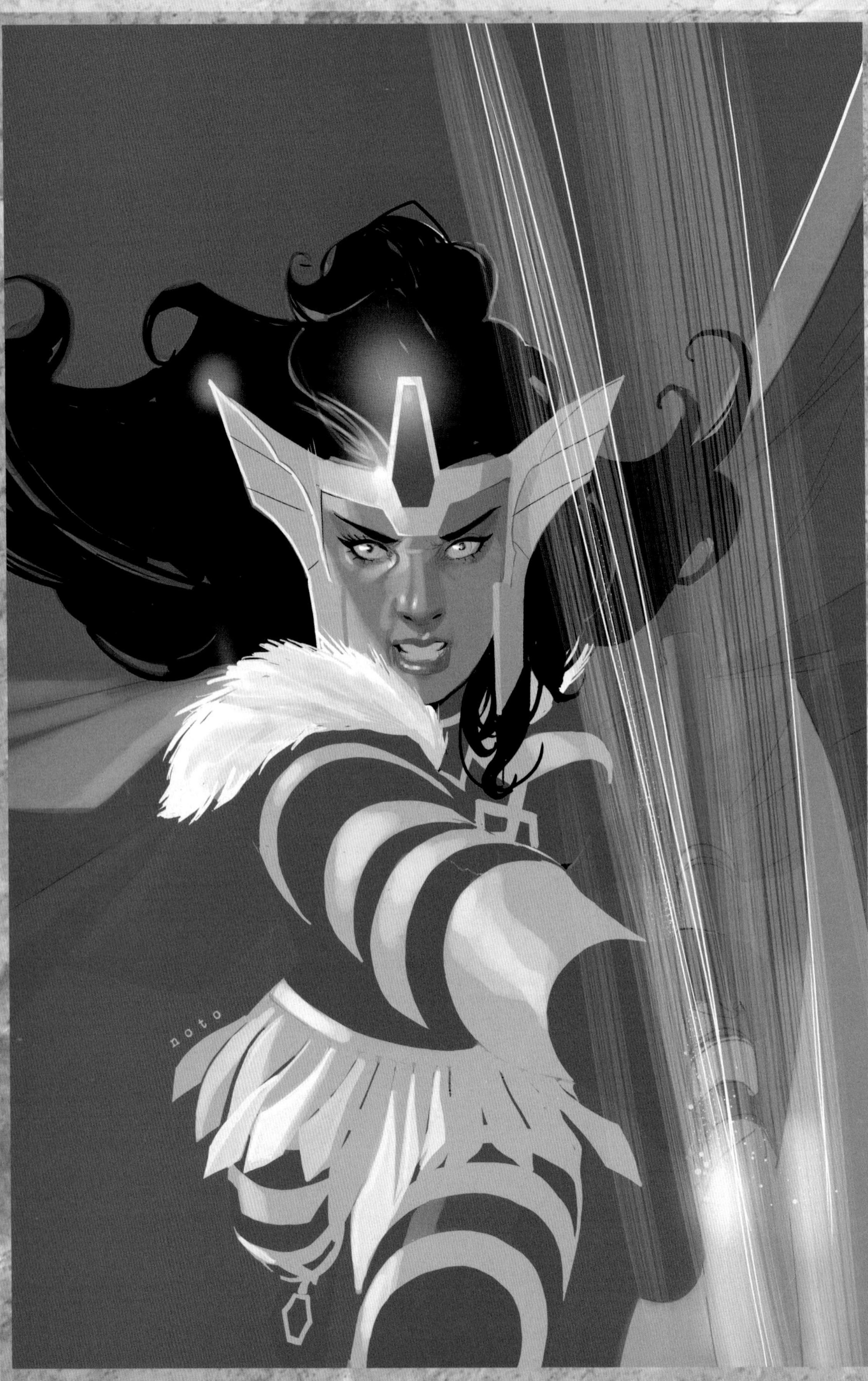
noto

#646 VARIANT BY PHIL NOTO

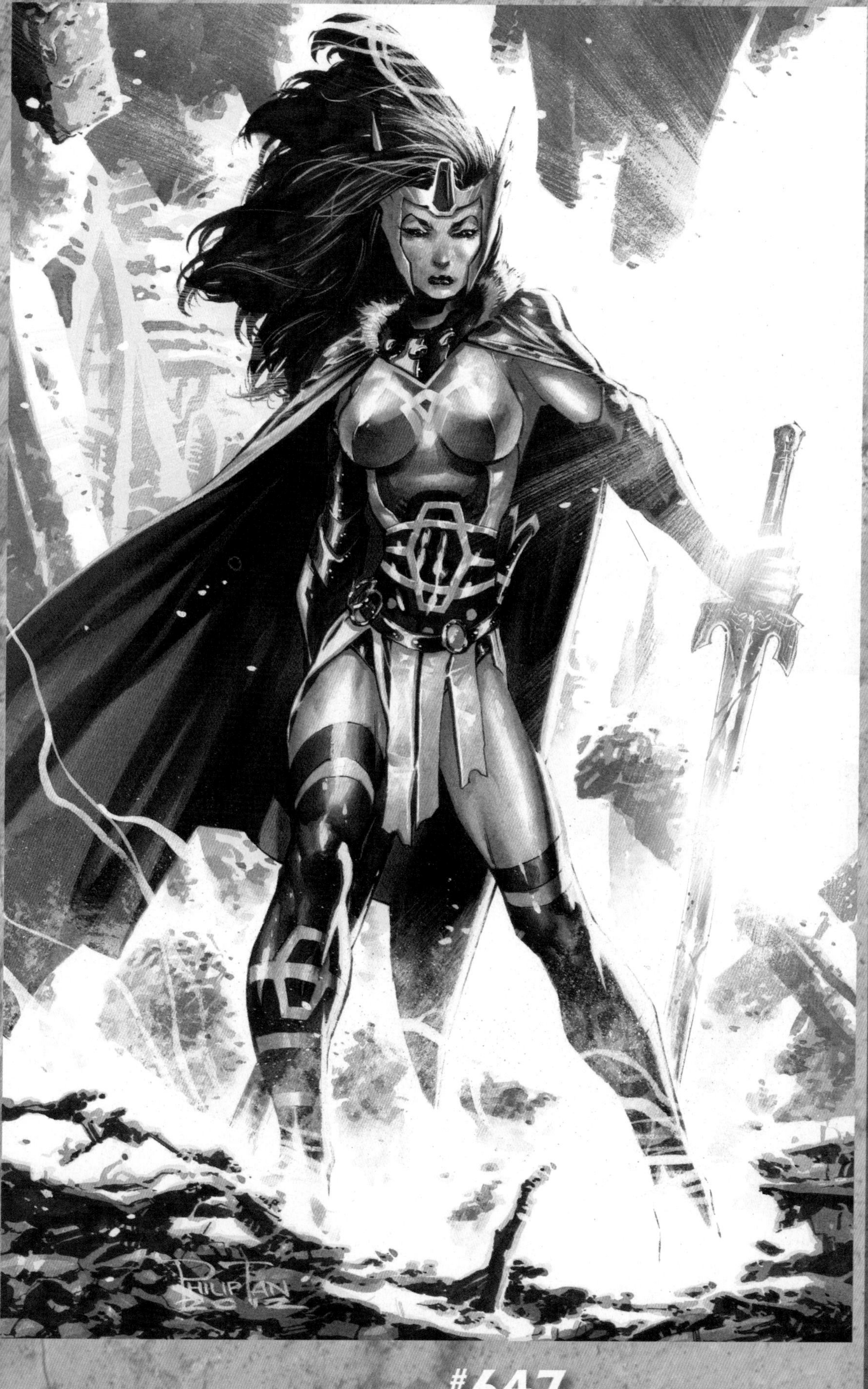
PHILIP TAN

#647 VARIANT BY PHILIP TAN

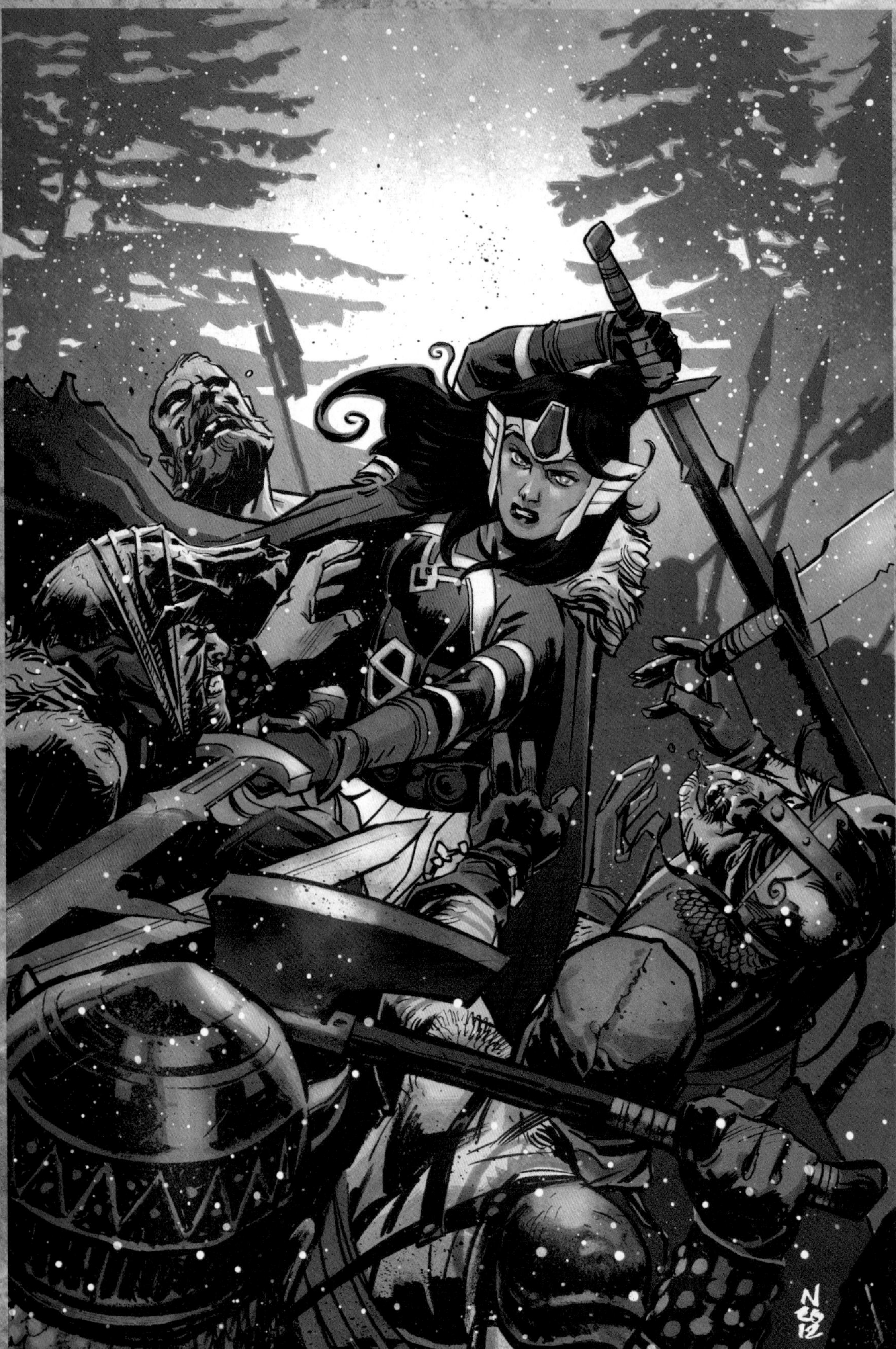

#648 VARIANT BY NIC KLEIN

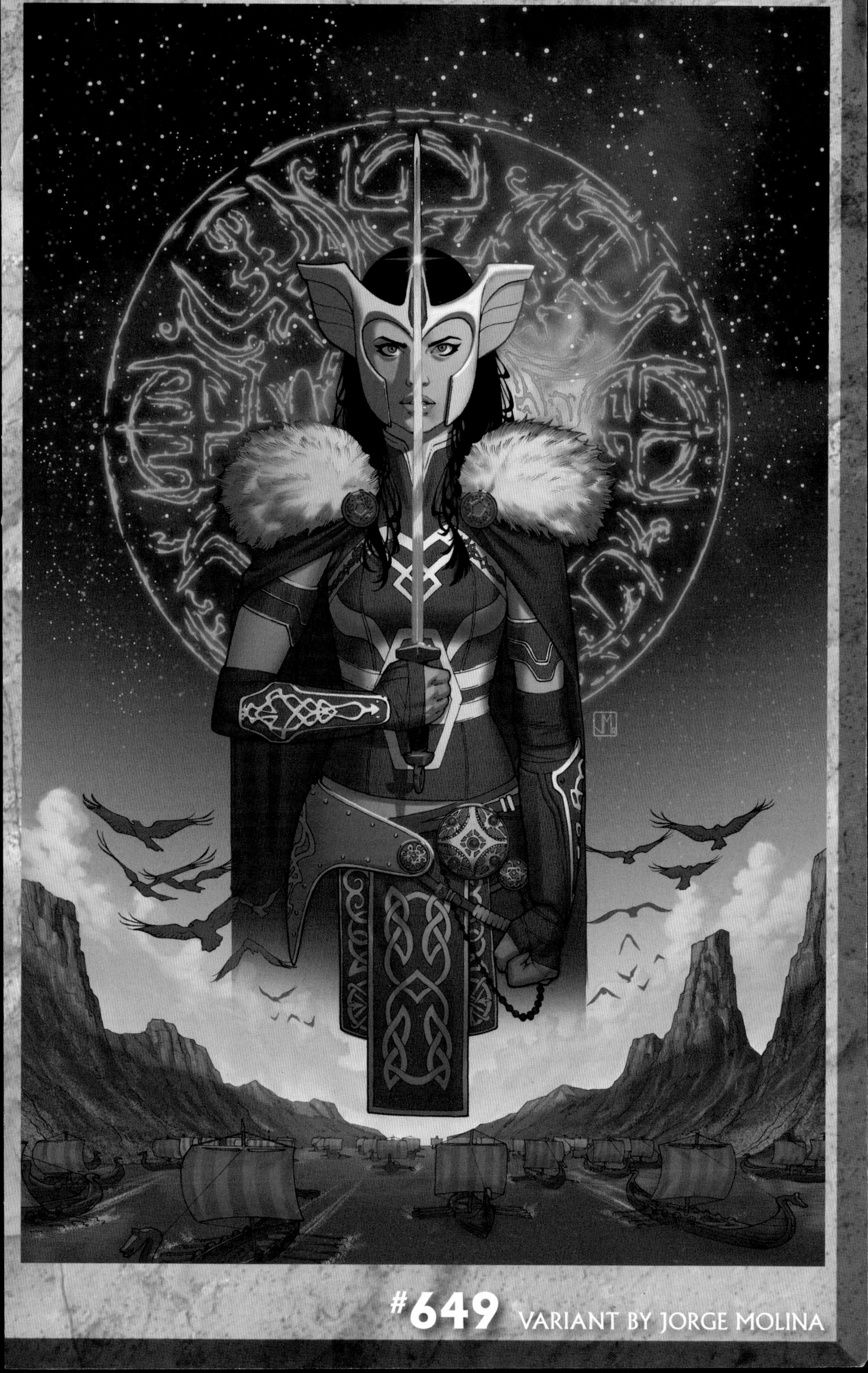
JM

#649 VARIANT BY JORGE MOLINA

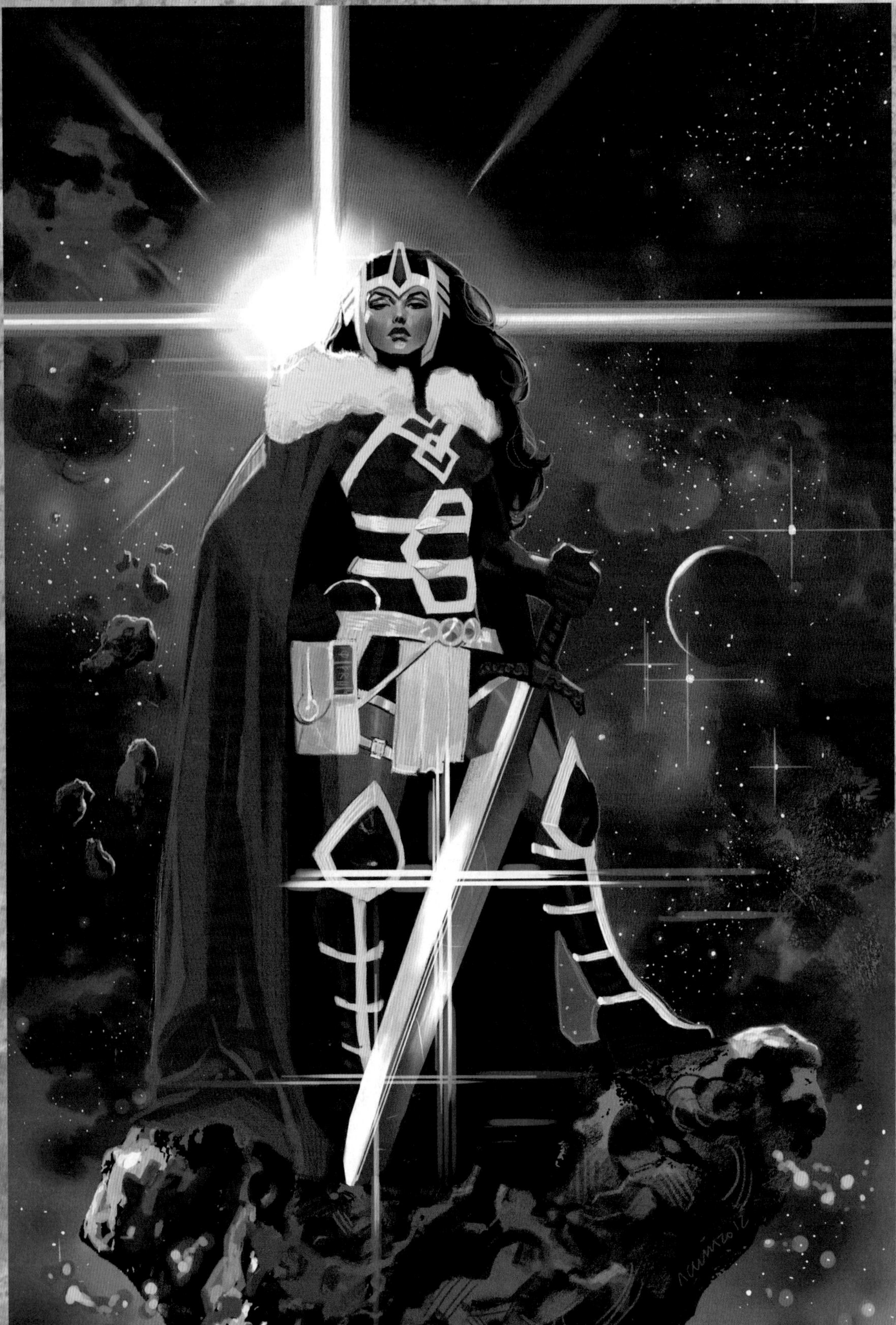

#650 VARIANT BY DANIEL ACUÑA

"ONE OF THE MOST ORIGINAL AND FUN TO READ COMICS"– SuperHeroHype.com

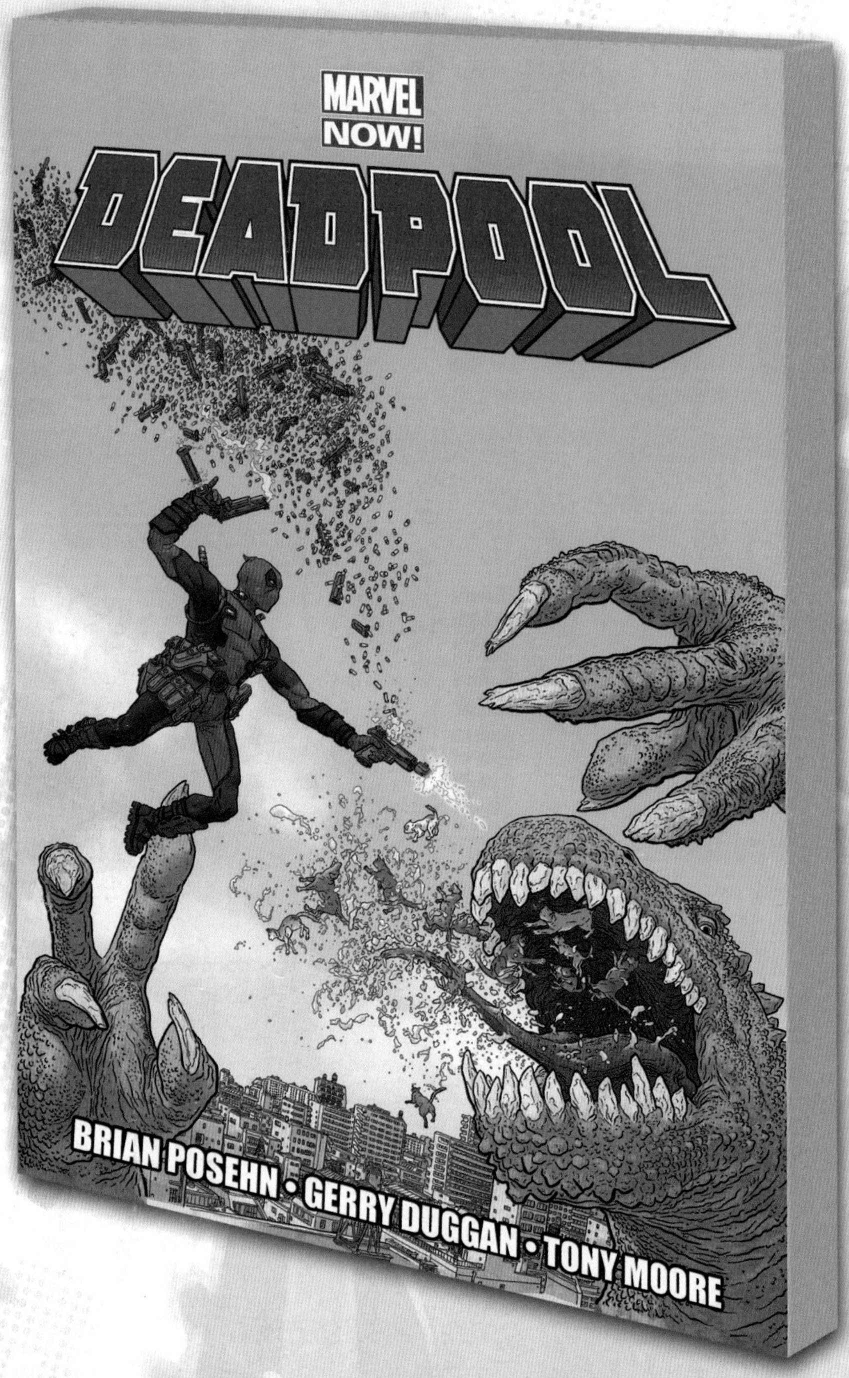
MARVEL
NOW!
DEADPOOL
BRIAN POSEHN • GERRY DUGGAN • TONY MOORE

DEADPOOL VOL. 1: DEAD PRESIDENTS TPB

978-0-7851-6680-1 • MAR130727

"A GREAT JUMPING ON POINT."– Comicvine.com

NOW!

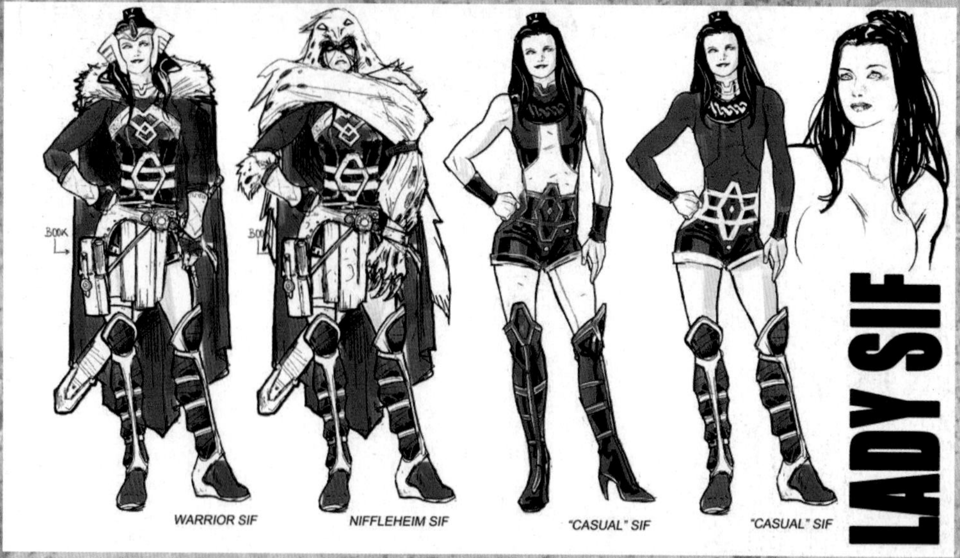
BOOK
WARRIOR SIF
NIFFLEHEIM SIF
"CASUAL" SIF
"CASUAL" SIF
LADY SIF

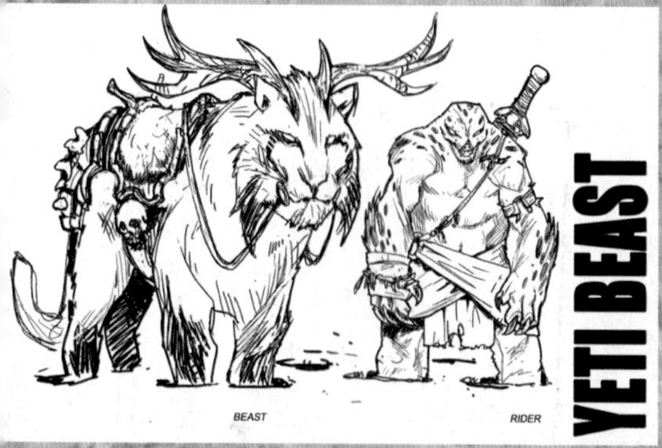
BEAST
RIDER
YETI BEAST

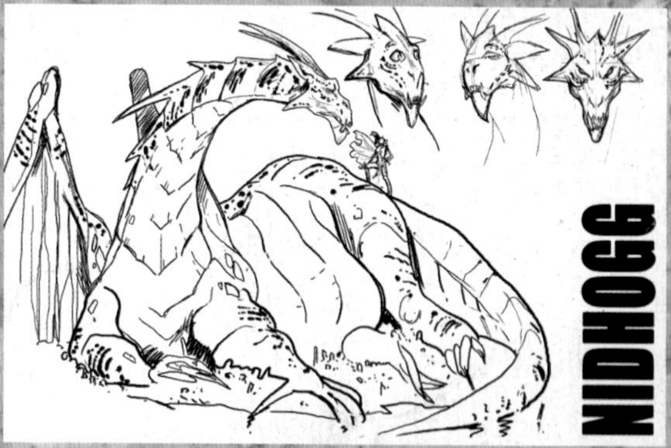
NIDHOGG

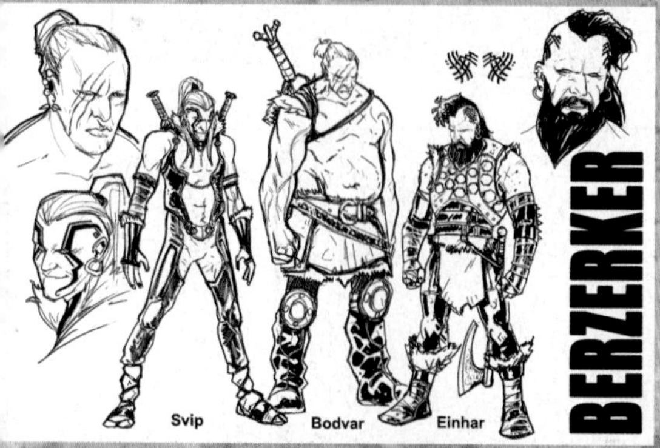
Svip
Bodvar
Einhar
BERZERKER

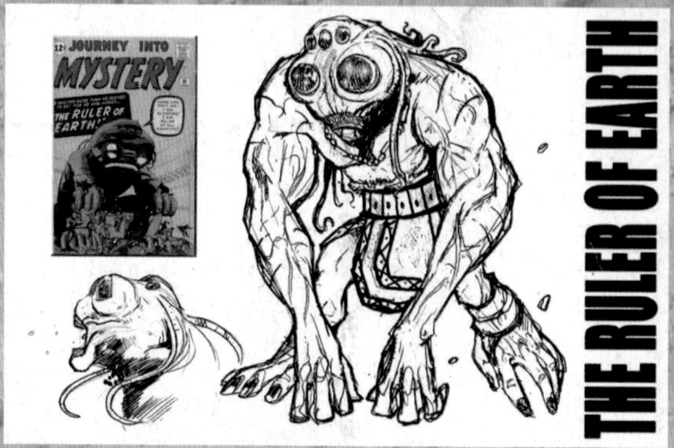
JOURNEY INTO
MYSTERY
THE RULER OF EARTH!
THE RULER OF EARTH

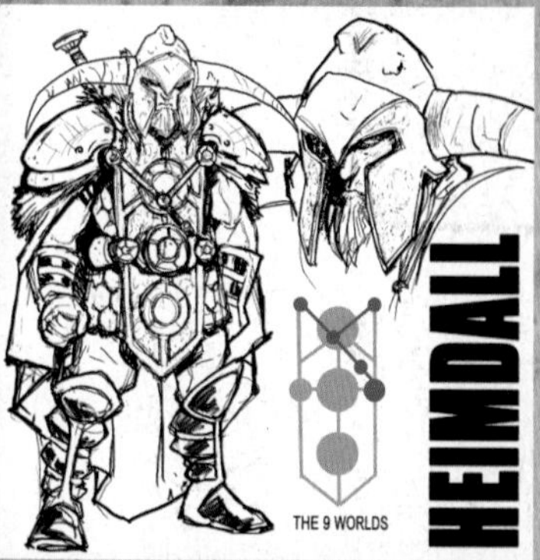
THE 9 WORLDS
HEIMDALL

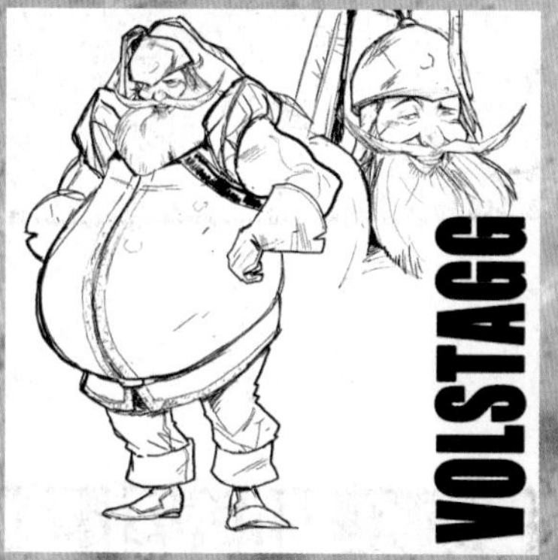
VOLSTAGG

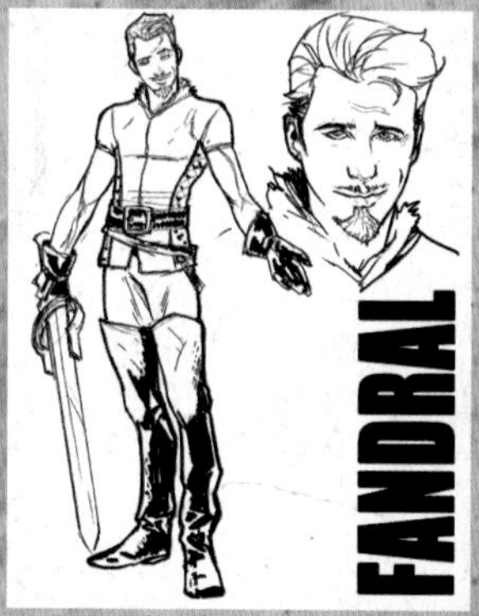
FANDRAL

CHARACTER SKETCHES BY VALERIO SCHITI